Final Journey

Martin Gilbert

The fate of the Jews in Nazi Europe

Steimatzky's Agency
Jerusalem, Tel-Aviv, Haifa

together with
The Jerusalem Post

Final Journey

First published by
George Allen & Unwin Ltd
Ruskin House, Museum Street
London WC1A 1LU

ISBN 0 04 940058 4

This book was designed and produced by
George Rainbird Limited
36 Park Street
London W1Y 4DE

House Editor: Erica Hunningher
Assistant House Editor: Clarinda Roothooft
Designer: Alan Bartram
Cartographer: T. A. Bicknell
Indexer: Martin Gilbert

Printed and bound by
Morrison & Gibb Limited,
Tanfield, Edinburgh

Contents

Prologue 7

1 Germany, the Jews, and the First Deportations 9

2 Journey to Lublin 26

3 Journey from Jassy 42

4 Towards the 'Final Solution' 51

5 Auschwitz 69

6 The City of Lodz 79

7 'Nobody Came Back . . .' 88

8 The Warsaw Ghetto 96

9 The Treblinka Death Camp 116

10 France: Convoy No 1 126

11 France: The Deportations Continue 134

12 The Children's Convoys 143

13 France: The Final Convoys 149

14 The Jews of Holland 157

15 Sophia's Story 168

16 A Belgian Story 174

17 A Single Train 178

18 'Our Hope' 181

19 The Jews of Italy 191

20 Eichmann in Hungary 194

21 Sara's Story 200

22 The Death Marches 209

Epilogue 214

Acknowledgments and Sources 216

Index 218

Three children in the Warsaw ghetto. This photograph was taken in 1941 by a Jewish photographer, Mr Forbert. A year later, both he and those whom he photographed were deported eastwards, to the death camp at Treblinka, where they were murdered, together with more than 300,000 Warsaw Jews.

The stories told in these pages are based on eye-witness accounts and on contemporary evidence. Wherever possible, I have given the precise date of every document quoted and have cited the actual words used at the time, both by the Nazis and by their victims.

I have tried to tell the stories of individuals, as well as of communities. On their own, the statistics are powerful and terrible. But the story of the Nazi attempt to murder the Jews of Europe concerned individual people; people with names, families, careers and futures, for millions of whom no one survived to mourn, or to remember.

helft! gebt
für die Berliner Winterhilfe
Bis Sonnabend früh
10 Uhr
hat das Judentum Bedenkzeit!
Dann beginnt der Kampf!
Die Juden aller Welt
wollen Deutschland vernichten!
Deutsches Volk!
Wehr Dich!
Kauf nicht beim Juden!
GRETA GARBO

1

Germany, the Jews, and the First Deportations

It has been calculated that more than twenty-five million civilians were killed during the Second World War: murdered in cold blood, with no chance of defending themselves; men, women, children, the sick and the elderly, cripples and babies. Of these twenty-five million, who included Russians, Chinese, Poles, Czechs, Serbs, Greeks, Belgians, Dutchmen, Frenchmen and Gipsies, six million were Jews.

The Jews of Europe had always known anti-semitism, and were no strangers to persecution, massacre and expulsion. Even the opening years of the twentieth century had been painful ones for them in many countries. Before the First World War, attacks, beatings and discrimination had dominated Jewish life in Tsarist Russia, the home of more than four million Jews, while anti-semitic political parties, literature and public outbursts were all too frequent in countries as civilized as France, as recently independent as Rumania, as familiar with minority groups as Austria-Hungary.

After the First World War, anti-Jewish violence had broken out again in Europe, driving many Jews to emigrate to the United States and to Palestine. In the Ukraine more than 80,000 Jews had been massacred during 1919 and 1920, while anti-Jewish attitudes and policies flourished in several of the newly independent, or enlarged States of inter-war Europe, among them Poland, Hungary, Rumania and the Baltic States. But it was in Germany, where more than half a million Jews formed an integral part of one of Europe's most modern societies, that hatred of the Jew was not only at its most violent, but became a part of the official policy of the State.

When, on 30 January 1933, Adolf Hitler became Chancellor of Germany, it was a turning point not only for the half million Jews of Germany, but for the seven or eight million Jews who lived elsewhere on the continent of Europe, the descendants of ancient Jewish communities, many of them dating back to Roman times; communities made up of hundreds of thousands of loyal citizens, of patriots, and of many who had submerged their Jewishness into the national life around them.

The boycott of Jewish-owned shops in Berlin. A poster *(opposite)* announces: 'The Jews of the world want to destroy Germany. Germans! Defend yourselves! Don't buy from a Jew.' Outside a leather goods shop *(below)* on the day of the boycott, 1 April 1933, a notice accuses the owners of being the 'parasites and gravediggers' of German artisans, and of paying them starvation wages.

'Whoever buys from the Jews is a traitor to his people.' ***Top:*** **copies of the anti-semitic magazine *Der Stürmer* were displayed on special public notice-boards in all German towns and villages.**

The parade ground at Sachsenhausen *(below)*, one of the camps in which Jews were imprisoned and ill-treated from the very first months of the Nazi regime.

Hitler was determined to destroy all this, to isolate the Jews, to impoverish them and to drive them outside the daily life, first of Germany and then of Europe. He expressed his deep hatred of the Jews in every speech, and by his speeches stirred the hatred of others, both inside and outside the German Reich.

By a series of laws, beginning in 1933 and culminating two years later in the Nuremberg Laws of 1935, the Jews were driven from German public life and denied all the rights and protections of citizenship.

Among the earliest of these laws was one of 7 April 1933 which forced the compulsory retire-

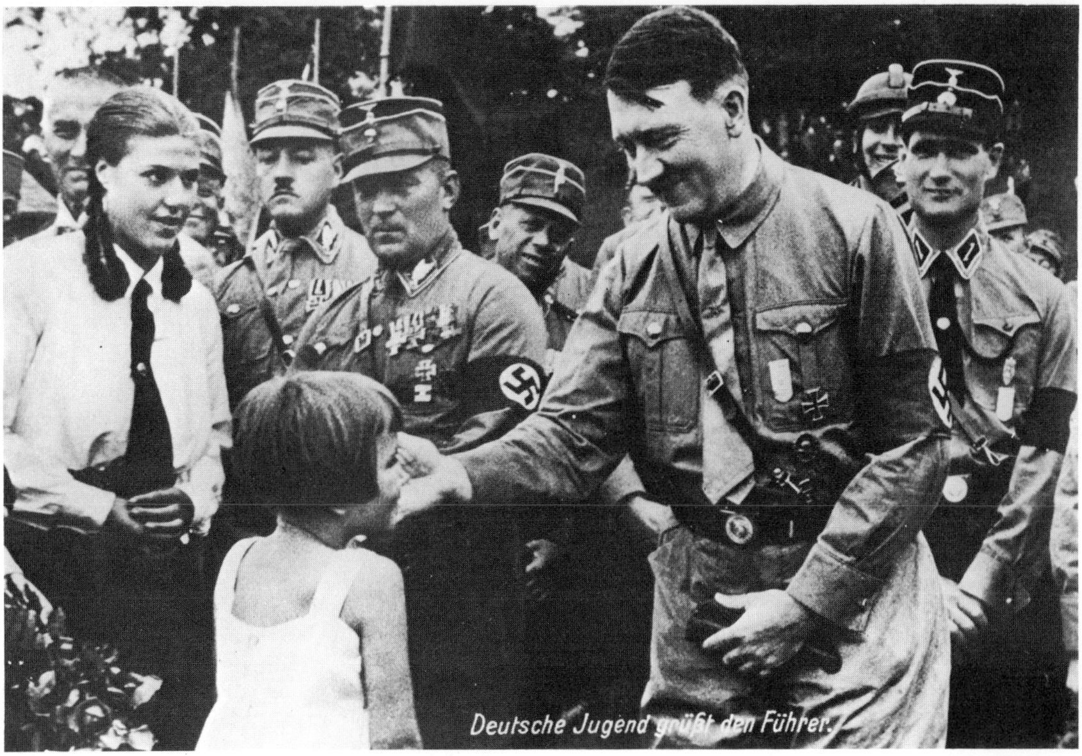
Deutsche Jugend grüßt den Führer.

Two propaganda postcards, published by Hitler's personal photographer, Heinrich Hoffman. *Above:* 'German Youth Greet the Führer.' *Left:* 'A Little Stormtrooper.'

ment of all 'non-Aryans' from professional life. By a further decree of 11 April 1933, a 'non-Aryan' was defined as anyone with Jewish parents, or with a single Jewish grandparent. 'Concentration' camps were established, in which Jews were among those imprisoned, beaten, terrorized and murdered. Anti-Jewish schoolbooks were published and Jewish children were forced to sit on separate benches at school.

Since the achievement of German unity in 1870, the Jews of Germany had been loyal and valuable citizens. In the days of the Kaiser they had contributed substantially to the prosperity, the culture and the welfare of the Empire. During the First World War 100,000 of them had served in the German army, and, among these, many had won the highest awards for courage. Twelve thousand had died on the field of battle. After the war the Jews had suffered, with their fellow citizens, all the rigours of inflation and economic chaos. In the fourteen years of the Weimar Republic, assimilation was widespread: by 1927 more than 44 per cent of all Jewish marriages were with non-Jews, and at least 1,000 Jews a year either converted to

Hitler, in Munich, surrounded by young Nazi admirers, shortly after he came to power in 1933.

Christianity, or dissociated themselves from the community. The urge to be exemplary citizens was strong in them. But none of this counted against the vitriolic hatred which Nazism now aroused.

No Jew could escape the Nazi determination to drive the Jews from German life, and to make them suffer in the process. Neither assimilation nor conversion could act as a shield. The story of one Jewess is typical of many. Bertha Pappenheim was seventy-five years old when Hitler came to power. Her life had been devoted to the cause of German orphans and delinquent women. Since 1895 she had been a pioneer of women's social welfare. A prominent Jewess, she was strongly and openly opposed to Zionism. After 1933 she spoke out against the emigration of Jews from Germany, fearing the disruption of Jewish family life. But in 1936, aged seventy-eight, she was taken by the Gestapo 'for questioning', and died as a result of her interrogation.

Neither quality of past service, nor respected position in society; neither ability nor age, could

Two anti-semitic slogans, photographed by a Dutch motorcyclist on his way from Holland to Berlin in the autumn of 1935: a street sign *(above left)* declares: 'Hyenas are never decent, neither are the Jews. Jews – clear out!' The sign on a bridge across the Elbe proclaims: 'The Jew is our misfortune. Let him get away from our corpse.' A third notice, outside the village of Oberstdorf, declares: 'Jews are not wanted here.'

protect a Jew in Nazi Germany. Everywhere, schoolchildren were taught that the Jewish people in their midst were the enemies of Germany. Villages competed with each other to declare themselves 'Jew-free'. Young men in uniform sang the new 'patriot' songs, in which race hatred predominated. One of the most popular of these songs proclaimed: 'When Jewish blood spurts from the knife, Then all goes twice as well!'

By the beginning of 1938, more than 200,000 German Jews had managed to find refuge elsewhere in Europe, some in France, Belgium, Holland, Austria and Czechoslovakia. Others had gone outside continental Europe altogether, to Britain, Palestine and the United States. But as the number of refugees rose each year, country after country began to restrict the numbers of those to whom it would grant admission.

It was not only the German Jews who tried to escape the violence of anti-semitism. In 1928 and 1929 there had been anti-Jewish riots in Hungary,

Europe, 1919 to 1937, showing the sites of some of the first concentration camps set up in Germany after 1933, and the towns referred to in the text.

Nazis taking over the Jewish communal offices in Vienna in March 1938.

followed by laws which discriminated against the Jews, many of whom were forced out of professional life. Between 1935 and 1937 not a single month passed in Rumania without Jews being attacked in the streets. In September 1935 several Jews had been killed during anti-Jewish riots in the Polish city of Lodz; riots which spread throughout Poland during 1936, when more than eighty Jews were killed. These Polish riots continued throughout 1937, when 350 separate attacks on Jews were recorded, and hundreds of Jews were injured.

For the Jews of central Europe, emigration became increasingly difficult. Even Palestine, in which Britain had established a Jewish National Home in 1922, imposed immigration restrictions after more than a quarter of a million Jews, the majority from Poland, but thousands more from Germany and the other States of Central Europe, had reached its shores. But while emigration became more and more difficult, the pressures against the Jews did not abate and the year 1938 saw a further, rapid deterioration of their hopes of a normal life.

On 15 March 1938 Hitler entered Vienna and direct Nazi rule was at once extended to Austria. Within only a few days, the whole apparatus of anti-Jewish persecution – from the imposition of

Nazi clerks register Jewish prisoners at Dachau.

the Nuremberg Laws to the beatings, the torture and deportation to Dachau concentration camp – was instituted in its most vicious form. Overnight more than 180,000 Jews were added to the German Reich, while an extra 40,000 people of Jewish descent – many of them baptized Christians – were declared to be, racially, Jews.

By the end of April more than 500 Austrian Jews had committed suicide. Others sought to flee across the borders into Czechoslovakia, Hungary and Switzerland; they were not always made welcome. In Vienna itself, the humiliations continued. One Jewish eye-witness of these events, the twenty-one-year-old Ehud Ueberall – later Ehud Avriel – recalled in 1975 in his book *Open The Gates!*:

'Jewish men, and especially women, were arrested in the streets and, under the scornful laughter of the Viennese, were forced to wash away the slogans painted during the desperate few weeks while Austria's fate lay in the balance. Jewish shops were broken into and plundered by the mob while Jews specially apprehended for the purpose stood in front (guarded by SA men, armed to the teeth) holding signs saying "Aryans, don't buy at the Jews".

'When dusk fell the emptied shops were abandoned by the looters. The SA then would collect the Jews who had been posted before the shops in one street, force them into a procession surrounded by Viennese of all ages and, while their Austrian neighbours shrieked and spat into the Jews' faces, lead them down the road into some dark alleyway where the Austrians were allowed to beat them viciously.

'Jews were evicted from their flats by their own landlords or by jealous neighbours. Jewish students were turned out of their schools. The prisons became full of innocent people simply because they were Jews.'

Throughout the spring and summer of 1938 the Jews sought to leave Austria. But it was not easy to do so. 'On the day Hitler took over Austria,' Ueberall recalled, 'there was a total of sixteen immigration certificates at the disposal of the entire Austrian Jewish community.' A few hundred visas were obtained during the summer for agricultural workers, who were able to proceed to England, Holland and Denmark. Those who left had, of course, to leave behind all their property, all their savings and almost all their belongings. For those who remained, as Ueberall wrote, 'turned down by one foreign consulate after the other, they realized that no country would take them in'.

German soldiers laugh at an elderly Jewish official as he leaves the Jewish communal offices in Vienna, March 1938.

Ueberall's recollections are fully borne out by contemporary records. On 31 May the British Consul-General in Vienna informed the British Ambassador in Berlin that 'the distress and despair amongst the Jews are appalling. This consulate-general is literally besieged every day by hundreds of Jews who have been told to leave the country and who come vainly searching for a visa to go anywhere.'

On 6 July an international conference opened at Evian, on the southern shore of Lake Geneva. For eight days, the representatives of thirty-two nations, including Britain and the United States, discussed the problem of those Jewish refugees seeking to escape from German persecution. Although each delegate present expressed his sympathy for the refugees, none of the major

On 1 December 1938 a group of Jewish children from Berlin take the train westwards, through Holland, to the Channel coast, and to safety in Britain. Between 1933 and 1939 Britain took in more than 65,000 Jewish refugees. This photograph was published in the Dutch newspaper, *Het Volk,* on 2 December 1938.

powers was prepared to increase its immigration quota. On the day the conference ended, one German newspaper declared:

'JEWS FOR SALE
WHO WANTS THEM?
NO ONE'

After the Evian Conference, the German Government intensified its anti-Jewish measures throughout Germany and Austria. On 8 August 1938 Jews were forbidden to open their safes, except in the presence of a tax inspector. Nine days later, on 17 August, a special decree forced all Jews to change their first names: every man to take the name 'Israel', and every woman the name 'Sarah'. All non-Jewish landlords were urged to get rid of Jewish tenants, while at the same time Jewish landlords were forced to sell their property. Jewish doctors and lawyers were barred from practice.

On 10 August it had been the main Nuremberg synagogue which became the target of Nazi hatred, for on that day the Nazi leader, or *Gauleiter*, of Franconia, Julius Streicher, having first opened a swimming pool, and then started a bicycle race, came to the synagogue. His official itinerary described what then occurred:

'On 10 August 1938 at 10 am the destruction of the synagogue will begin.

'*Gauleiter* Streicher will personally set the crane in motion which is to remove the Jewish symbol (Star of David etc).

'The affair is to be well publicized.'

The Nuremberg synagogue was demolished. In several other towns the Jews were told that the land on which the synagogues had been built must be 'returned' to the Reich. The Jews of Germany could see no way to alleviate their distress. As Jochen Klepper, a German Protestant writer, noted in his diary on 23 August: 'After it was revealed at the Evian Conference that the German Jews could not expect help from abroad, everything became far more tragic.' Klepper was married to a Jewess. Four years later, at the height of the Nazi extermination campaign, he was to commit suicide, together with his wife and their young daughter.

During September two of Germany's concentration camps, Buchenwald and Sachsenhausen, were enlarged. At Dachau, prisoners already in the camp were made to sew Stars of David on thousands of camp uniforms. Fears rose among German Jewry of some new and terrible event.

At the end of September Hitler, Chamberlain, Mussolini and Daladier, meeting at Munich, agreed to the transfer of the Sudetenland region from Czechoslovakia to Germany. Two weeks later the German authorities expelled tens of thousands of German-speaking Jews from the Sudetenland to Czechoslovakia. The Czech authorities refused to accept them, and deported them across the Danube. Several hundred were forced to remain on an island in no-man's-land. No one would give them refuge.

On 14 October a meeting of Reich leaders was held at the Air Ministry in Berlin. There, they were addressed by Marshal Hermann Goering himself, the overseer of the Nazi Four Year Plan. His message was blunt. The Reich, he declared, 'must eradicate doubtful elements from its population, namely the last remaining Jews'. On that same day, the French Government delivered a memorandum to the German Government in which it declared, in connection with the nations which had met at Evian: 'None of the States would dispute the absolute right of the German Government to take with regard to certain of its citizens such measures as are within its own sovereign powers.'

Not only in Germany was anti-semitism increasing. On 6 October the Polish Government had gone so far as to revoke all Polish passports if their bearers had lived abroad for more than five years. The order was to come into force on 31 October. It meant that at least 15,000 Polish Jews resident in Germany would cease to be Polish citizens on the last day of October.

The Germans were in a dilemma. They did not want 15,000 stateless Jews in their midst: people whom, it was clear from the Evian Conference, almost no country would be prepared to admit. They therefore told the Poles that these Jews would be expelled unless Poland formally agreed to allow them to return whenever they chose. On 27 October the Poles refused to accept these conditions. In only four days, the Jews they did not want would cease to be Polish citizens.

The Poles were prepared to wait until 31 October. The Germans were not. That same evening the order went out from Berlin: all Jews with Polish passports were to be expelled within forty-eight hours. The method chosen: deportation by train.

The trains were to depart at eleven on the following night. They were to have locked doors and armed guards. Across the Reich – in Berlin, Essen, Stuttgart, Bochum, Dortmund, Duisburg, Düsseldorf, Cologne, Hanover, Hamburg and Vienna – the trains were made ready. As for the Jews, they were first to be arrested, then taken to local police stations, and then moved in trucks and lorries to the railway stations. A witness of their plight was Ottilie Schoenwald, a leading

Polish-born Jews being deported from Germany to Poland in October 1938. The map (*opposite*) shows some of the towns from which they were taken.

member of the Jewish community of Bochum, herself a German citizen. As she recalled:

'It was a freezing October day. As if adhering to a Jewish tradition, the trouble began on the eve, not in the evening, but in the afternoon. The door bell rang constantly. Our library was soon teeming with a complete cross-section of the Congregation. Amid the confusion of voices and stories I could not tell what had happened.

'"All Jews from the east are to be arrested."'

In Hanover, among those caught up in the deportation order, was a Polish-born tailor, Sendal Grynszpan. He had lived in Hanover since 1911, with his wife and children. He later recalled:

The borders of Greater Germany, following the annexation of Austria in March 1938 and the Sudetenland in October 1938.

'It was a Thursday, 27 October 1938. A policeman knocked on our door and told us to report to the police station with our passports. He said, "Don't bother to take anything else, you'll be right back." When we reached the police station, my wife, my daughter, my son Marcus and myself, we saw a number of people sitting or standing. Some were weeping. The police inspector was shouting at the top of his voice, "Sign here. You are being deported." I had to sign like everyone else.

'We were taken to the concert hall beside the Leine, where about 600 people were assembled from various parts of Hanover. We were kept there for about twenty-four hours until Friday night, when police vans took us, about twenty at a time, to the station. The streets of Hanover teemed with people shouting, "Send the Jews to Palestine." '

That night thousands of Jewish men were arrested, and their wives and children ordered to join them at the station on the following day. Ottilie Schoenwald's account continued:

'Early next morning we carried our provisions to the prison. We simply marched past the speechless guards straight into the courtyard where the poor Jews had been lined up just as we arrived. The guard on duty, whom I knew, advised me to distribute the food at the station. He offered to carry the steaming boiler in his own car.

'A crowd of shouting and weeping women and

children was already assembled at the station. In the square outside trucks unloaded their unhappy passengers. Bochum was the assembly point for the surrounding villages.

'Most of the women and children herded into the third-class waiting-rooms had been dragged out of bed without being allowed to pack. After my husband agreed that the Congregation would bear the expenses, the fleet of cars set out to search Jewish shops for covers and underclothing. The lists of requests was unending, but under the circumstances displays of human weakness were merely heartbreaking.

'The stationmaster informed me that the special train would not leave before eleven that evening.'

All over Germany, the stationmasters made ready to organize the deportation trains, helped in their task by the Gestapo, and as the trains pulled out the stationmasters reported their success to the authorities. The stationmaster in Hanover reported that all had proceeded without a hitch. As he told the Gestapo:

'Special train SPECIAL HANOVER 4199 made up at 19.30 – about two hours before departure. Consisting of 14 well-lit carriages each with 55 seats, of which 35 to 40 were occupied.

'The departure of the Jews, carrying large quantities of hand luggage, proceeded on platform 5, which had been closed to the public before the train was assembled. The Jews were allowed to purchase food and tobacco.

'The special train departed on schedule at 21.40 from track 11, platform 5.'

The trains moved eastwards through the night. One, with 2,000 deportees on board, reached the Polish frontier station of Chojnice (Konitz). There the German guards disappeared, after threatening to shoot anyone who tried to leave the train, or even look out of the windows. At the same time, heating and lighting were turned off. When the Polish railwaymen approached the train, they let the Jews go for shelter into the two station waiting-rooms. There, in the crush and heat from so many terrified people seeking an escape from the cold, four Jews suffocated to death. Two days later the Poles allowed the 2,000 to continue to Cracow, where local Jews provided food and medicine.

The 2,000 were indeed fortunate, by comparison with those whose trains took them to another frontier station at Neu Bentschen. Here the deportees were forced to leave their trains four miles from the Polish frontier town of Zbonszyn. Then, threatened by Storm-troopers, they were made to walk to the frontier itself, where their only shelter was in the stables and pigsties of a frontier farm.

The first train reached Zbonszyn on the night of Friday 28 October, at the start of the Sabbath. But for 2,000 men, women and children it was an evening of uncertainty and fear. Some went mad with fright.

On the morning of 29 October more trains arrived, bringing a further 6,000 people, all of whom had been forced to leave behind all but the few possessions they could carry in their bags and briefcases.

It was seven o'clock in the morning. The German frontier police forced the Jews out of the train and pushed them towards the Polish frontier post with their rifle butts. The Polish guards confronted them with bayonets. 'Go on', the Germans shouted, 'Don't worry. They wouldn't dare shoot you.' The Polish guards fired into the air. Panic-stricken, the Jews pushed past the barrier into Poland. Exhausted by their journey, frightened and bewildered, they sat for three hours in the mud and rain until, at ten o'clock, the Polish authorities marched them into Zbonszyn's main square.

Sendal Grynszpan and his family were among those who had reached the frontier on the Saturday morning. As he later recalled:

'There were trains from all over Germany: Leipzig, Berlin, Cologne, Düsseldorf, Bielefeld, Essen, Bremen. We were about 12,000 in all. That was Saturday 29 October. When we got to the border we were searched. We were only allowed to take 10 marks; any excess was confiscated. That

Jews expelled from Germany, waiting in the stable yard of the Polish frontier station at Zbonszyn, November 1938, uncertain of whether they will be allowed into Poland or not.

was German law; we were told: "You didn't have more than that when you arrived in Germany, and you can't take any more away with you now."

'We were kept under guard and not allowed to communicate with anyone. The SS told us we would have to walk about two kilometres to the border. Those who couldn't walk were beaten until the road was wet with their blood. Their baggage was taken away. We were dealt with cruelly and barbarously. It was the first time that I realized how barbarous the Germans really are. They made us run while they shouted "Run! Run!" I was struck down at the roadside, but my son Marcus took me by the hand and said, "Come on Papa, run. They'll kill you if you don't."

'Finally we reached the border. We crossed it. The women went first because they began firing at us. The Poles had no idea why we were there or why there were so many of us. A Polish general and some officers came to examine our papers. They saw that we were all Polish citizens – we had special passports and they decided to let us into Poland.'

Slowly, as the days passed, the Jews in Zbonszyn were allowed to travel into Poland. Many of them were able to join their relatives. Behind them they had left their shops, their homes, their work, their belongings and their livelihood. In front of them lay whatever fate was in store for Polish Jewry.

Sendal Grynszpan and his family were to be sent to Lodz: and on 1 November his twenty-two-year-old daughter Berta sent a postcard to their son

A Jewish shop front destroyed in Hanover in November 1938. The shop was selling clothes.

Herszel, who was living – without a valid passport – in Paris. In her card, Berta told her brother of the family's plight:

'They shoved an expulsion order into our hands, saying we had to leave Germany before 29 October. We were not allowed to go home. I pleaded to be allowed to fetch a few things and a policeman accompanied me. I packed a case with the most important clothes, but that was all we could salvage.'

Her postcard ended: 'We haven't a penny. Could you send us something at Lodz?'

Berta Grynszpan's postcard reached her brother in Paris on Thursday 3 November. News of the deportations had already begun to appear in the Press and on 4 November the Yiddish daily paper, *Parisian Day*, published a detailed account of the distressing conditions of the deportees: '1,200 of them have fallen ill' the newspaper reported, 'and several hundred are without shelter'.

Herszel Grynszpan was filled with fury. On 5 November he bought a gun, determined to do something about the humiliation which his family, and his people, had suffered. Two days later he went to the German Embassy, intent on shooting the Ambassador. But the Ambassador was not there. Grynszpan had with him, he told the porter, 'an important document'. The Third Secretary at the Embassy, Ernst Vom Rath, agreed to see him, and Grynszpan was ushered into the room. 'Did you have an important document to give me?' Vom Rath asked. 'You are a filthy Boche', Grynszpan replied, 'and here, in the name of twelve thousand persecuted Jews, is your document.'

Grynszpan then fired five shots, two of which struck Vom Rath. He was rushed to a nearby clinic and for two days French and German doctors fought to save him.

Grynszpan made no attempt to avoid arrest. 'I was not motivated by hatred or by vengeance', he told his French police questioners on 8 November, 'but by love of my father and my people, who have endured unbearable suffering. I deeply regret having injured anyone, but I have no other way of expressing myself'. Grynszpan added: 'To be Jewish is not a crime. We are not animals. The Jewish people have a right to live.'

At four o'clock on the afternoon of 9 November, Vom Rath died. That evening Hitler and the Nazi leaders gathered at Munich Town Hall for their annual celebration of the Beer Hall *Putsch* of 1923. Shortly after nine o'clock a message was brought to the Führer telling him that Vom Rath was dead. Hitler at once left the meeting, his planned speech undelivered. Within three hours, the 'Night of Broken Glass' had begun. A Gestapo order was sent out from Berlin shortly before midnight. It began: 'Action will be taken against the Jews, particularly against their synagogues, throughout Germany. . . .'

The Gestapo order was obeyed. During the night hundreds of synagogues were set on fire and thousands of shops were looted. Throughout Germany Jewish homes were raided, their contents smashed and their occupants forced to watch the destruction of all their belongings. Hundreds of Jews were beaten by groups of Nazis roaming the streets in search of 'prey'. In one village, a Jewish mother and her son were stabbed to death by local peasants with pitchforks.

During 10 November, all over Germany, Jews were arrested. Once more the trains were on the move, this time taking their prisoners to concentration camps. In three days more than 10,000 Jews were brought to Dachau, from the Ruhr and Rhineland, from Heidelberg and Munich, from Graz and Vienna. A further 10,000 were taken to

Humiliating a whole Jewish community. Community leaders are marched through the streets of Baden-Baden (*top*). They are forced to carry a Star of David on which the Nazis have written: 'God will not forsake us!'

***Above:* the Jews of Baden-Baden, flanked by Nazi policemen, are led through the streets to the synagogue where they are forced to uncover their heads, in breach of Jewish religious practice, and to listen to readings from an anti-semitic newspaper.**

During the 'Night of Broken Glass', hundreds of synagogues were set on fire throughout Germany, Austria and the Sudetenland, among them the main synagogue at Baden-Baden.

Buchenwald from the towns and villages of Silesia. Yet another 10,000 were taken to Sachsenhausen from Berlin itself, from Hamburg and from the Baltic coast.

A Jew from Vienna recalled how, after he had been arrested, he was taken to the police station, where:

'Without having had anything to eat or drink we were loaded into omnibuses and taken to the South Station. Here we had to stand for some time in a draughty subway before we were taken to some third-class carriages waiting ready for us. The doors were locked behind us, and we were told that any attempts to open the windows would be met by immediate shots.

'The train travelled to Weimar non-stop. Here another wind began to blow as we moved from the hands of the police into those of the SS. Lorries took us from the station at Weimar to the camp at Buchenwald. . . .'

One of those deported to Sachsenhausen later recalled:

'A professor of mathematics, one of the new-comers, whose nerves could not stand the tension, became involved in a dispute with a guard. He was sentenced to a beating. The blows and the poor devil's shrieks of agony from the wooden horse to which he was fastened echoed throughout the night.'

By the end of the year, when most of those arrested were released, more than 1,000 had died at the hands of their tormentors.

Murder, burning and looting were not enough for the Nazis. New decrees were issued: no Jew was to be allowed in any public park, cinema, theatre or circus. No Jew was to be allowed to purchase jewelry or precious metal. In addition, all Jewish factories and workshops must be sold to non-Jews. Henceforth, no Jew could be either a manufacturer or a retailer.

Even on trains Jews were to be discriminated against. On 12 November while the embers of the burned synagogues were still warm, Goering summoned a high level conference at the Air Ministry. Among those present were five other Cabinet members: Joseph Goebbels, Minister of Propaganda; Walter Funk, Minister of Economics; Count Lutz Schwerin von Krosigk, Minister of Finance; Hans Frick, Minister of the Interior; and Franz Guertner, Minister of Justice. At one point during their discussion, Goebbels urged that if there were non-Jews in every compartment, any Jews on the train would have to stand in the corridor. The discussion continued:

Goering: 'I think it's much more reasonable to give them their own compartments.'
Goebbels: 'But not if the train is packed.'
Goering: 'Just a moment – there is only one Jewish carriage. If it's full, the others must stay at home.'
Goebbels: 'But let's assume that there aren't so many Jews travelling with the through train to Munich. Two Jews are sitting in the train and the other carriages are packed. Then these two Jews would have a private compartment. We must therefore say: the Jews can only claim a seat when all Germans are seated.'

Nazi youth watch as Viennese Jews are forced to scrub the streets in November 1938.

Jews being marched into Sachsenhausen concentration camp, in the striped uniform which all camp inmates had to wear.

Goering: 'I wouldn't make a special case of it but would prefer to give the Jews a carriage or a compartment. And if it ever did actually happen, as you say, that the train would otherwise be overfilled, then we don't need any law. The Jew will be chucked out, even if he has to spend the whole journey on the toilet.'

One final disaster followed in the wake of these events: the Jews were forced to pay a massive collective fine for all the damage done *against* them. Called by the Nazis the 'Jewish Atonement Fine', it stripped the Jews of Germany of virtually all their remaining assets: so much so that some of it had to be paid, not in cash, but in kind. The money seized was substantial: the equivalent of £100 million sterling, and it provided a much needed addition to the German rearmament budget.

2

Journey to Lublin

Hitler watches the advance of his troops into Poland on 1 September 1939.

On Friday, 1 September 1939, the German army invaded Poland; German aeroplanes bombed Warsaw and German tanks advanced deeply through the Polish countryside. The British Government, which had signed an alliance with Poland six days before, hoped, briefly, to avert the inevitable declaration of war by negotiations. The Soviet Union, which had just come to an agreement with Nazi Germany to partition Poland between them, likewise waited. The United States maintained its neutrality.

At various sea-front hotels in Hamburg, groups of more than a hundred German Jews were waiting to leave for the United States. The German authorities had granted them permission to leave, the United States authorities had granted them permission to land and they had bought tickets for a German boat. Now, in panic, they tried to buy tickets on a neutral boat, but could not do so.

On 3 September Britain and France declared war on Germany. The small groups of Jews on the Hamburg waterfront were forbidden to leave the hotels, and were then imprisoned. Although they had lived for almost the whole of the inter-war years in Germany, many of them had been born in Poland. As such, they were now declared to be 'enemy aliens'. On 15 September they were arrested, and imprisoned for five weeks, their only food throughout those weeks being bread and water. And then, shortly before midnight on 21 October, they began one of the first of what were to be so many war-time railway journeys across Germany and its conquered lands. One of the group, S. Mogilewer, who for twenty years had owned a small fur shop in Leipzig, and who had already spent some time as a prisoner in Buchenwald, recalled the course of that first journey:

'We are taken in wagons to a wayside depot somewhere off the beaten track, where they are loading freight cars. We are piled into one, all of us together. It is freezing cold and there is no light. We fumble around in the dark. The car stinks.

'Nobody has been allowed to take anything with him. The few belongings we had – the extra pair of shoes, a couple of shirts, a spare suit, the few clothes which one is allowed to take out of the Reich – have been seized as we left. Even our raincoats which we had carefully taken with us to the jail have become forfeit.

Top: German soldiers setting off for Poland. The writing on the carriage proclaims: 'We're off to Poland, to thrash the Jews.'
Below: Poland, 10 November 1939. A German soldier's 'sport', while all Jewish males over fifteen years of age were being rounded up for labour gangs, to clear the rubble caused by German bombardments.

'A clock strikes midnight. It begins to rain. We hear it pelting down on the roof of the car. The engine starts up and we are on the move. All around us there is a rattle of wheels. We seem to be hitched to a freight train.

'Presently, the movement stops and the train draws up at the tiniest and most insignificant wayside halt. We peer out of the window to catch a glimpse of what is going on. Trains are steaming in and out, laden with armaments. Tanks are lined up on the roadside. Troops keep pouring in on motorcycle and lorry. The whole of Germany has been turned overnight into a huge military camp. Every now and again the guards pass by outside our car and try the padlock.

'Twelve hours in the foul and filthy car. Not even a drop of water to drink. The few scraps of food we were able to buy at Hamburg with our last couple of marks have long since been exhausted. What we had has been divided among the women and children or given to the old people. We men have had nothing. For us it has been a real Day of Atonement.

'Suddenly the door of the freight car is opened. The captain of the guard pokes his head in and orders us all to get out. We form fours on the platform. The chief of the Berlin Gestapo calls the roll. One hundred and twenty-two "pieces of baggage." "No one dead?" he remarks ironically. "Wait till they get to Lublin, and we'll put them to bed with a shovel."

'It's the first time anyone has mentioned a destination. Now we hear it, we can scarcely believe our ears. What has Lublin to do with us? Naturally, we had heard of it. City in Poland. Once played a role in Jewish history. That's all. No one, of course, has the faintest idea that this is to be the capital of Hitler's "ghetto state", the republic that is somehow to rise from the ruins and smoke. For five weeks we have been cut off from the outside world and seen no papers.

'The formalities are over. We are herded back into the car, into our living grave.

'In heaven's name, we cry, what is to become of us? What does it all mean? Here we are, hungry and frozen, without a penny or a morsel of bread, without even a drop of water, and once again we are ordered out. This time they prod us in the back with the butts of their rifles. At four o'clock they stuff us in again and padlock the door. The train moves off. So there is no reprieve.

'In a corner of the truck, stifled sobbing. Every now and then a piercing shriek. Everywhere tears, everywhere terror. Presently pandemonium. People start knocking their heads against the walls. It goes on like this for a couple of hours. Then, a platform, crowds, human faces. People begin to hear us. They stop in their tracks. They look around.

'The bolt slides back. The Gestapo officer comes in. He is livid with rage. He wants to know the reason for the din. "We are hungry," cry some. "We want to know where we're going." "Where?" bellows the officer, foaming with rage. "To Lublin, of course, to the Jew state."

'Is the world gone crazy? It's the second time we've heard that name. Lublin. We are going to Lublin. A Jewish state. What does it all mean? Are we dreaming? Are we mad? A Jewish state in Lublin? Hitler the Saviour of the Jews? Hitler the Messiah?

'An order is rapped out. Whoever has money can buy food. Whoever hasn't can rot.

'We run through our pockets for our last few pennies and frenziedly hand them over. The Gestapo agent runs to the buffet. The place is cleaned out. Only sweets and chocolates. Better than nothing.

'The train moves on. Over and over again the

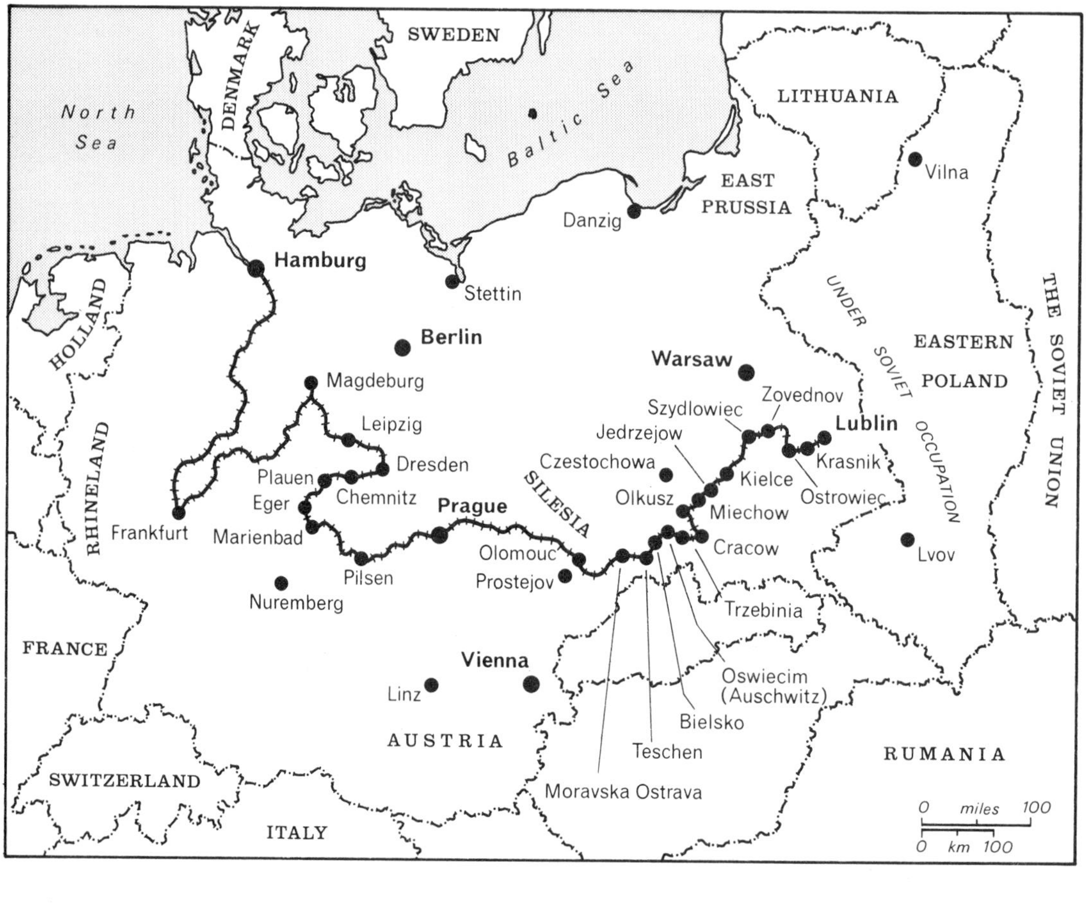

S. Mogilewer's journey from Hamburg to Lublin.

1939 / Folge 41 Illustrierter Beobachter Seite 1547

„. . . Zum siebenten: daß man den jungen starken Jüden und Jüdin in die Hand gebe Flegel, Axt, Karst, Spaten, Rocken, Spindel, und lasse sie ihr Brod verdienen im Schweiß der Nasen . . .“

Dr. Martin Luther

„Von den Jüden und ihren Lügen“

Sechzehn Mann hoch schieben einen Steinkarren.

Dem polnischen Bauern das reife Getreide und die fetten Schweine abzuhandeln, das haben sie besser verstanden. Jetzt verdienen sie sich das erstemal auf anständige Art ihr Brot.

Top: a German illustrated magazine shows a Jewish labour gang in Poland. The magazine quoted Martin Luther: 'Let the young and strong Jews and Jewesses be given the flail, the axe, the hoe, the spade, the distaff and spindle, and let them earn their bread by the sweat of their noses. . .' The caption read: 'It took sixteen men to pull one truckload of stones. Once they knew all too well how to haggle with a Polish peasant in order to get his grain – and his fat pigs. Now for the first time they are earning their bread in a decent way!'

Below: German soldiers watch as Jews are forced to sweep manure in German-occupied Poland.

word Lublin is muttered. But now it is not merely Lublin. It is the Jewish state. The words ring like magic. Now, at least, our journey has point. Instead of New York, Philadelphia or Chicago, they are taking us to Lublin. One hundred and twenty-two Jewish souls packed in a filthy freight car.

'We decide to choose a representative, someone who will speak for us. The choice falls on Dr K. of Plauen. Dr K. has a sister in Hollywood. He was going to join her, but like the rest of us got trapped in Hamburg. Dr K. accepts the office and agrees to become our spokesman.'

'The train rattles on, into eternity it seems. The greater part of us already are sick, prey to hunger, cold, and dirt. Frankfurt, Magdeburg, Leipzig flash by. We have been travelling for four days. At last we come to Dresden. It is early morning and bitterly cold. With the last remnants of our strength we hammer on the door and implore the guards to open it.

'So far, our Gestapo guards have at least been human. Their task is barbarous enough, to be sure, and their treatment none too gentle, but they are at least human beings. At Dresden all this is over. The Dresden guards are sadists, pure and simple.

' "Shoot us," pleads Dr K. "Shoot us, for mercy's sake, but spare us this barbarism. We are at the end of our strength."

'The answer, a blow till the blood runs.

' "Shoot me, you beasts," cries the doctor, his breath failing. "Shoot me, you murderers!"

'All this on the open platform, with hundreds of Germans carelessly looking on. Nobody lifts a finger. Mothers with half-dead children in their arms whine piteously. But no one takes any notice.

'We look awful. No one has had anything to eat or drink for days. No one has washed. We have "existed", in the most literal sense of the word, on the few sweets bought at the buffet.

'Weak and shivering with cold, we crawl out of the freight car and lie down on the bare rails. Those who are too ill to move stay inside, writhing and moaning in the darkness. The scene is like a battlefield.

'A large crowd of local Gestapo agents gather around our car, attracted by the cries from within. They start to investigate. There is something of a hubbub. It is not quite clear what is happening. Apparently some members of the Jewish community council in Dresden have arrived with food and clothing and with water to bathe our wounds.

'Suddenly, as they are helping the weaker ones from the truck, pandemonium breaks out. They have stumbled over two dead bodies lying among the sick and exhausted. One is that of a Hungarian, forty-two years old, Fritz L. of Castle. The other is a veteran of seventy on the way to his son in Chicago. We had been travelling with two corpses and had not noticed it.

'A group arrives from the Dresden Jewish Burial Society and removes the two victims to the local cemetery, to lie in that foreign soil, a witness forever to a people's sorrow.

'I should like to say here that many of the Dresden folk who witnessed the murderous assault on Dr K. would no doubt have reacted sympathetically if only someone had had the common courage to offer an open protest. Their expressions showed clearly what they felt, and several averted their eyes. But no one had the necessary courage. Nevertheless, it ought in fairness to be mentioned that it was these Dresden folk who actually called up the Jewish community and told them of our presence at the station.

'I should also like to make it clear that in speaking of the Dresden community I do so only metaphorically. In point of fact, with the single exception of Berlin, there is no formal Jewish community in any German city. Instead, there are merely small groups of Jewish members of the various burial societies who stay on to bury one another and to help the living whenever an "emergency" arises. Were it not for the help of our great-hearted brethren of Dresden, it is safe to say that we would all have died of hunger that very day.

'The Dresden Jews have already heard of the Lublin project, but they are not impressed. Healthy instinct has murmured the truth in their ears. "There won't be a Jewish state", whispers

February 1940: a German soldier stands guard as Polish Jews are forced to dig graves in the snow for the Jewish dead.

the head of the community, as the doctors lift down the bodies. "It will be another ghetto, an *all*-Jewish concentration camp."

'For the first time light dawns. So that is the Lublin idea. A giant camp in which to die. Then why this long journey? Why the trouble? I had just as well be one of the two men who had just been buried.

'The wheels of our freight car clatter once more. In every corner of the car men and women are lying, weals on their faces and their bodies bruised from the blows of the Nazi sadists at Dresden. Many have their heads swathed in bandages. Worst of all is the case of Dr K. He lies in a corner of the truck literally crumpled with pain. His entire face, hands and feet begin to swell and then slowly to shrink and shrivel.

'I stare at Dr K. There is a curious look in his one open eye. People have it when they are about to die. I tell some of the others. They notice it too.

'There are seven doctors among us. They can all do something, but they have nothing with which to work. They gather around him and feel his pulse. The worst becomes clear. He will go out like a snuffed candle unless relief comes quickly. The situation is critical and bewildering. Our train crawls along like a tortoise, stopping at every tiny station. What can we do?

'The train pulls up. We batter on the door. The Gestapo agent tears in, waving one hand like a madman and brandishing a pistol in the other. He threatens to kill us. They want no "revolutions" on this trip.

'"We are making none," we begin to protest. "There's a sick man here, and he needs help badly. We can save him but we need supplies."

'"You needn't bother," comes the answer. "Let him rot with the rest of you." And the door slams shut.'

'We have been going for five days and are only just on the line to Chemnitz. In normal times the journey from Hamburg to Chemnitz takes at most seventy-two hours by express. We begin to wonder whether we are really bound for Lublin. The route seems to be so roundabout. We ought to be travelling to Breslau. Everyone gets the jitters.

'All of a sudden one of the women lets out a piercing shriek. She has noticed a film forming over Dr K.'s eyes. Presently, there is a gurgling noise. The third victim of this journey to Lublin has fallen into everlasting sleep. *Baruch dayyan emeth!* Blessed be the Infallible Judge!

'We cover his bandaged face and begin to mourn. A young boy says *kaddish*, the mourner's prayer. His voice cuts like a knife. This is no *kaddish*. It is an oath, an oath to avenge a human life ended so pitifully and so alone, and a human being flung like a dog into a nameless grave.

'It is nearly 4 pm. We pull in to Chemnitz. The guards have already called up the local Jewish burial society. Two men come to fetch the body. The burial is a lonely business. There is no service and there are no mourners. Many of us actually envy our martyred comrade. He has paid his bill and left. In a corner of the Chemnitz graveyard he at least has found rest. But for us there is the endless road into exile.

'The burial society at Chemnitz makes us a gift of 100 marks and a little food. . . .

'At Chemnitz they change guards. The Gestapo are replaced by the Brownshirts. The difference is only one of colour; the nature is the same.

'According to plan we should be off again at seven. But when the time comes an order is issued to divide the transport in half. To relieve congestion, sixty of us are to go into another freight car. At last we can stretch our weary limbs.

'I am ordered to stay in the first car. The two are hitched together, and we start off.

'It is now the night of 26 October, and we are nearing Eger in Sudetenland. All of a sudden we discover that the second truck has vanished. To this day I don't know when it was unhitched or why. I only know that when we got to Eger and the door was opened so that the guard could come in and count us, I took a hurried glance at either side and there was no truck to be seen!

'I ask the guard, a young hooligan, and receive the dry reply: "They've been sent back."

' "Where to?" I am wild with curiosity. The answer is a shrug of the shoulders.

'I decide to find out the truth at all costs. I make him an offer. "Take 25 marks (part of the 100 given us at Chemnitz) and wire the Jewish community at Prague. Tell them to meet us at the station with food."

'The young hooligan does not want to take the risk. He says he will ask the commandant and makes off towards the waiting-room. A moment later he is back again. Everything is fixed.

'I begin to feel easier. The fellow may be all right. So I try him again about the missing truck. "They've shunted it to Nuremberg," he replies. More he doesn't know. He can't say what has happened to the people inside.

'The train puts on speed. Marienbad flashes by, an ethereal city of a bygone story. We came to Pilsen in Czech territory. About two kilometres from Pilsen is the border between Germany proper and the Protectorate of Bohemia and Moravia. We have to go through the customs. The door of our freight car slides back. Czech officials come aboard. With them are special officers of the Finance Department, which controls importation of money. They inspect the curious human baggage. I see in their eyes the impression it makes. They don't bother to ask us if we are hungry. They see it in our wan and pallid faces and in our staring eyes. They fetch us milk and tea and other refreshments from the canteen. While they are handing these out, their eyes fill with tears. But they say nothing. The Gestapo agent stands beside them, and they have to be careful.

'The formalities are over. We are off again. It is a brilliant shining afternoon and the territory of the Protectorate lies bathed in sunlight. We feel curiously light, almost sprightly. The sun is greater than Hitler, and more enduring.'

'Saturday, 28 October. About 10 am. We have reached Prague. Once again we are shunted to a siding to avoid exciting popular interest. Officials of the Jewish community in Prague are there to meet us. Everywhere, everywhere, in Dresden, in Chemnitz, in Pilsen and now in Prague, the scattered remnant of the community comes to our rescue. Everywhere there is the same Jewish brotherhood, the same solidarity of Israel. In a few moments our car is transformed into a canteen.

'But our luck is short-lived. In less than an hour we behold at that same station a scene which sends shivers down our spines. A group, surrounded by Nazi guards, is being herded toward our car. Presently, seventy persons step aboard, men, women and children. They have just come in from Vienna and are being shifted like us to Lublin.

'Again the old foul congestion.

'The newcomers make a shocking impression. Most of them look like us after our seven-week journey. They are all in tatters, hungry, thirsty, ill and broken. Without exception they look like living corpses. To come from Vienna to Prague has taken them five days! Like us, they too were bundled into a freight car as if they were the vilest criminals. And this only after tramping a good part of the way on foot. They spent a whole night in an open field, closely guarded by Gestapo agents. Three of them died there and were buried in a common grave, upon soil unknown and unmarked. Within two hours nothing was left of our provisions. Like hungry wolves they fell upon our bread, butter, cheese and eggs. Nothing was eaten, everything was devoured.

'They tell us that for the past two weeks Jews have been rounded up in Vienna and sent to Lublin. Throngs of Nazis poured into Jewish streets and houses and arrested the inhabitants *en masse*. They preferred to take the wealthier middle-class folk who owned property. These they fleeced of everything. Their wives and children had to go about barefoot and in rags. Only then were they regarded as suitable for emigration to Lublin. The seventy newcomers were, in fact, the aristocrats of the Vienna community.

'We are nearing Olomouc. Will we be met there? Are there still Jews in that city to have pity on our plight?

'At 2 am we eventually pull in. Wonder of wonders! Despite the hour, two aged members of the local burial society are there on the platform with food and a *Sefer Torah* (scroll) wrapped in a *tallith* (prayer shawl). "It is the last *Sefer Torah* in the city," they tell us, the tears welling in their eyes. "We too have been hounded like you. People are fleeing for their lives. Take this scroll as a memorial of our ruin. Take it as a gift on your wanderings, and may God deliver you out of their hands!"

'Scarcely have they finished speaking than the wheels begin to grind and we are off.

'And so we have a *Sefer Torah*, a memorial of older, happier days in the Moravian city of Olomouc. Time was when it housed a large Jewish settlement. Now there is nothing but a wilderness. The school was burned down the very night the Germans marched in. Jewish shops have been "Aryanized". The 2,000 Jews of Olomouc have fled. All that is left – watchmen of ruin – are a handful of old men.

'The two men tell us also that from the neighbouring city of Prostejov – formerly known as the Czechoslovakian Manchester and the seat of a prosperous community – all Jews have fled. Several of the more prominent manufacturers have been arrested, and many have already died.

'From Olomouc to Moravska Ostrava usually takes about an hour and a half by express. In our case it takes the better part of a day. The train stops not only at every wayside station, but also in midroute. Remember, it is the beginning of the German-Polish war. Armaments and troops are being rushed to the western front and the main lines are therefore closed. Trains are being held up for hours on end, and the congestion is especially heavy at Moravska Ostrava, which is a leading junction.

'Hour after hour a succession of freight trains flash by with Jews herded in the filthy cars and driven like us to the concentration camp-ghetto of Lublin. It is impossible to tell how many go by.

'On several of the cars there are legends scribbled in chalk: "Danger! Consignment of dirty Jews!" "Hands off! Jews in transit." On some of the cars yellow flags with a large black Star of David in the centre have been hoisted. On them are emblazoned the words, "Jews will be destroyed by German Kultur."

'To see these things through the tiny airhole of our locked car is far worse than going without food or drink. It is crueller than death and more bestial. It is death of the nerves. A man can be as tough as they come, but there are some things he just can't take. This is one of them. To this day I can't figure out how I kept sane.

'At last we come to Moravska Ostrava. We are

shunted, as usual, to a siding. But we are not alone. During the past few days similar transports have been pouring in from all parts of the Reich, and there are now about fifty lined up in a row. They are not locked as on the journey, but open, though heavily guarded by SA Brownshirts and by local Nazis distinguished by red armbands.

'I should say there are at least 4,000 Jews packed in the freight cars. The scene resembles nothing so much as a giant Gipsy camp. All around stand women wringing dirty clothes. Pots of tea are boiling over open fires. Men stand around in their light summer clothing, and women and children in tatters and barefoot shiver in the open cold. It is a sight which will live in my memory forever. No man forgets such things as long as he lives.

'Most remarkable of all, not one of the 4,000 souls utters a word. Conversation is forbidden and nobody dares to disobey. Even the children seem to sense the necessity for silence. After all, they come from the Reich. They have learned what Nazism is. Only their eyes speak, and in their eyes is the tale of all our yesterdays and – who knows? – all our tomorrows.

'People are dying all around us and not of natural causes. Many do away with themselves, usually the younger people, mere boys and girls. They slash their wrists at night when no one can see, and never wake up.

'The guards lift the dead from the cars with complete nonchalance. One day there are three; another five; a third, seven, and once, as many as sixteen. On the night of 30 October there were twenty-two suicides in those fifty freight cars. One of the suicides is a mother with her three-year-old child, Gertrude Clemenski. She lived in Vienna in the Storkgasse. Husband, forty-two years old, was bundled into another freight car. Disappeared *en route*. Body thrown out at Moravska Ostrava. Wife slashes her wrists. Takes the child with her. The world is too much with us.

'Still, we don't die of hunger. The Czechs help us as much as they can. No one is allowed to look into our car to see how things really are. So they have to guess our needs. They bring us bread, tea, potatoes and milk for the children. Also, most blessed gift, a piece of soap to wash our clothes. The Brownshirts scowl at them, but they are not frightened. Forbidden to come near, they throw the things in at us. They even bring old rugs and clothes. And all the while there are tears in their eyes.'

'Tuesday afternoon, 31 October. A sudden commotion outside our freight car. A group of Gestapo officers and Brownshirts, with captains of the Voluntary Labour Corps and about 100 sergeants of the special "Jew Police" drive up in limousines. We are ordered to get out and form fours, men and women separately. They run through the list of our names and check particulars.

'An order is barked out. "Doctors, engineers and technicians, one pace forward!"

'About 200 men answer. They are divided into squads. "You fellows are in charge until Lublin," raps out the commandant. "All aboard!"

'In a few moments we are back in the car. The door is slammed and locked. An hour later we hear an engine puffing in, and presently we are off. Some of our fellow travellers have been held at Ostrava for a fortnight. In our case, fortunately, it was only two days.

'Now it seems we are really bound for Lublin. The train is divided into two halves of twenty-five cars each, since a single engine cannot pull the lot. Presently we are at Teschen, the frontier between Czechoslovakia and Poland.

'From there we go on to Bielsko, the great textile centre of Polish Silesia. Then on to Oswiecim [Auschwitz], Trzebinia and Cracow. The stations make a dreary impression. There is not a soul on the platforms except soldiers and German police guarding the junctions. The normal hurry and bustle of a busy station is strangely absent. Cracow alone seems a bit more lively, but that is because it is a main junction and is being used for Jewish transports like ours.

'We wait in Cracow for about six hours, but no one is there to meet us. Not a Jewish face to be seen on the platform for love or money. The reason comes out later. Cracow is one of the places where the Nazis are especially strong. The

Jewish property is burned in the central square of the small Polish town of Myslenice while a German soldier stands guard. This photograph was taken by Hitler's personal photographer, Heinrich Hoffman, and was issued by him as postcard no 95 of his series 'The Soldiers of the Führer on Active Service', with the caption 'Lice-ridden Jewish beds being burned'.

Jews dare not show their faces. They spend their days huddled together in cellars and basements.

'Our route lies over the lands of the Polish peasantry. An autumn drizzle is falling. Everywhere a scene of desolation and rapine meets the eye. Cities and villages lie in ruins. Nothing remains of the houses but battered walls and broken chimney stacks outlined gauntly here and there against the evening sky.

'Olkusz, Miechow and Jedrzejow are at present pretty well intact. They have not suffered the same destruction as the other cities through which we pass. But as we pull in to the several stations the same spectacle confronts us at each one. There are no passengers waiting for trains and only a handful of soldiers. But there are crowds of Jews, men, women and children, working on the lines or carrying stones, all closely guarded by the Brownshirts.

'We reach Kielce, another spot where the lines

Lublin, capital of the Nazi-designated 'Jewish State'. An elderly Jew (*above*) is forced to stand by the synagogue gates with the synagogue's ornamental Star of David around his neck. *Opposite above:* Nazis watch while a Gestapo officer, named on the back of the photograph as Funker Griese, 'lectures' Lublin Jews with a stick, having first made the front row go down on their knees to be photographed.

cross. Here, as at Cracow there is a great deal of stir and bustle. Jewish transports from German Silesia and the Czestochowa zone come pouring in. It is the coordinating centre for the movement to Lublin.

'So far as I can see, the renowned German *Pünktlichkeit* – punctuality – is everywhere conspicuous by its absence. Instead, there is about this whole business nothing but muddle and confusion. Instructions seem to be issued wholesale without the slightest regard for the technical problems involved. There is a general order to get the Jews to Lublin, but not the faintest semblance of an organization to do so. People are merely pushed into trains and left to travel about aimlessly for weeks on end. . . .

'As we leave Kielce, the now familiar spectacle of ruin again presents itself. Everywhere you see shell holes and large cavities in the ground, sometimes also broken and discarded pieces of military equipment. In one place, not far from Zovednow we see a mass of Polish tanks lying abandoned in holes, with all kinds of ammunition scattered around.

'What strikes one most is the number of devastated churches. I should say, as a rough estimate, that of those we passed between Cracow and Lublin, at least 90 per cent were in ruins. It seems to have been an avowed aim of the German invaders to wreck every Polish place of worship they could find. This was especially evident in smaller towns like Szydlowiec, Krasnik and Ostrowiec.

'2 November, about 2 pm. At last we reach Lublin, capital of the new Jewish state.'

There is no pen wielded by man which can write even the thousandth part of the horror that is Lublin. Lublin is a vale of sorrows. No living beings are they who walk its streets. All are shadows, phantoms haunting a world that is ended. Nobody speaks in Lublin; nobody passes a greeting. They have even ceased to weep.

'Lublin has been turned into a vast concentration camp, the most terrible that the world has ever seen. In normal times Lublin has a population of 72,000 Gentiles and 40,000 Jews. Today, the number of Jews cannot be computed. It must run into at least 200,000, perhaps a quarter of a million. The congestion, the stench, the poverty, the disease and the chaos which reign in Lublin cannot be paralleled anywhere else on earth. Men live in the streets, in cattle stalls, in cellars, in carts and in the debris of devastated houses. You see their clothes hanging on trees along the main streets.

'Men die like flies in the thoroughfares, their bodies strewn on the roadway like burned out cinders. Shrouds are no longer used for the dead because none can be bought. At night everything is pitch black. The electric cables were smashed in the bombardment, and when they were repaired

Members of the SS enjoy the sight of two elderly Jews having their beards shaved off.

Polish Jews stopped at random in the streets of Lublin, and ordered to give the Nazi salute.

later, there was no coal to keep the power stations going.

'Chairs, wardrobes, even beds have long since been chopped up for firewood. Window panes have been shattered, and there is no glass to mend them. Icy winds whistle through the desolate houses. Foodstuffs are unobtainable. The whole city is girt with barbed-wire fences, and the Nazis allow no traffic to pass through. The water has turned foul and cannot be drunk. All the wells have become polluted.

'Cholera and typhus are already rampant when we reach Lublin. Men die like flies faster than one can bury them. Hundreds and thousands of bodies are thrown together into mass graves. Actually, there are sufficient doctors in the city to stem the epidemic, but they lack the barest necessities in the way of bandages, drugs, instruments and, above all, beds. The cemeteries are over-crowded. At least 1,000 Jews have fallen victim to the plague in the last two weeks. No one knows how it all will end.

'The authorities are well aware of what is going on. They feigned ignorance at first, but when the epidemic spread to their own ranks they had to sit up and take notice. The International Red Cross was at last allowed to bring in provisions and sanitary appliances. Drugs and medical instruments are distributed wholesale. Jewish doctors work day and night. Indeed, it is only their self-sacrificing labour and the open-handed help of the Red Cross that has saved Lublin from being turned within a few weeks into a morgue. But even they cannot reach everyone.

'The Jewish engineers and technicians, the very ones who were ordered at Moravska Ostrava to superintend the transport, have succeeded in clearing a space outside the city and in setting up a number of wooden huts as a protection from the cold. The work goes on feverishly for ten and more hours a day. The women band together and cook whatever they can gather. By poetic license we call the product "vegetable stew", but it has a million flavours. The communal soup kitchen run by the Jewish authorities can actually serve nothing but potato broth and stale black bread, but even this diet succeeds in sustaining thousands of lives.

'The refugees from Germany and Austria prove especially resourceful in building these wooden huts, constructed mainly from floorboards and posts retrieved from the general debris. Roofs are fashioned out of old straw and corrugated iron. The biggest problem is that of heating.

'Earlier arrivals begin to gather round in order to share the benefits of our efforts. All are in the sorriest plight, victims of the most wretched destitution. Hundreds have not slept for weeks, cramped and coffined in noisy freight cars. They wander about sad-eyed and distraught, like mourners at funerals. Many of them are alone, their wives or children having been killed in the bombardment. Brothers and sisters come without parents, wives without husbands, little children without father or mother, left utterly desolate in a brutal and rapacious world. Their situation is even worse than ours. One thing only is clear as day: the devil alone could have devised such hell. The seven tortures of the damned are there before your eyes. Lublin is a giant concentration camp where people spend their days trying to dig their way out of a living grave.

'Unobserved by the guards in and around Lublin, thousands of men, mostly youngsters, daily take their lives in their hands and try to escape from this ghetto-hell. Most of them make their way across the Soviet border, hiding in the fields by day and creeping on all fours at night. It takes them a week or more, but as a rule they get through. There are, however, exceptions. Sometimes the patrols catch them, and then these "deserters", as they are called, are invariably shot. . . .'

'15 November. I have been in Lublin for a fort-

Lublin: cutting the hair of a young orthodox Jew, for whom the wearing of long hair was part of his religious custom.

night. Suddenly my name is called. I tremble in every limb. My wife loses control of herself and begins to shriek. She is sure of the worst.

'A Nazi shouts at me to report at the superintendent's office. "Pack your stuff," he adds, "you're off."

'I think the fellow is kidding. The devil is having his joke. I must be going to Sachsenhausen or Spandau or Dachau or to my old "home", Buchenwald.

'The guard is serious after all. "Word has come from Warsaw", he explains. "You're to be let out. The wife and child can go with you. Seems you've got a visa for the United States, or something. The American Consul's intervened."

'I can scarcely believe my ears. Am I dreaming?

'Presently, one of the Red Cross, a Swiss, comes over and taps me on the shoulder. "It's all right", he says. "You're going to the United States all right. The Consul in Warsaw has spoken for you. He's got a ticket waiting and 100 marks for the journey. Get the express to Cracow and go on from there to Linz. Then you can catch the through train to Genoa. You'll have to wait, though, for the boat."

'There are moments in life when excitement can drive a man crazy. This is one of them. The Red Cross man understands. He tells it all over again. And then once more. He has to assure me it's true. Even that isn't enough. He tells me he'll go with us to Cracow.

'It takes me but a moment to collect my things. To tell the truth, there's precious little left. I say goodbye to the others, get my papers – and I am out of Lublin and hell.'

Mogilewer and his wife had escaped from 'Lublinland', and at the end of December they reached the United States. There, in the first week of January, Mogilewer published a full account in a leading New York Yiddish newspaper, of all that he had experienced and seen.

For those tens of thousands of Jews who remained in Lublin, or who had been deported from their homes in western Poland to other towns in the newly established General Government, unimaginable cruelties were still in store. Since 15 November 1939, following a conference under the chairmanship of the head of the General Government, Hans Frank, the entire railway network of the new State had been put at the disposal of the 'resettlement' policy. The aim of this policy was to deport all Jews, Gipsies and Poles from Germany itself, and from the Polish territories being annexed by Germany.

In January 1940, as the chaos of moving so many people began to subside, a memorandum prepared by the General Government expressed its 'willingness' to receive a million Jews within its borders: 400,000 were to be brought from Germany, Austria, the Sudetenland and the Protectorate, and 600,000 from the newly annexed territories of western Poland. Once Germany had been victorious in Europe, the memorandum declared, the Jews could be sent elsewhere, 'possibly to Madagascar', to make room for German settlers, while all 'superfluous Poles' could be sent to Siberia.

The Jews were now being driven out of cities and towns in which they had lived for centuries. At a conference held in Berlin on 12 February 1940, under the chairmanship of Goering and in the presence of Himmler, one of the Nazis present, the *Gauleiter* of Danzig, Albert Forster, proudly announced that he had only 1,800 Jews left in his city. Yet this was a Jewish community dating back to the fifteenth century which had numbered more than 9,000 before Hitler had come to power in Germany, and had, since the First World War, been protected by the minority rights statute of the League of Nations, under whose auspices Danzig had been made a Free City. But in 1937, Forster had dismissed the Jews from all the professions, and in 1938, on the Night of Broken Glass, he had ensured that the city's synagogues were a main target.

The powers to expel and to deport Jews were now substantial, and the areas available for 'resettlement' were increased. The fate of the Jews had fallen into the hands of a group of men, fanatical haters of all things Jewish, suddenly finding themselves with enormous power, backed by the full weight of a successful military machine.

In the region of the newly created General Government, Hans Frank made as his first aim the destruction of one of the largest and oldest Jewish communities in central Europe, the 60,000 Jews of Cracow, together with a further 20,000 Jews who had found refuge there. Frank's aim, as he himself told a conference of his Nazi subordinates on 12 April 1940, was to 'cleanse' the Jewish quarter in such a way that Germans could live there, breathing 'German air'. For the Jewish citizens of Cracow, the city had always been their home; it had been a flourishing Jewish centre for hundreds of years; it was their work and schooling, their family life, their culture and their religious centre.

For four months, Hans Frank encouraged the Jews to leave Cracow without compulsion, and even announced that they could take their belongings with them. But few could make use of the 'opportunity' to escape. They were not allowed to go to Germany or western Poland, and emigration

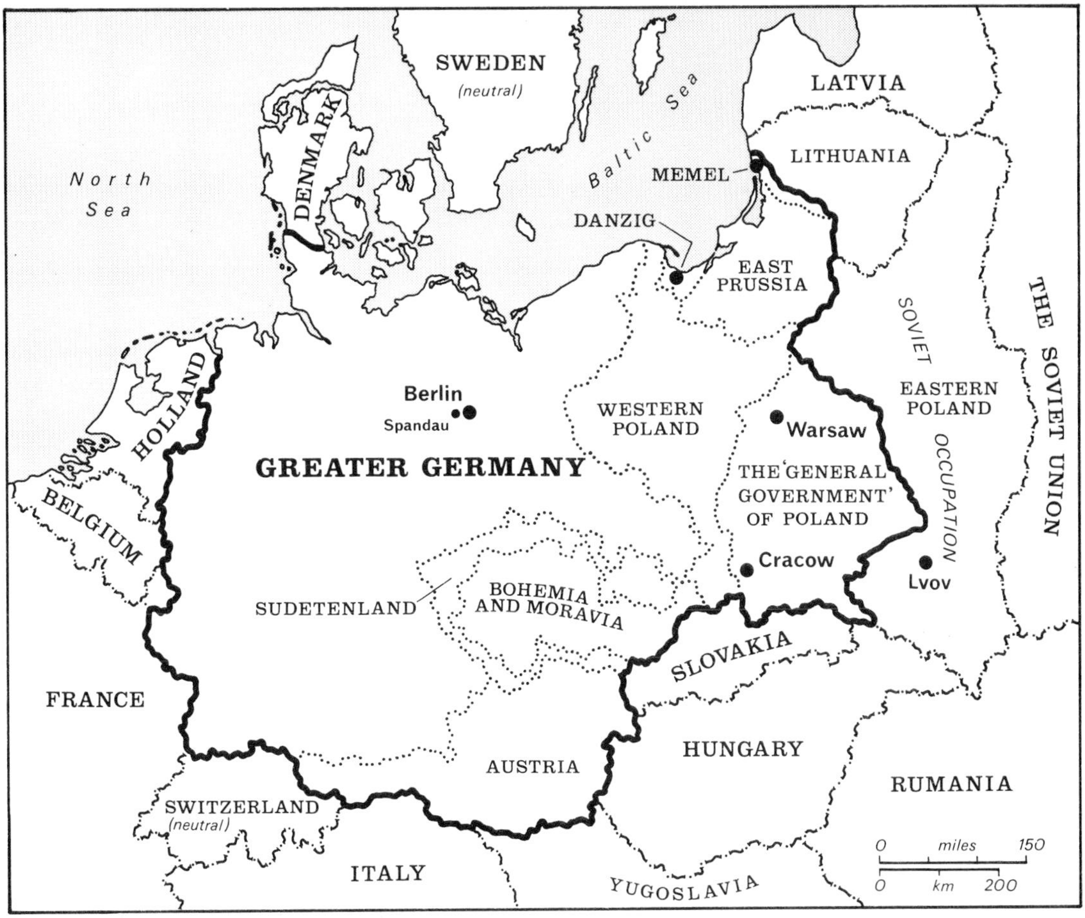

The borders of Greater Germany after the defeat and partition of Poland.

was impossible. To go east was to risk further deportation, and to court the uncertainty of perpetual flight.

The Nazis had no need to rely on voluntary movement, and on 6 August 1940 the General Government announced in the Cracow daily paper that any Jews still in Cracow in nine days' time would be subjected to what was called 'organized' expulsion, with only limited amounts of luggage, to places chosen by the administration. It was simply intolerable, Frank declared on the last day of the 'voluntary' policy, for the representatives of Hitler's Germany to live in a city which was 'crawling' with Jews to such an extent that no 'decent person' could step into the street.

By the end of September 1940 more than 32,000 Jews had been expelled from Cracow. But Frank was not satisfied with this rate of 'progress', and on 25 November 1940 a further 11,000 Jews were ordered to leave – to abandon their houses, shops and businesses, and leave behind all but a handful of their possessions. To ensure a greater efficiency than hitherto, the new expulsions were arranged alphabetically. All those heads of families whose surnames began with the letters A to D were to report for resettlement on 2 December; all those with letters E to J on 4 December, and so on.

In this way, yet more thousands of Jews began a journey, the end of which no one could forecast. Uprooted from their houses and streets, deprived of their means of earning a living, cut off from their schools and synagogues, the Jews of Cracow joined with the Jews of hundreds of other towns and villages, adrift in a hostile world from which there was little chance of escape. A few were able to cross into the Soviet-occupied eastern region of Poland. A tiny handful were able to flee into the Balkans. But neither Russia nor the Balkans was necessarily anything but a temporary resting place; the German army occupied Yugoslavia and Greece in April 1941, and invaded Russia two months later. Expulsion, followed by wandering from place to place, had become the pattern of life of tens of thousands of Jewish families.

3

Journey from Jassy

In 1941 the city of Jassy was the largest city in eastern Rumania. Its Jewish community had been founded more than 400 years before, and had provided a haven for Jews fleeing from the widespread Cossack persecutions of 1648. But in 1650, and again in 1652, the Cossacks had come to Jassy itself, and many Jews had been murdered in the city. Later, caught up in the wars between Russia and Turkey, the Jews of Jassy suffered further hardships and deportation. In 1726 the mob had plundered the Jewish quarter, set fire to the synagogue and tortured several of the older Jews, in order to obtain their money. In 1803, threatened with massacre, the Jews of Jassy had been saved at the last moment by the intervention of the Archbishop, who declared that the mob would have to cross his dead body to reach the Jews. In 1822 the entire Jewish quarter was burned to the ground. But even the anti-Jewish feelings of the later nineteenth century, and the continued emigration of local Jews to the United States and Western Europe, could not halt the growth of the community, and by 1917 there were 35,000 Jews in Jassy, out of a total population of 76,000.

For the Jews, Jassy had long been a spiritual centre, where biblical scholarship and religious learning had flourished. It was also a centre of modern Jewish culture. Both Hebrew and Yiddish newspapers were published in the city, and the Yiddish theatre was a focal point of talent, and entertainment.

But for the Jews of Jassy, daily life had its darker side, for the city had become a noted centre of anti-semitic activity. In 1882 and 1884, two 'economic congresses' had been held, aimed at imposing a boycott on all Jewish commerce and industry, and succeeding in forcing many Jewish shops to close down. The University of Jassy became a centre of Rumanian anti-semitism: in 1900 Alexander Cuza, the founder of the Universal Anti-Semitic Alliance, became a teacher there, and ten years later formed a political party, one of whose main aims was to remove all Jews from professional life, from the army, and from the villages.

Between the wars Cuza's influence grew, as did the anti-Jewish feeling. Extreme anti-semitism led to the formation in Jassy, in 1927, of the Archangel Michael League, later called the Iron Guard, which set about, as deliberate policy, forcing the Jews out of Rumanian life. During the 1930s many of the Jews of Jassy, for whom daily life was becoming an increasing struggle against boycott, prejudice and physical violence, sought refuge in emigration. They went to the United States, to western Europe and to Palestine, and by 1939 the Jewish population, which in 1921 had risen to over 43,000, had fallen back to 35,000.

When the German armies invaded Poland in September 1939, Rumania remained neutral. But just over a year later, on 6 November 1940, power was seized by Marshal Ion Antonescu, a violent anti-semite. On 8 November Jassy was proclaimed the capital of the Iron Guard. Immediately, Jews were arrested, tortured, forced to surrender their businesses and subjected to whatever indignity the whim of the Iron Guard dictated. It was only in return for an enormous ransom that the Iron Guard agreed to halt the persecution.

In the early months of 1941, Antonescu's government drew closer to Nazi Germany and German troops arrived in Jassy as part of the

The Rumanian city of Jassy, and the deportation journey which began on 30 June 1941.

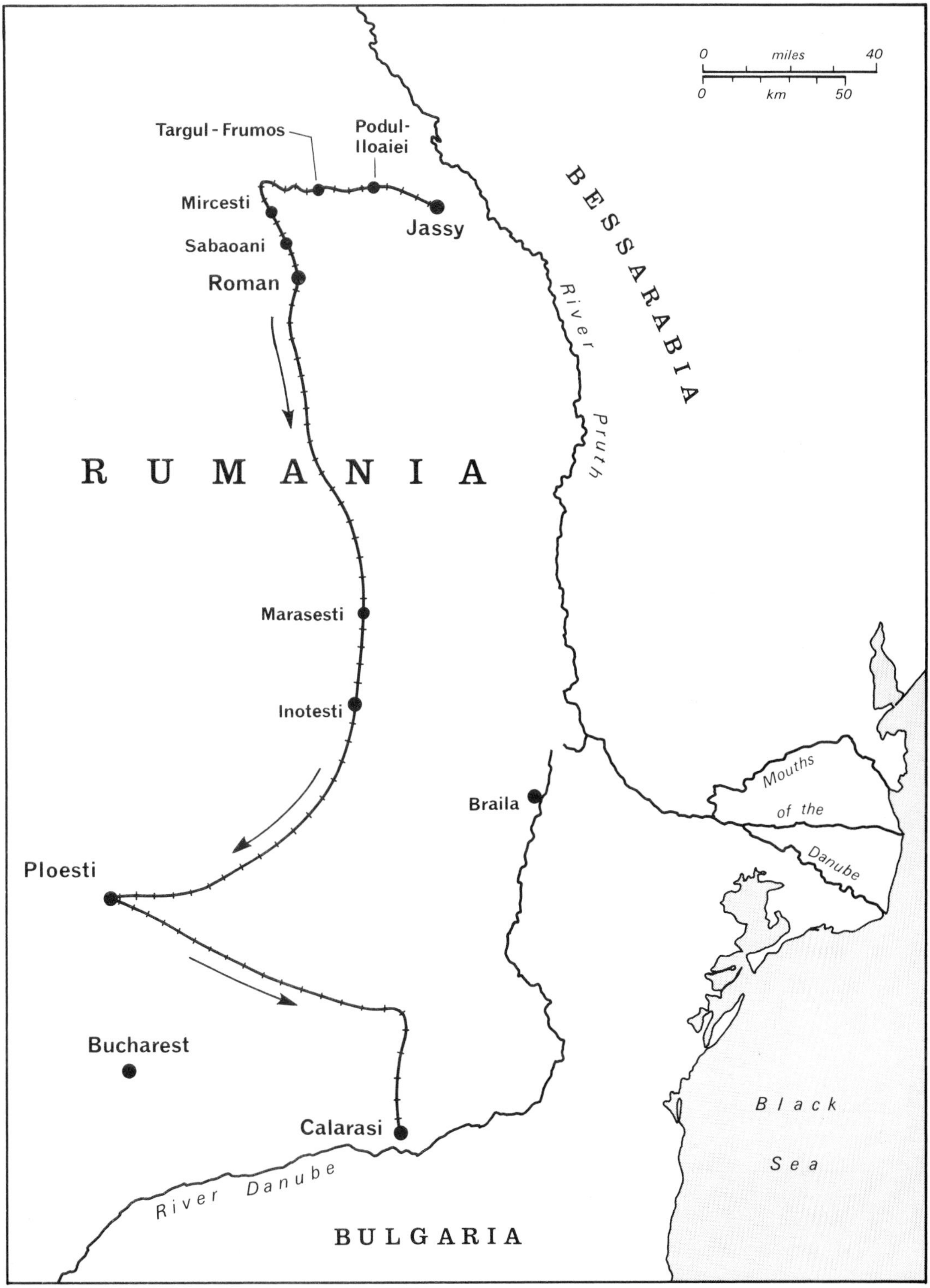

At a halt during the railway journey from Jassy, the bodies of Jews who have died during the journey lie at the side of the track, while those who have survived the journey so far are allowed briefly to leave the train.

forthcoming German offensive against the Soviet Union. Then, on the evening of 28 June 1941, Rumanian police, helped by local citizens, rampaged through the streets of Jassy, murdering several hundred Jews at random and arresting over 6,000 more.

The torment of the Jews of Jassy had begun. Now it was to reach a grim climax which few were to survive. One of those who escaped later described what happened to him, and to more than 6,000 others, on the morning of 29 June 1941. He himself had been ordered to the police station, to apply for a permit which would give him the right of 'free movement'. Such a permit, he was told, might save him from death. On his way to the police station he met a group of about 400 Jews, who were being marched to the police station, with their hands over their heads. In his recollections he wrote:

'Their faces were smeared with blood, testifying to the kind of ordeal through which they had passed. The policemen held pistols in their hands and pointed them at the victims. Near the police building five or six Germans of the Todt organization stood waiting for them with heavy sticks in their hands. As the group of Jews passed by they showered heavy blows on the unfortunate victims, aiming at their heads. Whoever stumbled and fell, was instantly shot.

'After six thousand Jews had finally been gathered in the yard of the police building, the policemen and gendarmes opened fire on them. Those who escaped the bullets were brought to the railway station before dark; but many were shot by the assassins on the way. After reaching the station, the Jews were told to lie down on the ground; then the murderers systematically started despoiling them of all their belongings: money, jewels, documents, etc.

'Eventually the victims were herded into railway trucks, 100 to 120 people in each. They were not given any food, nor a single drop of water. The heat and stench inside were fearful.

'Before our eyes our children fell, our parents and our friends. They might possibly have been saved if only we had had a few drops of water. There were some who drank their own urine or that of their friends. A little water was afterwards poured into the truck through its holes when the

Shortly after the train has continued on its way to Calarasi, Rumanians strip off the clothes of the dead in their search for money and valuables.

death train was halted at different stations.

'Meantime, the heat in the truck became fearful, it was literally an inferno. The journey of the living together with the dead lasted for four days; and then the train halted so that the corpses could be removed.

'After four days more the train reached the Calarasi. On the way the victims were robbed of all the clothes that had been left them. When they went out of the train most of them were nearly naked, wearing little more than their shirts.

'Another chapter of the torments began when we reached this place. We were left out in the open, hungry, tattered and filthy. Eventually the Jewish community at Calarasi succeeded in coming to our aid. As a result some of the victims were rescued, when they were on the verge of death.

'The following incident will illustrate the horror of this thirst which was experienced by the unfortunate victims. On the way to Calarasi the train stopped at Mircesti, near a pool of filthy water. The reckless victims or madmen, which ever we ought to call them, broke down the doors of the trucks and made for the pool. They paid no attention to the warnings of the trainmaster that they would be killed and refused to move away from the turbid water. Dozens of them were shot by the guards as they stood in the pool and drunk the filthy mess.'

Official statistics of this railway journey from Jassy were prepared, and certified, by the Rumanian police chiefs in the various towns along the route. Two trains had left Jassy on 30 June. The first had gone, with 1,900 Jews sealed into its wagons, to Podul-Iloaiei, twenty kilometres from Jassy. By the time it had arrived, 1,194 of the Jews were dead. The second train, with 2,500 Jews, had set off towards Calarasi, stopping six times, and taking four days to travel to its first stop, only sixty-four kilometres from Jassy, when 650 dead were removed from the train. A further 327 were removed at Mircesti, 172 at Sabaoani and 53 at Roman.

It was at Roman that the survivors of the journey so far had been forced to strip naked, in order to bath in a special 'sanitary' train. They had then been made to spend the night, most of them without clothes, on the ground by the train.

The railway journey from Jassy to Calarasi, the river Dniester, and the surrounding areas.

Also at Roman a voice had been raised in protest against the horrors of the journey. A local woman, Viorica Agarici, a Christian, head of the regional Red Cross, had insisted that measures be taken to lessen the torment of the journey. In part, her intervention was successful, and the death rate fell considerably.

From Roman the train had gone on to Inotesti, where forty more dead were removed, and then to Calarasi, where a further 25 bodies were taken out of the train. The final stop, on 6 July, was Calarasi camp.

The Rumanian police reports were detailed and precise. Reports No 1324 of 4 July, No 4457 of 6 July, and No 10,252 of 6 July gave a total of 2,530 deaths, station by station, in the two trains; and in the weeks that followed, hundreds more died as a result of starvation and beatings to which they had been subjected during their week-long journey.

On 1 September 1941 the German Minister to Rumania, Manfred von Killinger, reported to the Foreign Office in Berlin that some 4,000 Jews had died as a result of the killings at Jassy and the two train journeys. For Marshal Antonescu, who

One of the mass deportations of Jews across the river Dniester into Transnistria: these photographs were taken on 10 June 1942 at Vascaut.

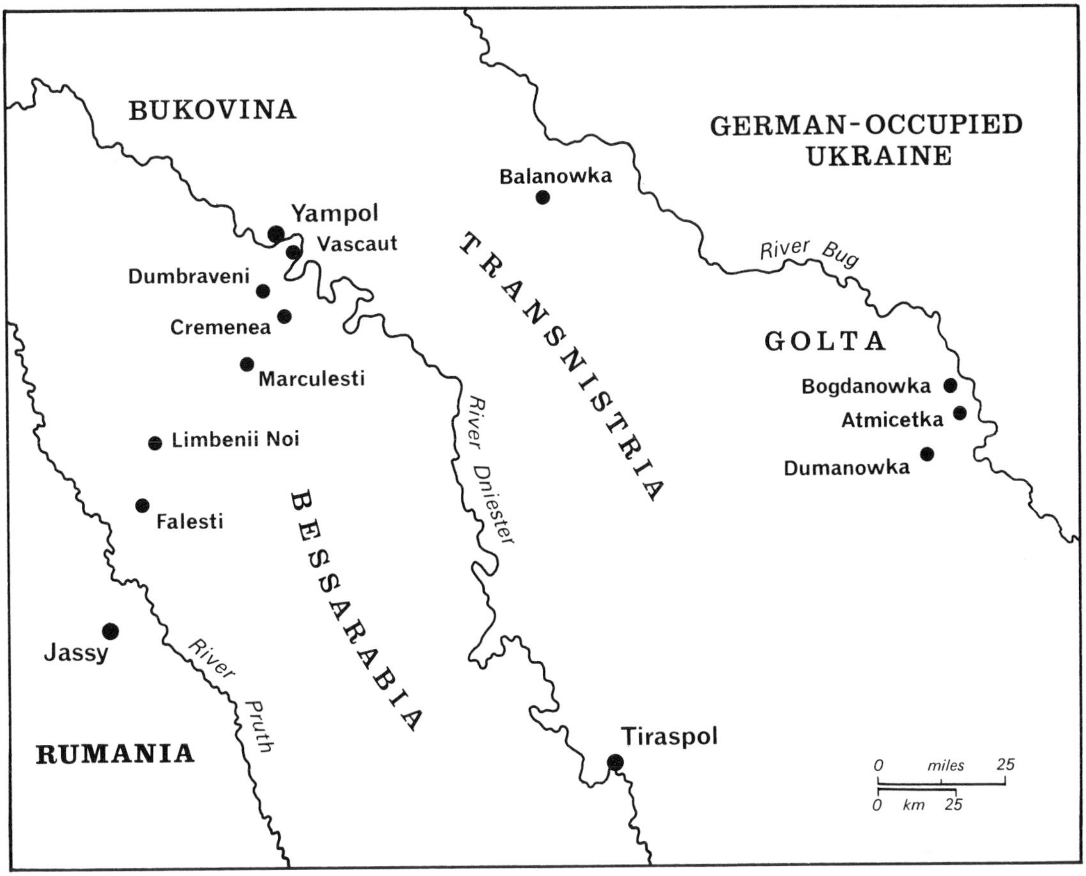

The deportation of the Jews from Rumania to the east.

had now annexed the former Soviet regions of the Bukovina and Bessarabia, this toll was not, apparently, enough, and it was the Gestapo's own representative in Rumania, Gustav Richter, who sent back to Berlin on 17 October 1941 a report that '110,000 Jews are being evacuated from the Bukovina and Bessarabia into two forests in the Bug river area'. The purpose of this deportation, Richter added, 'is the liquidation of these Jews'.

The deportations took place at once, amid scenes of looting and violence. On 2 December 1941 the German Military Attaché in Bucharest reported that Rumanian army officers on leave were weighed down with rings, furs, silks and other valuables seized from the deportees.

More than 185,000 Jews were deported eastwards by Antonescu during the last months of 1941. Sent to concentration camps in which the tortures were of diabolical ferocity, by May 1942 more than 100,000 had been killed. Yet their story is almost unknown, and even the names of the camps themselves find no place in most of the history books of the period. In one region, Golta, there were three camps: Bogdanowka, Dumanowka and Atmicetka, under the command of Colonel Modest Isopescu. At Bogdanowka alone 48,000 Jews were held. At Colonel Isopescu's whim, those who had managed to bring valuables with them were allowed to buy bread, for five gold roubles a loaf. When the gold ran out, the colonel ordered the shooting to begin. For three days,

Jews executed in a Rumanian town, and left hanging in the market place, guarded by a German soldier.

beginning on 21 December 1941, tens of thousands of Jews were driven into stables, and then shot. For others, another fate had been reserved, which the historian, Levai, has described. Marched in groups of 80 to 100 to the edge of a cliff above the Bug river, a few kilometres from the camp:

'They were stripped of their belongings, and their ring fingers were chopped off if the rings could not easily be removed. Even their gold teeth were forcibly extracted. After that, standing stark naked in a temperature of 40° below zero, they were shot. The corpses fell over the precipice into the river.'

The shootings ended on 30 December, leaving only 200 Jews alive. These survivors were then forced to burn the bodies which had remained at the cliff top. Then they too were shot. Meanwhile, at Dumanowka 18,000 Jews were killed, and a further 5,000 at Atmicetka.

One of those who witnessed the Bessarabian massacres was a Jewish schoolboy, Gedaliah Schneider, who lived in Falesti. He was only fourteen years old when Marshal Antonescu came to power in Rumania. Miraculously, he survived, reaching Palestine in July 1944. Three months later he recorded his recollections:

'At the beginning of the Russo-German war in 1941 the front line was only twenty kilometres away from our village. When the terrible bombardment began, our family fled to the neighbouring village of Limbenii Noi, but there the Rumanian peasants were not prepared to let us into their houses until the bombardment was over. (It should be remarked that those villagers did know us, for they used to come to my father and order their clothes from him.) Since no alternative was left to us, we had to return to our village. The place was repeatedly bombed and there were many casualties.

'A week later the Germans entered the village. We fled to Dumbraveni village which was about sixty kilometres away. Three days later the Germans entered Dumbraveni, and set the village on fire; they began to loot. The Jews who tried to put out the fire were shot on the spot by the Rumanians and Germans.

'During a single night 280 Jews were murdered. When we saw what was going on we fled back to Falesti on the following morning. On the way we were caught by the Rumanians, who beat us cruelly and led us to slaughter. The Rumanians cut off the beard of my seventy-year-old grandfather and made fun of him.

'Our group numbered fifty people, including fifteen children. We were robbed of everything we had. When my mother broke into tears and began to wail, a Rumanian officer put the barrel of his pistol into her mouth. In this way we were led about for ten days without food. Many died on the way. Then we were taken into an empty room and left there for three days without food. At last we were brought back to Falesti.

'When we entered our house we found it empty; everything had been stolen. There were still 1,500 Jews left in the village.

'Three days later all the Jews were driven to the camp at Limbenii Noi. All the inhabitants of Falesti were ordered to assemble in the morning; members of the militia and the police surrounded us and brought us to the camp, which was fenced with barbed wire. There were 2,500 Jews in the camp including people from the neighbouring villages. Conditions were bad. We received no food. Against *bakshish* the Rumanian officer permitted people to leave the camp for a few hours. Thus the artisans among us could earn a few pence and the food they bought had to suffice for all of us.

'We slept on the bare earth and in the open. It was the beginning of autumn. Heavy rains poured down, turning the soil into mud. The sick were put into the only stable in the place. As a matter of course they were given no medicines. Dr Shar, the young doctor of our village, also fell ill. Two hundred and ten people in the camp died of illness and hunger.

'After three and a half months we were driven to Marculesti. Eighty people died on the way.

'Jews from another three camps were concentrated in the ghetto of Marculesti. Altogether we were about 10,000 people. When we reached there we found the bones of thousands of people near the sewage drains. In Marculesti there were no local Jews, since these had already been murdered. The Rumanians used to drag us to work while beating us cruelly.

'A fortnight later we were expelled to Transnistria. In the small hours of 10 October 1941 we were driven from our houses into the streets without any warning. We then numbered 10,000 people. There was a torrential rain, and we waded through mud for three days and three nights. Many fell down, including a large number of children. When we reached the forest, near Cremenea village, several thousand Jews were flung into pits. The Rumanians did not even permit us to bury them.

'On reaching the banks of the river Dniester we were released. I did not find my family and arrived alone in Yampol.

'During the first year my situation was very bad. I had no clothing or footwear. I managed to get some food. After ten months I was informed by a friend from my home town that my parents and my sisters had died of hunger and sickness in Balanowka village. That friend also informed me that many other Jews had died in that village.

'After a year had passed I began to earn somehow, and could afford to buy clothes. There were only a few Jews living in Yampol, although formerly 2,000 Jews had been living there; but many were sent to the camp at Pinara and only 700 people were left. . . .'

Another schoolboy who had been deported through Marculesti was the twelve-year-old Jona Malleyron. 'Marculesti', he later recalled, 'was the last railway station to which the cattle train had taken us from our native Czernowitz on our way to a concentration camp in Nazi-occupied Ukraine.'

A week after Gedalia Schneider and those with him had been driven out of the town, Jona Malleyron arrived. On 17 October he wrote in his diary:

'They have taken us off the cattle train. The place is called Marculesti. I have never heard of it. We are huddled together on the outskirts of it and the soldiers tell us we may be allowed to enter the houses tomorrow.... We have spent another night in the open again, in the freezing cold and rain of this muddy place. I am hungry and I wish they would let us take shelter in those houses....

'18 October 1941: they are driving us into the houses now. The houses are of a kind I had never seen before. Small, dilapidated huts with big frightening holes in them; they are empty and dirty and surrounded by barbed wire. There is no room for all of us in them, some people are lying down on the ruins of other houses. Among graves. Open, messy graves. I can see bones, bones of butchered Jews, people say... I do not want to be inside this house. Mice are crawling all over me, or are these creatures rats?

'19 October 1941: it is raining heavily. I wish they would leave us in Marculesti just one more day.... But here they come, they are chasing us out of the dilapidated houses. They are screaming and beating us to hurry up. Some people do not have the strength to move. They use clubs and rifles, *Vorwaerts!* Move on! 250 more kilometres to go, they scream.... We are leaving Marculesti.'

Herman Iwanir, aged fifteen, arrives in Palestine in July 1944. Born in Czernowitz, he had escaped from one of the Transnistrian death camps and made his way across Europe to Turkey, and then to Palestine.

Out of Rumania's pre-war Jewish population of more than 600,000, it has been estimated that more than 260,000 were murdered. Yet even this death toll was not sufficient for the Nazis, who considered their Rumanian policy a failure. As early as July 1943 Marshal Antonescu had authorized certain Rumanian Jews to return from Transnistria, including old people, widows, wounded veterans of the First World War, and former officers in the Rumanian army. Foreseeing the eventual defeat of Germany, the Rumanian Government now hoped to create a favourable impression with the western Allies.

On 31 May 1944 the German military commander in the Jassy region, General Wöhler, reported with disgust that Jews had actually tried to buy food and clothing from his men. 'I ordered the arrest of these creatures', Wöhler commented, and added angrily: *'Jews must disappear.'* But the Rumanian Government was no longer willing to agree to German demands.

During the spring and summer of 1944, the Nazi designs on the Jews of Rumania were finally defeated by the advance of the Red Army. This did not prevent the German authorities from several 'last minute' killings, as their troops withdrew. As the Red Army approached the town of Tiraspol, on the Dniester, the Germans murdered a thousand Jews who had been held in the prison there. But on 22 August 1944 Soviet troops entered Jassy and on the following day, less than four months after General Wöhler's outburst, the Rumanian Government accepted the Russian armistice terms, announced the end of all hostilities, broke off relations with Germany and, on 25 August, entered the war on the side of the Allies.

4

Towards the 'Final Solution'

It was Adolf Hitler who had sworn to annihilate the Jews from Europe. On 30 January 1939 he had set out, in a speech in Berlin, his designs towards what he called 'the Jewish world-enemy', telling his listeners, and the world:

'One thing I should like to say on this day which may be memorable for others as well as for us Germans: In the course of my life I have very often been a prophet, and have usually been ridiculed for it.

'During the time of my struggle for power it was in the first instance the Jewish race which only received my prophecies with laughter when I said that I would one day take over the leadership of the State, and with it that of the whole nation, and that I would then among many other things settle the Jewish problem. Their laughter was uproarious, but I think that for some time now they have been laughing on the other side of their face.

'Today I will once more be a prophet: if the international Jewish financiers in and outside Europe should succeed in plunging the nations once more into a world war, then the result will not be the bolshevization of the earth, and thus the victory of Jewry, but the annihilation of the Jewish race in Europe!'

Thousands of individuals were encouraged to turn against the Jews as a result of Hitler's anti-semitic policies. Not only German anti-semites, but individual Austrians, Poles, Ukrainians, Lithuanians, Rumanians and many others emerged between 1939 and 1945 as murderers of the Jews.

For the Jews themselves, no one person came to represent the active forces of evil so much as Adolf Eichmann, whom many had met personally during the early years of his official career.

Eichmann (on the left, looking towards the camera) standing with other Nazi officials outside the Jewish communal offices in Vienna, immediately after the German annexation of Austria in March 1938.

Adolf Eichmann was born in Germany in 1906, the son of a clerk. At the outbreak of the First World War, when he was eight years old, his family moved to Linz, in Austria. At the age of twenty-two he became a travelling salesman for the Socony Vacuum Company. Four years later he joined the Nazi Party.

Eichmann's early years as a Nazi marked him out for rapid promotion. In 1933 he joined the SS and left Austria for Germany. In 1934 he was serving as a corporal in Dachau concentration camp, and by 1935 he was working in the Nazi Secret Service as a member of the Jewish Section. His work took him to Palestine where he observed the Jews in their 'national home'. He studied Judaism, Zionism and the work of the various Jewish community organizations. He even began to learn Hebrew and Yiddish. By 1937 he was one of the Nazis' acknowledged experts on Jewish affairs.

In March 1938, when the Germans annexed Austria, Eichmann was sent to Vienna, to organize Jewish emigration. The Jews with whom he came into contact there were struck by his single-minded determination to see an end to Vienna's Jewish community, which could trace its origins to Roman times. So successful was his Centre for Jewish Emigration, that a similar office was set up in Prague when German troops entered the Czech capital in March 1939.

Eichmann returned to Berlin, where he was promoted to the rank of Captain and put in charge of the German Centre for Jewish Emigration. Shortly after the outbreak of war he went to Poland, where he organized the expulsion of thousands of Jews to the Nisko region: the 'Lublinland' to which S. Mogilewer had been sent, and whose journey there had been so harrowing.

Jews being deported from Cracow: a photograph published in a German magazine, *Berliner Illustrierte*, early in 1940.

The aim of the Nisko project was to transfer the Jews from the towns of Greater Germany to a remote corner of Poland. The first deportees were 1,000 Jews from the former Czechoslovak town of Moravska Ostrava who, locked in goods wagons, were met at Nisko railway station by Eichmann himself, who told them:

'Here, six or seven kilometres from this place, across the San, the Führer has promised a new homeland to the Jews. There are no apartments or houses; if you will build them, you will have a roof overhead. There is no water. The wells are infected with cholera, typhoid and dysentry. If you drill and find water, you will have it. Once you cross the river you will never come back.'

Once they had reached the place marked out for them, the deportees were ordered to put up their first building: barracks for the SS guards.

At a conference held in Lodz, on 30 January 1940, the Nisko project was expanded, again under Eichmann's supervision. More than 190,000 Jews, Poles and Gipsies were to be expelled from the newly annexed German territories, all of which were to become 'clear of Jews' as soon as possible. 'In fifty years', the German Minister of Labour, Dr Robert Ley, told the meeting, 'this will be a flourishing German country, with not a Pole or a Jew in it.'

Among the Jews deported to the Nisko area were those from the Baltic town of Stettin. A full account of their deportation was published on 17 February 1940 in a Danish newspaper, *Politiken*, by its Stettin correspondent. Men, women, children, war veterans and old people were all awoken by the Gestapo in the middle of the night, forced from their beds and told to bring with them only a single piece of hand luggage. Everything had to be left behind: clothes, furniture and means of livelihood. At dawn they were marched to the railway station. Asked whether housing would be made available to them in the new area, an SS man told them: 'You will be unloaded in the open fields and you will take care of yourselves.'

The Stettin correspondent of *Politiken* was able to report on the fate of the deportees, a fate which

Central Europe, showing the places mentioned in this chapter.

was shared by tens of thousands of other deportees to this, Eichmann's first so-called 'resettlement' project. Brought to a railway station in the Nisko region, the deportees were then ordered to walk more than ten miles in the snow, with the temperature 22°C below freezing.

'The march lasted over fourteen hours; seventy-two people were left on the road to freeze to death. Among them was a woman, found with a three-year-old baby in her arms, both frozen to death, the mother's last movement being to protect the child with her clothing.'

In March 1941 Eichmann received the job which he was to keep until the end of the war: head of

Section IVB4 of the Gestapo, responsible for Jewish affairs throughout German occupied Europe, and in the countries friendly to Germany.

In June 1941 Hitler launched his attack on the Soviet Union. Within six months, the Red Army had been driven back almost to Moscow. Vast areas of European Russia, including White Russia, the western Ukraine and the Baltic States, were under German military control. And as the German army advanced, special killing squads – *Einsatzgruppen* or Strike Commandos – massacred the Jews in every town and village.

Eichmann remained in Berlin, receiving full reports of the work of the *Einsatzgruppen* and summarizing them for his own Gestapo chief, Reinhard Heydrich. The numbers of those murdered were on a scale previously unknown, and yet the statistics were presented with bureaucratic precision: in the last three days of August 1941, 23,600 Jews were executed in Kamenets-Podolsk. In the last three days of September, 33,777 Jews were murdered in Kiev.

For more than a year these killings continued: diligently accounted for in report after report. One of these reports was sent to Berlin from the Lithuanian city of Kovno on 1 December 1941. It was marked 'Secret Reich Matter!', and in it Group 3 of the *Einsatzgruppen* sent a day-by-day account of the number of Jews, Russians, Poles and Lithuanians who had been murdered by one of its sections between 4 July and 25 November

Towns in German-occupied Lithuania in which the *Einsatzgruppen* killings took place during August 1941.

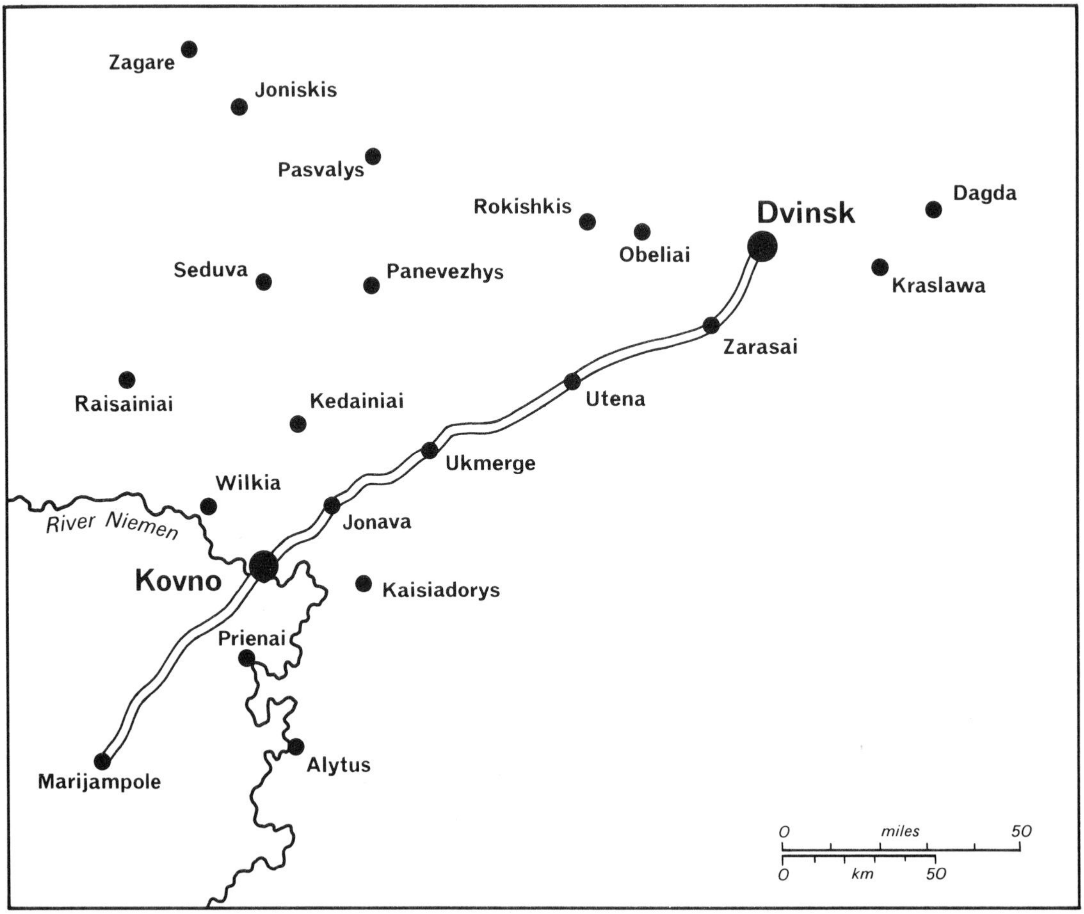

1941. The section was described as 'a raiding party under the direction of SS First Lieutenant Hamaan and 8 to 10 trustworthy men of *Einsatzgruppe* 3 . . . in cooperation with Lithuanian partisans'. Five copies of the report were prepared. Set out below is the section from 2 to 28 August, listed under date, town or village, category of those killed and, at the end of each line, the total deaths for the day. The very first line shows two American citizens among the victims:

2.8.41	Kovno, Fort IV	170 Jewish men, 1 USA Jew, 1 USA Jewish woman, 33 Jewish women, 4 Lithuanian communists	209
4.8.41	Panevezhys	362 Jewish men, 41 Jewish women, 5 Russian communists, 14 Lithuanian communists	422
5.8.41	Raisainiai	213 Jewish men, 66 Jewish women	279
7.8.41	Utena	483 Jewish men, 87 Jewish women, 1 Lithuanian who robbed corpses of German soldiers	571
8.8.41	Ukmerge	620 Jewish men, 82 Jewish women	702
9.8.41	Kovno, Fort IV	484 Jewish men, 50 Jewish women	534
11.8.41	Panevezhys	450 Jewish men, 48 Jewish women, 1 Lithuanian and 1 Russian communist	500
13.8.41	Alytus	617 Jewish men, 100 Jewish women, 1 criminal	719
14.8.41	Jonava	497 Jewish men, 55 Jewish women	552
15 and 16.8.41	Rokishkis	3,200 Jewish men, Jewish women, and Jewish children, 5 Lithuanian communists, 1 Pole, 1 partisan	3,207
9 to 16.8.41	Raisainiai	294 Jewish women, 4 Jewish children	298
27.6 to 14.8.41	Rokishkis	493 Jews, 432 Russians, 56 Lithuanians (all active communists)	981
18.8.41	Kovno, Fort IV	698 Jewish men, 402 Jewish women, 1 Polish woman, 711 members of the Jewish intelligentsia from the ghetto as reprisal for an act of sabotage	1,812
18 to 22.8.41	Raisainiai District	466 Jewish men, 440 Jewish women, 1,020 Jewish children	1,926
19.8.41	Ukmerge	298 Jewish men, 255 Jewish women, 1 Politruk, 88 Jewish children, 1 Russian communist	645
22.8.41	Dvinsk	3 Russian communists, 5 Latvians, including 1 murderer, 1 Russian guard soldier, 3 Poles, 3 gipsy men, 1 gipsy woman, 1 gipsy child, 1 Jewish man, 1 Jewish woman, 1 Armenian man, 2 Politruks (prison inspection at Dvinsk)	21
22.8.41	Aglona	Mental patients: 269 men, 227 women, 48 children	544
23.3.41	Panevezhys	1,312 Jewish men, 4,602 Jewish women, 1,609 Jewish children	7,523
25.8.41	Obeliai	112 Jewish men, 627 Jewish women, 421 Jewish children	1,160
25 and 26.8.41	Seduva	230 Jewish men, 275 Jewish women, 159 Jewish children	664
26.8.41	Zarasai	767 Jewish men, 1,113 Jewish women, 1 Lithuanian communist, 687 Jewish children, 1 Russian communist woman	2,569
26.8.41	Pasvalys	402 Jewish men, 738 Jewish women, 209 Jewish children	1,349
26.8.41	Kaisiadorys	All Jews (men, women, and children)	1,911
27.8.41	Prienai	All Jews (men, women, and children)	1,078
27.8.41	Dagda and Kraslawa	212 Jews, 4 Russian prisoners-of-war	216
27.8.41	Joniskis	47 Jewish men, 165 Jewish women, 143 Jewish children	355
28.8.41	Wilkia	76 Jewish men, 192 Jewish women, 134 Jewish children	402
28.8.41	Kedainiai	710 Jewish men, 767 Jewish women, 599 Jewish children	2,076

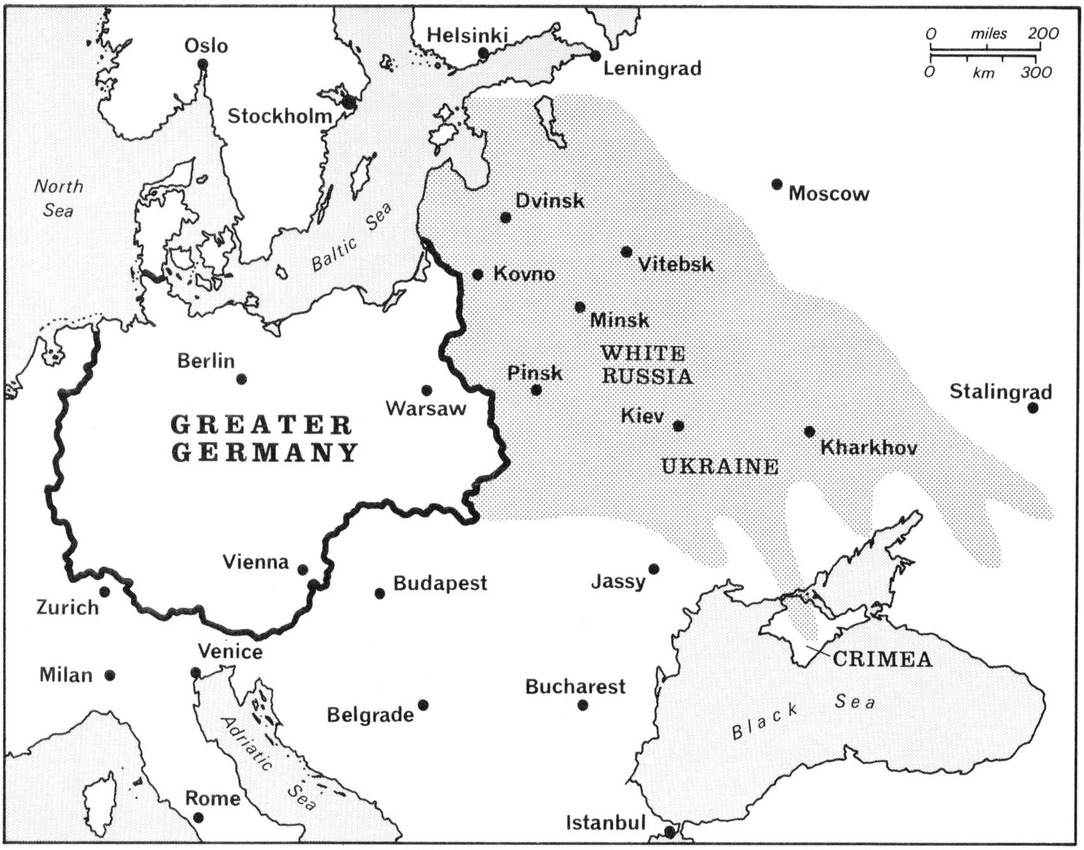

General area (shaded) in which *Einsatzgruppen* killings took place between June 1941 and the end of 1942.

Among those listed in Lieutenant Hamaan's report for September, October and November were '100 mental patients', and '1 female German national who was married to a Jew', all of whom were murdered at Marijampole on 1 September 1941; 1,608 Jews, including 581 children, all described as 'sick people and suspected carriers of epidemics' murdered at Kovno on 16 September; 150 Jews 'shot right away' because they had begun 'a mutiny' at Zagare, on 2 October; and 'one Reich German who had converted to Judaism and attended a rabbinical school', killed at Kovno on 29 November.

Lieutenant Hamaan's section concluded its report by listing its 'grand total': 137,346 people killed.

These massacres were carried out by *Einsatzgruppen* in every village in Lithuania, eastern Poland and western Russia. One of the few people who survived them was Rivka Yosselevska, a young mother from Zagrodski, a small village near Pinsk. On 8 May 1961 she was to give an account of her experiences in court, in Jerusalem, at Eichmann's trial, telling the court, under questioning, as the official transcript recorded:

'... We were told to leave the houses – to take with us only the children. We were always used to leaving the ghetto at short order, because very often they would take us all out for a roll-call. Then we would all appear. But we felt and realized that this was not an ordinary roll-call, but something very special. As if the Angel of Death was in charge. The place was swarming with Germans.

As the German armies advanced eastwards, the *Einsatzgruppen* searched out Jews even from the smallest villages and hamlets. A German soldier photographed this family with their hands up, shortly before they were led away to an execution site.

Some four to five Germans to every Jew.'
Attorney-General: 'Then all of you were driven out, and were taken to this square – weren't you?'
Witness: 'No, we were left standing in the ghetto. They began saying that he who wishes to save his life could do so with money, jewels and valuable things. This would be ransom, and he would be spared. Thus we were held until the late afternoon, before evening came.'
Presiding Judge: 'And did the Jews hand over jewels and so on?'
Witness: 'We did not. We had nothing to hand over. They already took all we had before.'
Presiding Judge: 'I see.'
Attorney-General: 'Yes. And what happened towards sunrise?'
Witness: 'And thus the children screamed. They wanted food, water. This was not the first time. But we took nothing with us. We had no food and no water, and we did not know the reason. The children were hungry and thirsty. We were held this way for twenty-four hours while they were searching the houses all the time – searching for valuables.

'In the meantime, the gates of the ghetto were opened. A large truck appeared and all of us were put on to the truck – either thrown, or went up himself.'
Attorney-General: 'Did they count the Jews?'
Witness: 'Yes – they were counted. They entered the ghetto again, and searched for every missing person. We were tortured until late in the evening.'
Attorney-General: 'Now – they filled up this truck.

And what happened to the people for whom there was no room in the truck?'
Witness: 'Those for whom there was no room in the truck were ordered to run after the truck.'
Attorney-General: 'And you ran with your daughter?'
Witness: 'I had my daughter in my arms and ran after the truck. There were mothers who had two or three children and held them in their arms – running after the truck. We ran all the way. There were those who fell – we were not allowed to help them rise. They were shot – right there – wherever they fell.

'When we reached the destination, the people from the truck were already down and they were undressed – all lined up. All my family was there – undressed, lined up. The people from the truck, those who arrived before us....

'There was a kind of hillock. At the foot of this little hill, there was a dugout. We were ordered to stand at the top of the hillock and the four devils shot us – each one of us separately.'
Attorney-General: 'Now these four – to what German unit did they belong?'
Witness: 'They were SS men – the four of them. They were armed to the teeth. They were real messengers of the Devil and the Angel of Death.'
Attorney-General: 'Please go on – what did you see?'
Witness: 'When I came up to the place – we saw people, naked, lined up. But we were still hoping that this was only torture. Maybe there is hope – hope of living. One could not leave the line, but I wished to see – what are they doing on the hillock? Is there anyone down below? I turned my head and saw that some three or four rows were already killed – on the ground. There were some twelve people among the dead. I also want to mention what my child said while we were lined up in the ghetto, she said, "Mother, why did you make me wear the Shabbat dress; we are being taken to be shot"; and when we stood near the dug-out, near the grave, she said, "Mother, why are we waiting, let us run!" Some of the young people tried to run, but they were caught immediately, and they were shot right there. It was difficult to hold on to the children. We took all children not ours, and we carried them – we were anxious to get it all over – the suffering of the children was difficult; we all trudged along to come nearer to the place and to come nearer to the end of the torture of the children. The children were taking leave of their parents and parents of their elder people.'
Presiding Judge: 'How did you survive through all this?'
Attorney-General: 'She will relate it.'
Presiding Judge: 'Please will you direct the Witness.'
Witness: 'We were driven; we were already undressed; the clothes were removed and taken away; our father did not want to undress; he remained in his underwear. We were driven up to the grave, this shallow ...'
Attorney-General: 'And these garments were torn off his body, weren't they?'
Witness: 'When it came to our turn, our father was beaten. We prayed, we begged with my father to undress, but he would not undress, he wanted to keep his underclothes. He did not want to stand naked.'
Attorney-General: 'And then they tore them off?'
Witness: 'Then they tore off the clothing off the old man and he was shot. I saw it with my own eyes. And then they took my mother, and we said, let us go before her; but they caught mother and shot her too; and then there was my grandmother, my father's mother, standing there; she was eighty years old and she had two children in her arms. And then there was my father's sister. She also had children in her arms and she was shot on the spot with the babies in her arms.'
Attorney-General: 'And finally it was your turn.'
Witness: 'And finally my turn came. There was my younger sister, and she wanted to leave; she prayed with the Germans; she asked to run, naked; she went up to the Germans with one of her friends; they were embracing each other; and she asked to be spared, standing there naked. He looked into her eyes and shot the two of them. They fell together in their embrace, the two young girls, my sister and her young friend. Then my second sister was shot and then my turn did come.'

Attorney-General: 'Were you asked anything?'
Witness: 'We turned towards the grave and then he turned around and asked "Whom shall I shoot first?" We were already facing the grave. The German asked "Whom do you want me to shoot first?" I did not answer. I felt him take the child from my arms. The child cried out and was shot immediately. And then he aimed at me. First he held on to my hair and turned my head around; I stayed standing; I heard a shot, but I continued to stand and then he turned my head again and he aimed the revolver at me and ordered me to watch and then turned my head around and shot at me. Then I fell to the ground into the pit amongst the bodies; but I felt nothing. The moment I did feel I felt a sort of heaviness and then I thought maybe I am not alive any more, but I feel something after I died. I thought I was dead, that this was the feeling which comes after death. Then I felt that I was choking; people falling over me. I tried to move and felt that I was alive and that I could rise. I was strangling. I heard the shots and I was praying for another bullet to put an end to my suffering, but I continued to move about. I felt that I was choking, strangling, but I tried to save myself, to find some air to breathe, and then I felt that I was climbing towards the top of the grave above the bodies. I rose, and I felt bodies pulling at me with their hands, biting at my legs, pulling me down, down. And yet with my last strength I came up on top of the grave, and when I did I did not know the place, so many bodies were lying all over, dead people; I wanted to see the end of this stretch of dead bodies but I could not. It was impossible. They were lying, all dying; suffering; not all of them dead, but in their last sufferings; naked; shot, but not dead. Children crying "Mother", "Father"; I could not stand on my feet.'
Presiding Judge: 'Were the Germans still around?'
Witness: 'No, the Germans were gone. There was nobody there. No one standing up.'
Attorney-General: 'And you were undressed and covered with blood?'
Witness: 'I was naked, covered with blood, dirty from the other bodies, with the excrement from other bodies which was poured on to me.'
Attorney-General: 'What did you have in your head?'
Witness: 'When I was shot I was wounded in the head.'
Attorney-General: 'Was it in the back of the head?'
Witness: 'I have a scar to this day from the shot by the Germans; and yet, somehow I did come out of the grave. This was something I thought I would never live to recount. I was searching among the dead for my little girl, and I cried for her – Merkele was her name – Merkele! There were children crying "Mother!", "Father!"– but they were all smeared with blood and one could not recognize the children. I cried for my daughter. From afar I saw two women standing. I went up to them. They did not know me, I did not know them, and then I said who I was, and then they said, "So you survived." And there was another woman crying "Pull me out from amongst the corpses, I am alive, help!" We were thinking how could we escape from the place. The cries of the woman, "Help, pull me out from the corpses!" We pulled her out. Her name was Mikla Rosenberg. We removed the corpses and the dying people who held on to her and continued to bite. She asked us to take her out, to free her, but we did not have the strength.'
Attorney-General: 'It is very difficult to relate, I am sure, it is difficult to listen to, but we must proceed. Please tell us now: after that you hid?'
Witness: 'And thus we were there all night, fighting for our lives, listening to the cries and the screams and all of a sudden we saw Germans, mounted Germans. We did not notice them coming in because of the screamings and the shoutings from the bodies around us.'
Attorney-General: 'And then they rounded up the children and the others who had got out of the pit and shot them again?'
Witness: 'The Germans ordered that all the corpses be heaped together into one big heap and with shovels they were heaped together, all the corpses, among them many still alive, children running about the place. I saw them. I saw the children. They were running after me, hanging on to me. Then I sat down in the field and remained sitting with the children around me. The children

The *Einsatzgruppen* at work. These three photographs, taken by German soldiers, show *(below)* women and girls at Dvinsk being forced to undress, and families being led, naked, to their execution at Misocz. *Opposite:* A woman and her child are killed as they run across the fields.

who got up from the heap of corpses.'
Attorney-General: 'Then the Germans came again and rounded up the children?'
Witness: 'Then Germans came and were going around the place. We were ordered to collect all the children, but they did not approach me, and I sat there watching how they collected the children. They gave a few shots and the children were dead. They did not need many shots. The children were almost dead, and this Rosenberg woman pleaded with the Germans to be spared, but they shot her.'
Attorney-General: 'Mrs Yosselevska, after they left the place, you went right next to the grave, didn't you?'
Witness: 'They all left – the Germans and the non-Jews from around the place. They removed the machine guns and they took the trucks. I saw that they all left, and the four of us, we went on to the grave, praying to fall into the grave, even alive, envying those who were dead already and thinking what to do now. I was praying for death to come. I was praying for the grave to be opened and to swallow me alive. Blood was spurting from the grave in many places, like a well of water, and whenever I pass a spring now, I remember the blood which spurted from the ground, from that grave. I was digging with my fingernails, trying to join the dead in that grave. I dug with my fingernails, but the grave would not open. I did not have enough strength. I cried out to my mother, to my father, "Why did they not kill me? What was my sin? I have no one to go to. I saw them all being killed. Why was I spared? Why was I not killed?"

'And I remained there, stretched out on the grave, three days and three nights.'
Attorney-General: 'And then a shepherd went by?'
Witness: 'I saw no one. I heard no one. Not a farmer passed by. After three days, shepherds drove their herd on to the field, and they began throwing stones at me, but I did not move. At night, the herds were taken back and during the day they threw stones believing that either it was a dead woman or a mad woman. They wanted me to rise, to answer. But I did not move. The shepherds were throwing stones at me until I had to leave the place.'
Attorney-General: 'And then a farmer went by, and he took pity on you.'
Witness: 'I hid near the grave. A farmer passed by, after a number of weeks.'
Attorney-General: 'He took pity on you, he fed you, and he helped you join a group of Jews in the forest, and you spent the time until the summer of 1944 with this group, until the Soviets came.'
Witness: 'I was with them until the very end.'

The work of the special murder squads continued. More than 90 per cent of the Jews of Lithuania, eastern Poland and western Russia were killed: a total of 1,400,000 people.

Eichmann himself had inspected the *Einsatzgruppen* at work. At his trial in Jerusalem in 1961 he told the court of how, near Minsk, he had seen the young troopers shooting into a pit already full of writhing bodies: 'I can still see', he said in his interrogation, 'a woman with a child. She was shot and then the baby in her arms. His brains splattered all around, also over my leather overcoat.'

While these killings continued in the east, the Nazi officials in Berlin began to consider what should be the fate of the Jews elsewhere in Europe: not only in Greater Germany itself, and in those countries already under German rule – among them France, Belgium, Holland, Luxembourg, Norway, Denmark, Yugoslavia and Greece – but also in the countries still neutral, or as yet unconquered. On 31 July 1941 Marshal Goering sent Eichmann's superior, Heydrich, instructions as to how future policy should be conducted. The instructions read:

'In supplementing the task assigned to you on 24 January 1939, to bring the Jewish problem to a possibly satisfactory solution through emigration and evacuation in accordance with circumstances obtaining at the time, I hereby commission you to make all necessary preparation, in the organizational, material and financial sense, to bring about a total solution of the Jewish problem in the German sphere of influence in Europe.

'Wherever other government agencies are concerned, they are to be called upon to cooperate. I further commission you to submit to me as soon as possible an over-all plan concerning the organizational, substantive and financial measures for the execution of the desired final solution of the Jewish problem.'

Goering's instructions had in fact been drafted by Eichmann himself, and it was Eichmann and his Gestapo Section IVB4 who undertook the task of carrying them out. But before a 'final solution' could be devised, Eichmann found himself called upon to give his opinion as to what should become of the Jews of Serbia who, since the German conquest of Yugoslavia in April 1941, had been under German military occupation. In the parts of Yugoslavia conquered by the Hungarians, many Jews had already been executed: 250 in Subotica on the first day of the Hungarian occupation, 500 in Novi Sad – Jews and Serbs included – on the third day. But the Germans, having used the Jews to clear the damage caused by the Luftwaffe's own air attacks on Belgrade, placed them in a concentration camp, together with hundreds of Gipsies whom the Nazis had also sworn to 'eradicate'.

In September 1941 the senior German diplomat in Belgrade, Fritz Benzler, asked whether the Jews of Serbia could be deported either to the General Government or to the newly conquered areas of Russia. On 13 September 1941 a member of Eichmann's section, Franz Rademacher, noted on Benzler's letter: 'Eichmann says no possibility of reception in Russia and General Government. Even German Jews cannot be disposed of there. Eichmann proposed shooting.'

After the war, during the Nuremburg trials, Rademacher was questioned about this note. He still remembered, he said, 'talking on the telephone' to Eichmann, 'and writing down the main words of Eichmann's reply'. Rademacher added: 'When I questioned him again, he simply said: "Kill by shooting" and hung up.'

Rademacher travelled to Belgrade, accompanied by two other members of Eichmann's section, SS Major Suhr and SS Lieutenant Stuschka. On their arrival in Belgrade, he reported back to Eichmann, they had found 'only 4,000 Jewish males, 3,500 of whom will be shot by the end of the week'. That same week the Chief of Staff of the Military Government, Harald Turner, wrote to a friend:

'That the devil is loose here you probably know. . . . I had 2,000 Jews and Gipsies shot during the last eight days in accordance with the quota of 1:100 for bestially murdered German soldiers, and another 2,200, again almost exclusively Jews, will be shot in the next eight days. This is not a pretty business. The Jewish question solves itself most quickly this way.

The 'final solution', for which Eichmann had been asked to make his preparations in July was intended to involve not thousands, but millions of Jews. Random shootings as in Belgrade would clearly take a very long time indeed. But mass shootings as in Russia would be much more difficult to carry out, if not impossible, in countries like France, Holland, Belgium, Norway or Italy, where the local population might be sympathetic to the Jews, would certainly be disgusted by the work of the *Einsatzgruppen*, and might even be provoked to protest. There were only a few countries where the local population could be relied upon to do the work themselves, as happened in the Croatian region of Yugoslavia, where local fascists murdered more than 20,000 Jews.

During the autumn and winter of 1941 a more centralized, organized and efficient system had begun to emerge. At the outbreak of the war in 1939, as part of the Nazi plan to kill people who were mentally defective or incurably sick, exhaust fumes from a lorry had been used to murder many thousand inmates of German lunatic asylums. In 1941 similar experiments were tried in the Lublin region, against Jews, and at a camp near Lodz, in the village of Chelmno, mobile gas vans were used; Eichmann himself watched one of these experiments. Gas vans had also been used to murder some of the Belgrade Jews: so 'successful' had they been that they were specially requested by the Gestapo in Riga, for use there. Eichmann knew of these experiments and had discussed them with Rudolf Hoess, the Commandant of a concentration camp which had been established on Polish soil, at Auschwitz. Gradually, as these experiments and discussions continued, the plan of the 'final solution' became clear.

On 25 October 1941 a senior official in the Ministry for the Eastern Territories, Dr Erhard Wetzel, reported to his superiors that, during discussions with Eichmann, and with a member of Hitler's Chancellery, Colonel Victor Brack, the three men had decided to use poison gas for killing Jews. Colonel Brack, Hitler's special adviser on euthanasia, promised to set up the necessary installations and to send one of his own experts, Dr Walter Kallmeyer, to Riga, to help with the programme.

Eichmann steadily prepared the ground for the 'final solution' of the Jewish question. In September 1941 Hitler's consent had been obtained to force all German Jews to wear the yellow Star, hitherto worn only in Poland, and in November Goebbels published an article in which he declared: 'Jewry is now suffering a fate which, though hard, is more than deserved. No compassion and certainly no sorrow is called for. In this historic conflict every Jew is our enemy.'

The time had come for Eichmann's section to draw up a comprehensive plan which could then be carried out by all the departments of the German Government and in all the countries under German rule. A meeting of senior civil servants was called for 9 December 1941. Two days earlier, however, the Japanese attacked Pearl Harbor, and on 11 December Germany declared war on the United States; Eichmann's meeting was therefore postponed. But it was not postponed for long; on 20 January 1942 fifteen high-ranking German Government officials met in the Berlin suburb of Wannsee, to hear from Heydrich how the 'final solution' was to be attained.

The senior officials present at the Wannsee Conference were from the Ministry for the Eastern Territories, the Ministry of the Interior, the Justice Ministry, the Foreign Office, the General Government of Poland, the Chancellery, and the Race and Resettlement Office. All were asked by Heydrich to cooperate 'in the implementation of the solution'.

After listing, country by country, the number of Jews 'involved in this final solution', and noting that Estonia was already 'free of Jews', Heydrich went on to explain, from a draft prepared by Eichmann, that:

'In the course of the final solution, the Jews should be brought under appropriate direction in a suitable manner to the east for labour utilization. Separated by sex, the Jews capable of work will be led into these areas in large labour columns to build roads, whereby doubtless a large part will fall away through natural reduction.

'The inevitable final remainder which doubtless constitutes the toughest element will have to be dealt with appropriately, since it represents a natural selection which upon liberation is to be regarded as a germ cell of a new Jewish development. (See the lesson of history.)

'In the course of the practical implementation of the final solution, Europe will be combed from west to east. If only because of the apartment shortage and other socio-political necessities, the Reich area – including the Protectorate of Bohemia and Moravia – will have to be placed ahead of the line.

'For the moment, the evacuated Jews will be brought bit by bit to so-called transit ghettos from where they will be transported farther to the east.'

It was intended, according to the statistics which had been prepared by Eichmann for the Wannsee Conference, that a total of eleven million Jews should 'fall away', including those in countries which were yet to be conquered, including Britain, Ireland, Spain and Portugal. The conference discussed the various problems involved. 'In Slovakia and Croatia', they were told, 'the situation is no longer all that difficult, since the essential key questions there have already been resolved.' As for Hungary, 'it will be necessary before long', Heydrich told the conference, 'to impose upon the Hungarian Government an adviser on Jewish questions'. Rumania posed a problem, as 'even today a Jew in Rumania can buy for cash appropriate documents officially certifying him in a foreign nationality'. Speaking of the occupied and unoccupied zones of France, however, Heydrich commented that there 'the seizure of the Jews for evacuation should in all probability proceed without major difficulty'.

The representative of the General Government, Dr Joseph Bühler, stated that his administration 'would welcome the start of the final solution in its territory, since the transport problem was no overriding factor there and the cause of the action would not be hindered by considerations of work utilization'. Bühler added:

'Jews should be removed from the domain of the General Government as fast as possible, because it is precisely here that the Jew constitutes a substantial danger as carrier of epidemics and also because his continued black market activities create constant disorder in the economic structure of the country. Moreover, the majority of the two and a half million Jews involved were not capable of work.'

Bühler had, he said, 'only one favour to ask', and that was 'that the Jewish question in this territory be solved as rapidly as possible'.

The meeting was drawing to its end. 'Finally', the official notes recorded, 'there was a discussion of the various types of solution possibilities.'

The officials present at the Wannsee Conference had agreed with Heydrich's suggestion that the 'final solution' should be carried out in coordination with his 'department head', Eichmann himself. The result of this was that Eichmann's representatives now went to all the occupied capitals. Although they were attached to the German embassies, they received their instructions direct from Eichmann's section in Berlin and reported back to Eichmann, by telegram, as each deportation was planned and carried out.

These deportations began in March 1942 and were to continue for more than two years. In order to achieve the 'final solution' as quickly as possible, death camps had to be designed, staffed and operated: all of them situated in remote areas of what was once Poland, at Auschwitz, Treblinka, Belzec, Sobibor, Chelmno and Majdanek. Throughout German-dominated Europe, the concentration camps now became places where brutality, and even medical experiments, led to thousands of deaths. In Croatia, the camps set up in 1941 continued to be places of the mass murder of thousands of men, women and children. In addition, several hundred labour camps were built to make use of the slave labour of several hundred thousand able-bodied Jews and Jewesses.

To transport a total of more than three million people by rail across Europe to the death camps and labour camps of the east, railway timetables had to be devised, wagons hired, frontier crossing-points organized, shunting arrangements perfected, and whole communities uprooted by means of registration centres, confinement to special

The death camps of Greater Germany and German-dominated Europe.

The Jasenovac concentration camp.

sections of towns, deportations to special holding camps, and a regular system of despatch 'to the east'.

In addition to the technical arrangements involving thousands of trains and tens of thousands of miles, a complex system of subterfuge had to be created, whereby the idea of 'resettlement' could be made to appear a tolerable one.

All this was done by Eichmann's section, whose representatives were to be active in France, Belgium, Holland, Luxembourg, Norway, Rumania, Greece, Bulgaria, Hungary, Poland and Czechoslovakia. Regular meetings were held in Berlin to coordinate the despatch of full trains and the return of empty trains. One of the railway documents which survives is dated Berlin, 13 January 1943. Signed by Dr Jacobi of the General Management, Railway Directorate East, in Berlin, it took the form of a 'telegraphic letter' addressed to the General Directorate of East Railways in Cracow; the Prague Group of Railways; the General Traffic Directorate, Warsaw; the Traffic Directorate, Minsk; and the Railway Directorates in fourteen cities, including Breslau, Dresden, Königsberg, Linz, Mainz and Vienna. Copies were to be sent in addition to the General Management, Directorate South, in Munich, and to the General Management, Directorate West, in Essen: a total distribution of twenty copies. The subject was: 'Special trains for resettlers during the period from 20 January to 28 February 1943.'

The table shows some of the details given for the first seven days of February 1943:

1 February	Rumanians, train No 3	*dep* Gleiwitz	*arr* Czernowitz
	Jews, train No 109	*dep* Theresienstadt	*arr* Auschwitz
2 February	Jews, train No 15	*dep* Berlin 17.20	*arr* Auschwitz 10.48
	empty, train No 110	*dep* Auschwitz	*arr* Myslowitz
3 February	Poles, train No 65	*dep* Zamosc 11.00	*arr* Auschwitz
4 February	empty, train No 4	*dep* Czernowitz	*arr* Ratibor
	empty, train No 16	*dep* Auschwitz	*arr* Theresienstadt
	empty, train No 66	*dep* Auschwitz	*arr* Myslowitz
5 February	Polish Jews, train No 107	*dep* Bialystok 9.00	*arr* Auschwitz 7.57
6 February	Polish Jews, train No 109	*dep* Bialystok 9.00	*arr* Auschwitz 7.57
7 February	Polish Jews, train No 111	*dep* Bialystok 9.00	*arr* Auschwitz 7.57
	empty, train No 108	*dep* Auschwitz	*arr* Bialystok

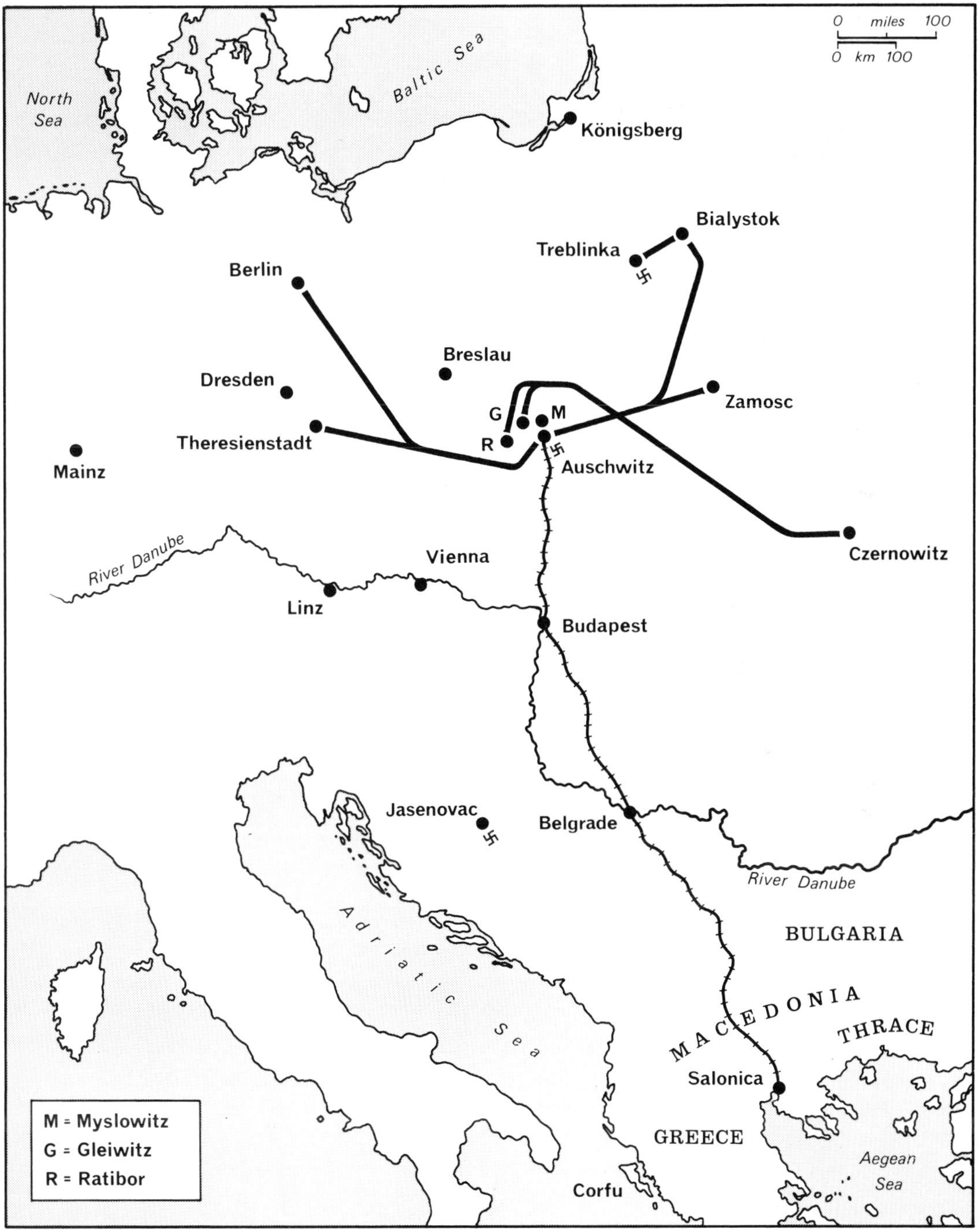

Railway routes described in Dr Jacobi's instructions of February 1943, and the railway deportation route of Greek Jews from Salonica to Auschwitz later that same month.

Also under Dr Jacobi's schedule, a deportation of Polish Jews, in train No 127, was despatched from Bialystok at 9 am, 9 February 1943, reaching the death camp at Treblinka at 12.10, and returning empty that same evening from Treblinka, as train No 128, leaving Treblinka at 9.18 pm and reaching Bialystok ninety minutes after midnight. The instructions of 13 January 1943 had referred specifically to the return of the empty trains. The last paragraph of the instructions read:

'Train formation is noted for each recirculation and *attention is to be paid* to these instructions. After each full trip, cars are to be well cleaned, if need be fumigated, and upon completion of the programme prepared for further use. Number and kinds of cars are to be determined upon dispatch of the last train and are to be reported to me by telephone with confirmation on service cards.'

Each aspect of the railway deportations involved a substantial number of people. Gestapo bureaucrats hired trains from the various regional directorates, railwaymen took charge of the shunting and signalling whereby each train was forwarded to its destination. Bills of lading were prepared, checklists of trains and of passengers, were signed and countersigned, and return tickets were issued for the train guards.

Not only were profits to be made from the belongings of those who were murdered, but even the cost of the railway journeys were to be paid for by the Jews themselves. At the time of the deportations of the Jews of Greece from Salonica to Auschwitz, the Gestapo had ordered special trains from the Greek State Railways, at a cost of nearly two million Reichsmark. A year after the deportations – in which more than 40,000 people were sent to their deaths – payment had still not been made. This led to an angry letter being sent from Dr Rau, of the Ministry of Transport in Berlin, to the Army High Command. The letter was dated 1 March 1944. In it Dr Rau pointed out that Himmler himself, the Gestapo chief, had agreed over the telephone that the costs of deporting the Jews from Salonica 'were to be borne from confiscated Jewish property'. It was the Military Commander of the Aegean area who was in charge of all confiscated Jewish property; hence this letter. Dr Rau continued:

'The fare owed to the Greek State Railways as dispatcher of the trains, for the benefit of all participating railways, is 1,938,488 Reichsmark..

'Repeated attempts were made to collect this amount from the above-mentioned office [the Military Commander], unfortunately without result so far. Now, on Feb. 1, '44 [the Army's] Field Railway Command 6, which has been primarily occupied with this situation, informed Reich Railway Directorate Dresden – which I deputized to carry out the negotiations – as follows: "The Economic Attaché at the German Legation [in Athens], Mr Höfinghoff, reported personally that payment of the transport costs of the Jewish special trains could not be made out of German-Greek clearing funds because there were no credits in this account. For the payment of *c* 1.9 million Reichsmark one would first have to obtain authorization from the Reich Finance Ministry. The Special Plenipotentiary of the Reich [in Greece] refused to request this authorization and indicated that the transport cost should be raised at the Reich Finance Ministry."

'This suggestion obviously ignored the position of the Reichsführer-SS [Himmler] that the transport costs must be met from confiscated Jewish property.

'I ask that this matter be cleared up with the Reichsführer-SS and Chief of the German Police/ Command Security Police and possibly with the Reich Economy Minister and that care be taken to assure transmittal of the transport costs to the Directorate of the Greek State Railways. Kindly inform me about the progress of negotiations.'

The Jews of these deportations had been murdered nearly a year before. Nevertheless, the process of making them pay for their final journey continued.

5

Auschwitz

Auschwitz: the ovens in the crematorium.

The evil done to the Jews of Europe between 1939 and 1945 was done in every region where Nazi tyranny was established. No city, town, village or hamlet escaped. The massacres took place everywhere, from France to the Crimea. Death camps, labour camps, mass executions, forced marches and starvation all took their toll. But it was on the outskirts of one single town, Auschwitz, that barbarism reached its most diabolical depths.

Auschwitz itself had once been a small town in the Austro-Hungarian empire, with its own Jewish community; a place of no special interest or significance. Under its Polish spelling, Oswiecim, it appears briefly in Baedeker's 1905 guide to Austria-Hungary, as a junction on the Vienna to Cracow railway, with a branch line to Breslau. Forty years later it was to become the most terrible railway terminus of all, to which, for more than two years, trains from every corner of Europe had brought Jews, Gipsies and others to their death, some killed while working in the nearby factories and labour camps, others shot at random, but the majority, possibly as many as two million, gassed within a few hours of their arrival.

The gas chambers at Auschwitz were designed by German firms and experts, who submitted their plans on a competitive basis. A processing unit had to be designed with the capacity to dispose of 2,000 bodies every twelve hours. A tall chimney had to be designed to provide the necessary draught for five furnaces, each with three doors, as supplied under contract by the German firm of Topf and Company of Erfurt. According to the specification plans, use could be made in the furnaces of body fat as fuel. The gas chambers themselves were designed by another firm,

A Gipsy woman, one of tens of thousands gassed at Auschwitz, photographed by the Germans on her arrival in the camp.

German Armaments Incorporated, who prepared the chambers, described in the firm's specifications as 'Corpse Cellars', with 'metal fittings and gas-proof doors with rubber surround and observation post of double 8 millimetre glass, type 100/192'. The gas to be used was a commercial pesticide, Zyklon-B, supplied in tins by the German Vermin Combating Corporation. Each tin contained pellets which, when shaken through a roof grill into 'The Corpse Cellar', gave off hydrogen cyanide – prussic acid gas.

The murder of two million people was embarked upon as if it were a mass production programme at a factory.

No one living in Nazi-occupied Europe was unaware of the deportation of the Jews, as train after train travelled eastward. One Polish-born Jewess who survived the war, Luba Krugman, a graphic artist, illustrator and fashion designer, has recalled in her memoirs, *The Death Train*, how:

'At night the rumbling of the train woke me up. I rushed to the door and found it wide open, with father watching the dark monster, which had only one brightly illuminated car behind the locomotive. . . . "It's a real Cyclops", I said. "I can't hear you", replied father.

'Our voices were drowned out by the clatter of the wheels and penetrating whistle of the engine. The train was of gigantic proportions and its load stupendous. I counted sixty-two cars. Father was breathing heavily, and his temples were moist with sweat. He wiped his forehead and opened his shirt. "Please, close your shirt", I implored. "It's bitterly cold." He did not hear; his eyes were fixed on the train.

'A few windows opened. Our gentile neighbours were awakened by the noise. The train passed, leaving behind a cloud of smoke. Windows were closing when one harsh voice came through loudly: "Those damned Jews – they won't even let one sleep at night". . .'

One of those being deported was a twenty-six-year-old French woman, Fania Fénelon, a pianist. In her memoirs she recalled how the deportation journey began in a truck being driven through the streets of early-morning Paris:

'. . . Our truck was covered with tarpaulin and open at the back. The few chilly early-morning passers-by hardly bothered to cast a glance in our direction. And yet our convoy must have been rather unusual, with women wearing fur coats, men of all ages, old people and children.

'Awaiting us at the marshalling yard was a very old train which had seen action in World War I and a wheezing engine which certainly didn't deserve its insolently large, immaculate white V, Churchill's victory sign that had been expropriated by the Germans after Stalingrad.

'We staggered beneath the weight of our luggage. Everyone had brought everything he'd managed to get together: clothing, food, drink, cigarettes, jewellery, money. There were a hundred of us, from all walks of life, all ages and races, crowded into the pitch-black interior of a carriage meant for cattle. There was clean straw on the floor. The quick thinkers – and the strongest – did what they could to stake claims to

The deportation of Slovakian Jews to Auschwitz.

their own corners: they dug in, flapping, shuffling their bottoms into the straw like chickens, acting as though they were going to be there for an eternity.

'The enchanting young mother was quietly advocating various subtle points of etiquette to her children: "Don't make too much noise, there are other people here." Already there were quarrels of the "I was here before you" type.

Below: **Jews deported from Hungary arrive at Auschwitz.**

Opposite: **the 'selection' at Auschwitz: women, children and babies are assembled to be led off to the gas chambers, while the men (on the right) are selected to go to the camp. Both these photographs were taken by two SS officers, Walter Bernard and Ernst Hoffman, as part of a collection of 200 photographs which were intended for an 'official' record of 'The Resettlement of Hungarian Jews' subsequently to be published as pro-Nazi propaganda, but never in fact released.**

Laughable. People started telling stories, jokes, groaning, complaining, making conclusive but unfounded statements: "We're going to a work camp in Bavaria, with little German bungalows, quite clean and decent, and comfortable, with little gardens for those with children." "He's crazy!" "I'll say. That camp is the worst of all, I know that for a fact."

'Me, I . . . I, me . . . One opinion followed another.

'The smell of the improvised lavatory soon became unbearable. At every jolt, there was a worrying ploshing noise. The straw around it was already filthy. A child sitting on the floor in the middle of the carriage kept repeating in a piercing little voice, "I can see things moving everywhere."

'A woman called out, "Make that filthy brat shut up." "It's obvious you've got no children," shrieked the mother. "You're wrong – I've got six." "Where are they then?" "I'm not saying." "Are you afraid I'll expose you?"

'It was outrageous, but no one laughed. Quite the contrary – the two women leapt at one another. The tension was exhausting.

'The time came to eat: it seemed like a picnic without the bonhomie. The whole crowd chewed; it wasn't an elevating moment, but it was restful. . . .'

Fania Fénelon found someone to talk to, a girl called Clara, and began to tell her of her life in Paris as a singer. But the conversation was soon interrupted:

' "We're trying to sleep." "You wouldn't sing if you knew what you were in for," one woman commented prophetically.

'Another brightly volunteered a juicy piece of inside information: "I didn't want to mention it earlier, but I happen to know that we're going to be murdered in the train! They're going to machine gun us right here, all of us!" "They're going to electrocute us.". . .

'We'd been travelling for over fifty hours. The smell was frightful, the door hadn't been opened once. At first, under the supervision of the SS, the men in each carriage had taken out the buckets to empty them. Since then, our bucket had emptied itself by overturning.

'We were desperately thirsty; all the bottles – water, coffee, wine, spirits – were empty. The stinking air was unbreathable, the ventilation nil; we were beginning to suffocate.

'My watch was at twelve when the train stopped – midnight. Our door was opened. "Quick, fresh air", and everyone rushed for the door. "Get out. Leave all luggage in the train." The orders were in French.

'The younger ones jumped out, others managed as best they could. Searchlights lit the platforms, their blinding glare making the night seem darker still. There was a dizzying succession of images. Clara was beside me; there were cries and shrieks, and orders barked in a guttural German: *"Raus! Los! Los! Schneller!"* Out! Out! Faster!

'Shouts in the dark: "Mama, where are you?" "Françoise, Jeannette, where are you?" "Here", called a child's voice. "Mama, we're here." "Where's here?"

"SS soldiers climbed into the carriages and threw the ill, the stiff, and the exhausted out on to the platform with kicks and rifle blows; last of all went a corpse.

'Living skeletons in striped uniforms, their skulls shaven, moved among us like silent shadows, climbing on to the train; these strange "porters" took out our luggage, piled it on to trolleys, and took it away. The snow was thick and dirty, but Clara and I tried to melt some in our hands to drink.

'There was a rumble of vehicles, military trucks, but with enormous red crosses set in white circles.

' "The Red Cross is here", exclaimed Clara. "We're not in any danger."

'The SS thrust the crowd towards the vehicles. Old people and children moving too slowly for the SS stumbled and picked themselves up, clung to one another and were hustled brutally.

'Caught up in an eddy, I was about to climb up in my turn. A sergeant stopped me. "How old are you?" I told him and he pushed me back. "You can walk."

'The mother and little girls called to me from the

back of the truck. I too could have climbed up there and joined them, under cover of darkness, but Clara stopped me. "Don't get in there, we've been cooped up for days in that terrible atmosphere; it'll do us good to walk, even in the snow."

'Two columns had formed, fifty men and fifty women; everyone else from the train had got into the trucks with the red crosses. The convoy moved off, skidding over the snow, sending up violent flurries of slush. From the back of the last truck the little girls waved goodbye to me; the older one fluttered her handkerchief. I smiled at them until they were out of sight.

'At a barked command our column moved off, flanked by soldiers and guard dogs. We walked at a brisk rate, Clara and I arm in arm, almost cheerful. It was very cold and snowing heavily, but I had my fur coat and was comfortably shod in furlined boots. "I wouldn't actually come here for a Christmas holiday, of course", I said jokingly. "The staff haven't quite been licked into shape yet; they're not what you'd call considerate." '

***Below and opposite:* three more 'official' photographs taken by the SS to record the arrival of Hungarian Jews at Auschwitz. The men *(below)* are being led away to forced labour; the women and children *(opposite)* are being sent past the men's huts to the gas chambers.**

At Auschwitz station, still a provincial main-line railway junction, as it had been in 1905, the special trains, mostly sealed goods wagons and cattle trucks, had been shunted on to the branch line which led to the camp. One of the railwaymen who received these trains was Willi Hilse. At a time when the number of trains had become too much for the manager of the Auschwitz goods depot to handle by himself, Hilse had been appointed Deputy Manager. Hilse later recalled the first day at his post:

'The train was standing right by the goods depot and I saw that a woman, a young woman, was holding a small child in her arms and kept on crying out for water. So I filled a jug with water, and as I had my uniform on and was recognizable as a railwayman, I went over and was going to hand the jug of water through the ventilation flap.

'I hadn't even got to the wagon – I was standing on the next track – but already an SS man came up towards me and asked me what I wanted.

'So I said to him I wanted to give the water to the woman and child.

'His answer was that "If you don't get out of here immediately I shall shoot you down." '

On their arrival at Auschwitz the Jews, exhausted, starving, frightened, not knowing where they were, were divided by the Gestapo into two groups. The able-bodied men, and some of the women, like Fania Fénelon and her friend, were sent to the barracks, to work, in conditions of terrible hardship, in the many factories and

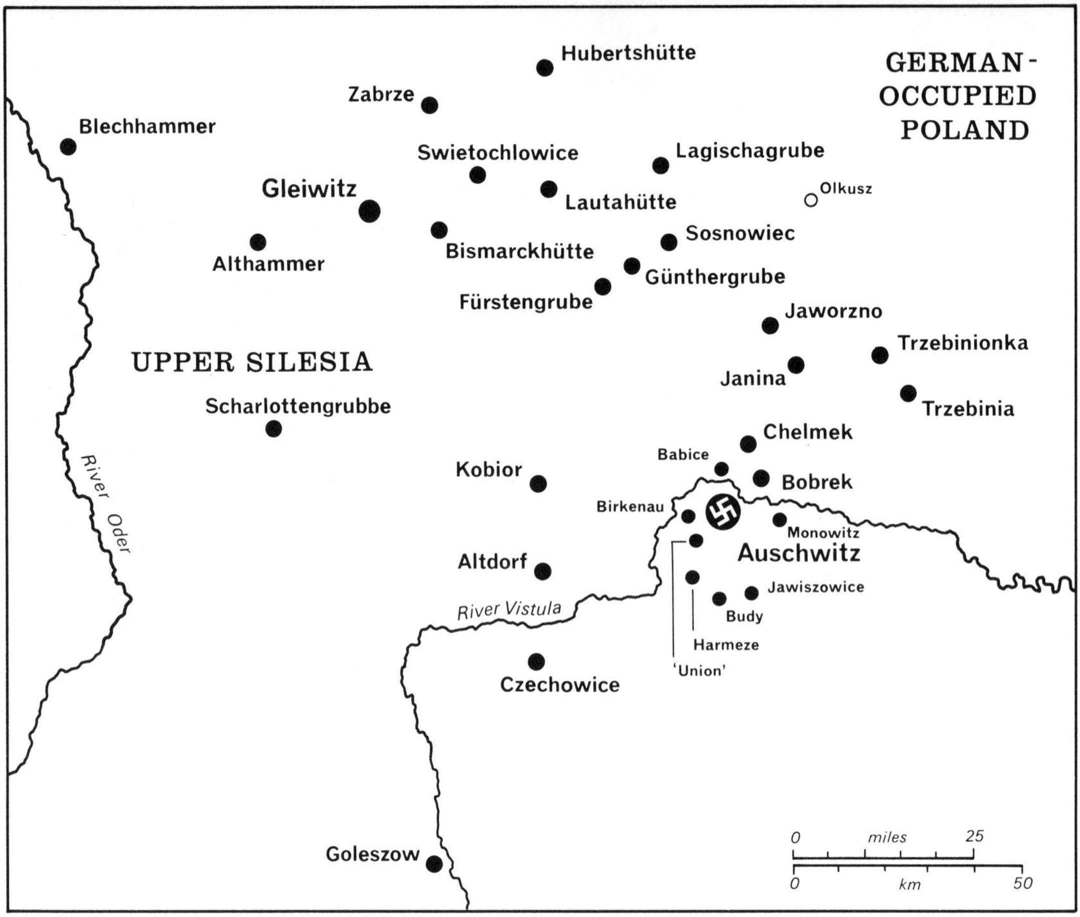

Labour camps in the Auschwitz region, in which hundreds of thousands of Jews died.

labour camps that had sprung up in the neighbourhood of the camp. The rest, the children, mothers, old people and the sick, were sent to the gas chambers. Their destination, they were told, was a shower bath. After their long journey, they would have to be deloused. Some were reassured by the sight of an ambulance standing by the 'shower'. It was, in fact, a truck in which the tins of poison gas were being taken to the gas chambers.

One of the Germans who witnessed these events was a Corporal in the SS, Richard Böck, a member of the transport section at the camp. One evening a friend of his, Karl Hölblinger, one of the drivers of the 'ambulance', took him to watch an 'action' at the gas chamber. Böck later recalled:

'... we went into the hall and the so-called prisoners, the new arrivals, had to get undressed. And then the order came: "Prepare for disinfection."

'There were enormous great piles of clothing in there, and there was a board running round so that the piles didn't all collapse. And the new arrivals, Dutch people, they had to stand on top of this great heap of clothes and get undressed. Lots of them hid their children under the clothes and covered them up.

'Some of them stood with the clothes pulled up round their legs because it was very cold – it was the beginning of winter. Well, then they shouted "Get ready" and they all went out. And then they had to run, naked, approximately twenty metres from the hall across to Bunker One.

'There were two doors there standing open, and they went in there and when a certain number had gone inside they shut the doors. And that happened about three times.

'And every time Höblinger had to go out to his ambulance and one of the SS block leaders took out a sort of tin and he climbed up the ladder and then at the top there was a round hole and he opened a little iron door and held the tin there and shook it. And then he shut the little door again. Then a fearful screaming started up – approximately I would reckon after about ten minutes, it slowly went quiet.

'I said to Höblinger "Can we get a bit nearer when they take them out?" so we went over a bit closer. They opened the door – that was the prisoners squad who did that – then a blue haze came out. And I looked in and I saw a pyramid. They had all climbed up on top of each other until the last one stood on the very top, all one on top of the others – it was a pointed heap, it all came up to a point. And then the prisoners had to go in and tear it apart. I tell you... all tangled. One had his arm down by another's foot, and then round it and back up again and his fingers were sticking in someone else's eye, so deep.

'They were all so tangled. They had to tug and pull very hard to disentangle all these people.

'Then we went back to the hall, and now it was the turn of the last lot to get undressed – the ones who had managed to hang back a bit all the time. One woman said something – meaning that it was cold, perhaps – something like that, and then I did understand a word, that she wasn't used to this sort of thing, and I thought to myself "Dear Lady, I believe you that you're not used to this sort of thing!" And one girl with beautiful black hair, a beautiful girl – she was crouching there and didn't want to get undressed. And an SS man came up and said "I suppose you don't want to get undressed?" And she tossed her hair back and laughed a little. Then he went away and came back with two prisoners and they literally tore her clothes off her, then they each grabbed an arm and they dragged her out and across to Bunker One and pushed her in there.

'Then the prisoners had to check where small children had been hidden and covered up; they pulled them out and opened the doors quickly again and booooomph! They threw all the children in and slammed the doors. "Brrr. I'm going to be sick", I said. "Oh my!", I said, "Karl, I've never seen anything like it in my life. It's absolutely terrible."

And just imagine – when they threw the children in how the people inside screamed, because then they suddenly realized what was happening. And I said "Karl, can we leave soon – I can't stand it any more." And he said "Yes, I feel like that too, but I must stay until they have collected up all the empty tins and put them in the ambulance – I have to take them back."

'Hölbinger said he didn't like doing this duty at all, and he really didn't enjoy it, but he preferred being in the transport section to being in the guard company. "But", he said, "You do get used to anything in time." '

Later, Richard Böck was ordered to take part in a gassing, but he refused to do so, despite threats of punishment.

In February 1945 a Polish woman who had survived seven months at Auschwitz sent an account of her experiences to the President of the Polish Government in Exile in London:

'The fate of the women in the camp was frightful. Six crematories were in action uninterruptedly, and day by day we saw trains bringing in Jews from Bulgaria, Greece, Italy, Holland, France, Poland and Russia as well. The trains were crowded with men, women and children.

'Ten per cent of each group of women were brought to our camp and detained there; each woman was given a number. The remainder were sent direct to the gas chambers....

'It should be noted that all the victims do not die in the gas chambers; some of them only lose consciousness. Those in charge of the gas chambers have been ordered to save gas, which is rather expensive. The quantity used was only small, but enough to kill the weak; the strong, however, were burned alive.

'The ten per cent of the women who were left at the camp were not kept alive for long. Their death was only postponed. Every month a selection was made. The women were forced to undress and to line up in the open, whatever the weather. The commanders of the camp selected a certain number who were left alive, while the others were sent to the crematory.

'The selection usually lasted for several days. During that time those sentenced to death were housed in Hut No 25, the 'death hut', naked and without food waiting for death.

'Their screaming was only interrupted by the arrival of the death lorry, on which they were thrown by the guards.'

The records kept by the camp administration at Auschwitz were precise and voluminous. Three examples will give their tone and nature. On 22 June 1943 a sealed train arrived at the camp siding with 3,650 people. Among them was Jakob Gordon, from Vilna, who was one of the 345 who were 'selected' to survive, as slave labour, and who were marched off to the camp barracks. The remaining 3,305 were 'selected' to die, marched to the gas chamber, gassed, and their bodies burned, all within a few hours.

Among those who were killed were Jakob Gordon's seventy-three-year-old father, his sixty-four-year-old mother, and his son, aged four and a half.

On 5 December 1943 another sealed train arrived with 1,200 Jews, from Flossenbürg concentration camp, in Germany. It was late in the evening, and the temperature was falling rapidly, reaching 20° below zero. Another 'selection' was made, whereby the eighty weakest-looking were left lying in the snow. During the night, cold water was poured over them to speed up the freezing process. Some of those lying there were carried away by other prisoners, to the comparative shelter of the barracks. But forty-two could not be rescued, and all but one of them were dead by morning. This one man had survived the night by hiding under the corpses of three others, but he too died during the following day.

On 15 January 1945 the German authorities at Auschwitz sent an official report to Germany, listing the 'confiscated' properties which they had been able to send to Germany in the previous six weeks, since 1 December 1944. These included 222,269 sets of men's suits and underwear; 192,652 suits of women's clothing and underwear, and 99,922 suits of children's clothing and underwear.

A 'selection' over, the Nazis walk away from the trains; only bundles of clothes are left, awaiting to be taken away, sorted, and sent to Germany.

6

The City of Lodz

The city of Lodz, a centre of the Polish textile industry, had a population of more than 600,000 at the time of the 1931 census. Of these, 200,000 were Jews: a busy, prosperous community, with an active cultural and civic life. Two years later, in April 1933, local Polish thugs began a series of attacks on Jews, and in the municipal elections of 1934 a coalition of anti-semitic parties won a majority on the town council. Their platform: to purge the city of Jews.

There were further attacks on Jews, and several deaths, in September 1935. In 1938 local anti-semitism intensified; Polish 'controllers' were imposed on several of the larger Jewish textile factories and several wealthy Jews were arrested and imprisoned.

On 8 September 1939 the German army entered Lodz, which was given a German name – Litzmannstadt – and annexed to the Reich. In October a Jewish Council was set up by the Germans: an advisory body of thirty-one distinguished Jewish citizens. But the council's life was a short one. On 11 November 1939 the Nazis deported all its members to a nearby detention camp. The great synagogue was burned down, and many Jews were deported from the city, their houses and shops handed over to the local German-speaking minority.

Early in 1940 the Germans decided to expel the Jews from all the main sections of the town, and to confine them in a small dilapidated area. On 1 March 1940, as a prelude to creating this ghetto, the Gestapo organized a series of violent assaults on Jews, several of whom were killed. Thousands of Jews were then forced to leave their homes and to settle in the ghetto, leaving behind all their belongings save those which could be put together hastily in a bundle or a handcart.

Some of the Jews of Lodz managed to flee from their city: to Warsaw; even across the River Bug to the relative safety of the Soviet Union; and to other towns and villages. But on 3 April 1940 the Lodz ghetto was suddenly and completely sealed off from the outside world, surrounded by barbed wire, wooden fences and guards. Inside it were 164,000 people, prisoners in their own city.

At first it was intended to deport the Jews of the ghetto eastwards, to the 'Lublinland' reservation. Later in the year the German Government considered deporting them out of Europe altogether, to the distant island of Madagascar. But by the end of 1940 no hope was held out for the inmates except starvation.

Hundreds died of starvation in Lodz during 1941. At the same time, house searches and torture were common occurrences: any valuables which a Jew might have kept were regarded as a legitimate object of German rapacity.

Under appalling conditions of hunger, forced labour and violence, the Jewish Elder, Chaim Rumkowski, organized an administrative structure of schools, hospitals, pharmacies and public kitchens. The community even obtained money by purchasing Jewish property at low prices and selling it to the German authorities. Jewish police supervised law and order within the ghetto, and a ghetto factory network was organized, mostly to produce clothes for the German army. Every attempt was made by Rumkowski to organize a 'normal' existence out of the existing intolerable conditions. But the daily deaths from starvation were a grim reminder of the reality.

The Jews of Lodz being driven out of their homes with whatever furniture they could take with them, and forced to move into the ghetto.

Below: Young Jews in the Lodz ghetto.

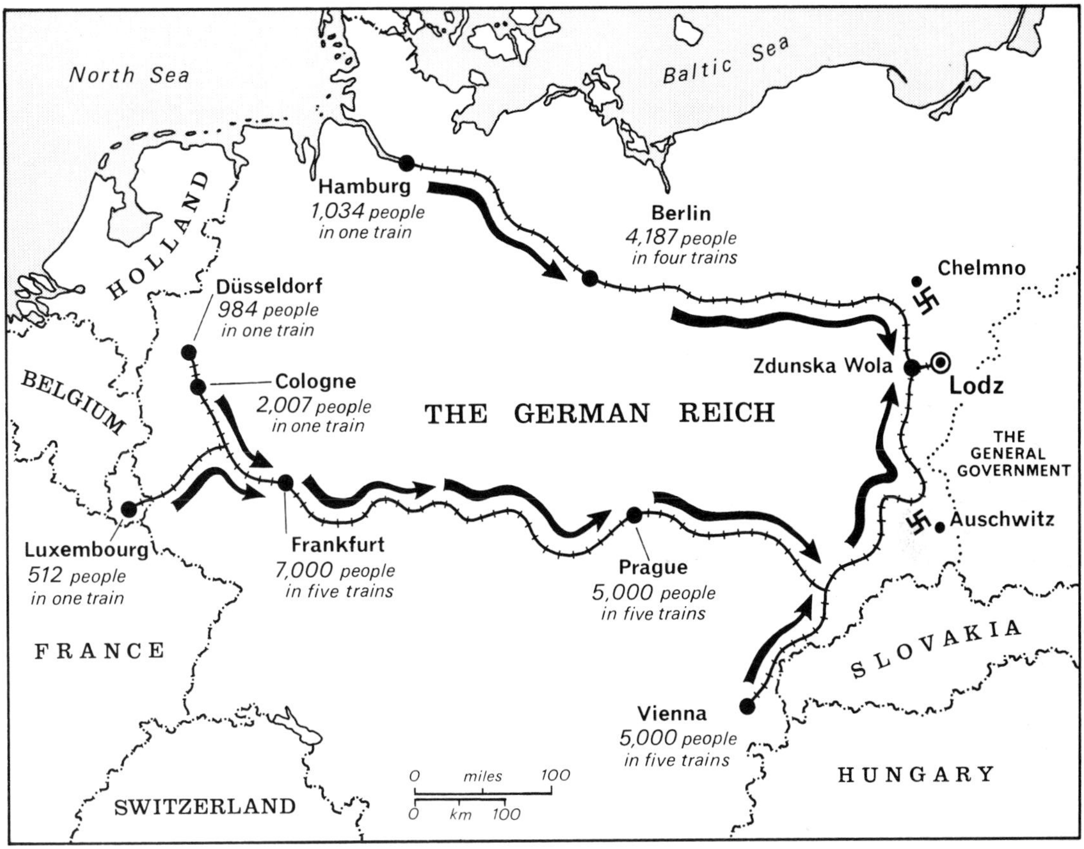

Deportations to Lodz during the autumn of 1941.

In the autumn of 1941 the Germans decided to make use of the Lodz ghetto for the old and sick, and other 'unwanted' Jews, from the cities of western Europe. Suddenly, with ruthless efficiency, railway timetables were prepared and trains made ready: and from Berlin and Prague, from Luxembourg, from Frankfurt and Vienna, more than 20,000 Jews were forced out of their homes, taken to the railway stations and deported to the east.

Even before their deportation, the Jews of these towns had been harried and restricted. In Frankfurt, a city whose Jewish community dated back a thousand years, they had been obliged, during 1941, to wear a yellow Star of David on their coats, with the word 'JEW' in the centre. One witness of their plight was a United States citizen, Edwin Van D'Elden, secretary of the American Chamber of Commerce in Frankfurt, who had remained in the city until being deported in May 1942. On his arrival in the United States in July 1942, Van D'Elden had reported how, in the autumn of 1941, Jews had been forbidden to engage in any kind of business activity, even with fellow Jews, and that no non-Jewish doctor, dentist or lawyer had been allowed to have a Jew as a client. At the same time, Jews had been forced to leave their homes in the city and move into buildings occupied entirely by Jews: most of the uprooted families were allowed only one room. No taxi or tram was allowed to take a Jewish passenger and railway travel out of Frankfurt was strictly forbidden.

Two boys in the Lodz ghetto.

Van D'Elden's report told also of the last few months before the deportation: of the continual searches of homes and confiscation of linen, clothing, shoes, furniture and food, of the desecration of the Jewish cemetery; of the cutting off first of medical and then of food supplies to the Jewish hospital; and of Jews walking in the street being forced to hand over their coats. During 1941, he estimated, more than 500 of the 10,000 Jews of Frankfurt had committed suicide. Many hundred others had been taken off to concentration camps in Germany and were never seen again. 'It was a frequent occurrence', Van D'Elden wrote, 'for Jewish families in Frankfurt to receive from the Nazi authorities the ashes of relations who died or were cremated in concentration camps', and he added:

'It is a standing rule in concentration camps that prisoners guilty of the slightest disobedience render themselves subject to summary execution, this applying not only to Jewish but non-Jewish prisoners as well.

'Execution in concentration camps generally is by means of hanging by strangulation since the victim is lifted from the ground by a rope encircling the neck. Executions at concentration camps generally are performed in the presence of all the other inmates of the camp.'

The first deportation from Frankfurt to Lodz took place on 19 October 1941. Van D'Elden reported that while he was still in the city, from October 1941 to May 1942, five separate trains had left Frankfurt, each with about 1,400 people on board. Among the deportees known to him personally was Dr Ascher, former chief of the city's Health Department; Miss Glaser, former superintendent of the Jewish Community Hospital; and Miss Alice Rosenbaum, a distinguished pianist who had played before the war in London and other European cities.

Van D'Elden noted in his report that some of the deportees were people 'who had already received visas for emigrating to foreign countries'. Some had made all their preparations for leaving Germany altogether 'and were on the verge of actual departure from the country'. His report continued:

'Jewish persons of all ages were included in the deportation, from newly born babes to persons over eighty years of age. They were allowed to take with them only as much baggage as they personally could carry. They could not take with them more than 40 Reichsmarks per person and all of their other money, possessions, furniture, etc., were confiscated by the Reich.

'The deportees were required to march through the streets in groups to the Central Market Hall. Many were physically unable, due to advanced age, infirmities, etc., to carry their effects the long distance of at least five kilometres from their homes to the Market Hall. These persons were not allowed to stop *en route*, and were compelled to discard the luggage that they were unable to carry, so that many of the deportees had already lost most of their effects before they even reached the Market Hall, where they had to spend the night in cellars, sleeping on the stone floor.

'In these quarters, they were subjected to a

thorough search to insure against their taking with them any money or property not approved by the authorities. Women and girls were subjected to abominable indignities.'

On the following morning special deportation trains drew up to the Market Hall and the deportees, as Van D'Elden reported, 'were crowded into the carriages like so many cattle, many of them not having seats in the over-crowded quarters'. So it was that each of the trains set off for the Lodz ghetto. Yet even this destination was not for all the trains. Van D'Elden concluded his report with a terrible account of the fate of three of the trains:

'Of the five convoys leaving Frankfurt prior to my departure, I learned from incontestable sources that only one reached its destination at Lodz and that three never reached their destination.

'These three convoys were compelled to leave the train in open territory in Poland, were stripped of their clothing and then were summarily executed by Nazi firing squads who mowed the victims down by machine-gun fire.

'Unbelievable as this information may appear, I nevertheless can guarantee its accuracy for I learned of these events from Aryan friends of mine who secured the information from soldiers who actually participated in the executions in Poland and who subsequently returned to Frankfurt on leave.

'I was unable to learn of the fate of the fifth deportation since I left Frankfurt only two days after this convoy left Frankfurt and too soon to receive information.'

Those Frankfurt deportees who reached the Lodz ghetto were forced to live in unheated barns and barracks. The winter of 1941 was a severe one – on the eastern front it was causing havoc with the German advance into Russia – and in Lódź itself 5,000 of the deportees from the west had died of starvation and of typhus by the spring of 1942. Then, in May 1942, as the policy of the 'final solution' laid down at the Wannsee Conference began to be put into effect, those western deportees who had survived the winter were seized and deported again. Their new destination: Auschwitz. Their fate on arrival there: immediate death.

As trains left the Lodz ghetto to the death camps, new trains reached Lodz, bringing more Jews from elsewhere, some from neighbouring Polish towns from which they had been expelled. An eye-witness of these events – whose report was smuggled out of Europe two years later – recalled how, in May 1942, 1,000 Jews, expelled from Zdunska Wola, had reached Lodz by train, deported from their home town in sealed goods trucks. 'When the train reached Lodz', the eye-witness reported, '200 were found to be choked to death.'

During the spring and summer of 1942 the Nazis focused their deportation plans on the original inhabitants of the ghetto. The first of these to be deported were all those who were sick or dying of starvation, all those who were over sixty and children up to ten years old. For more than 80,000 people, the final journey had begun. It is now known that 44,000 of them were sent direct to the extermination camp at Chelmno. At the time all that was known was that once they were taken away, they were never heard of again. The same eye-witness wrote, after the massive deportation of May 1942:

'People were taken away and kidnapped without any lists, and children exceeding the age of ten were also included. The nurses were compelled to take out the little babies and hand them over to the Germans who carried them off in whole groups by their little hands. The Germans even looked for children in the cisterns; and found them there.

'Nobody knows to what place the 50,000 were taken away.

'One woman hid her five-year-old daughter in rags, throwing her over the other side of the fence where there was a rag warehouse. Three days later she took her out and brought her back home. The child was like a wild animal with the fear and hunger she had experienced and bit everybody who endeavoured to approach her. The woman also succeeded in hiding her second

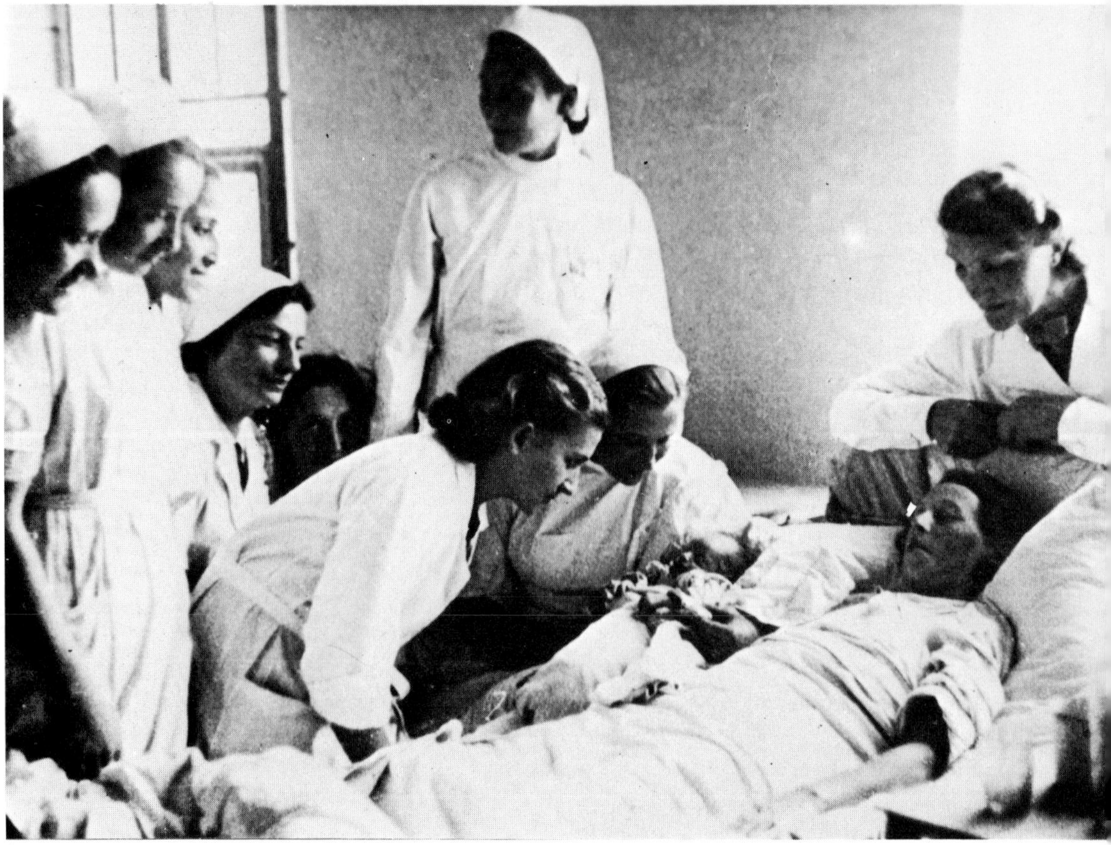

child in a niche in the wall behind a curtain.

'In addition there were repeated expulsions of smaller groups consisting of a few hundred, or including prisoners or those who were being punished, for slight transgressions of administrative regulations; or of patients who were taken out of hospitals. No trace of all those persons is known.'

In September 1942 the deportations ceased, and hunger became the main enemy. The Germans had turned the Lodz ghetto into a vast labour camp, serving the needs of the German army. By August 1943 more than a hundred factories were in operation, employing almost 80,000 of the 89,000 surviving Jews of Lodz. All men and women had to work, as did all children over the age of eight. As for the ghetto administration, it too was liquidated. The children's homes, old people's homes, hospitals, schools and orphanages, which Rumkowski had created, were closed down: their inmates put to work, or left to die. All that the Germans wanted now was forced labour. All who were too weak to work would die of hunger. The eye-witness wrote of how:

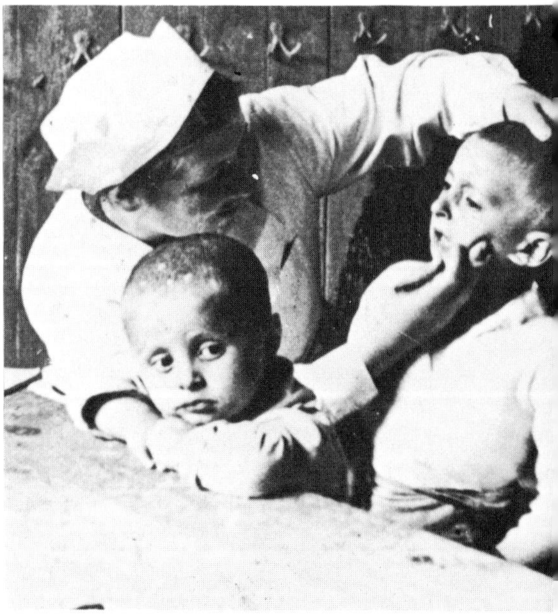

The Lodz ghetto: the hospital *(above)* and *(top)* a baby is born.

Opposite above: **women and children search for food in the ghetto rubbish dump.** ***Opposite below:*** **a brother and sister photographed by Mendel Grossman.**

'Each resident of the ghetto, irrespective of age or whether he works or not receives 250 grams of bread per day. The workers must work ten hours daily with an interval of an hour at noon. They receive soup once a day.

'The supervisors and those engaged in difficult work receive two soups twice a week.

'Recently they have stopped giving any soup at all to sick people.

'The children receive half a litre of soup per day at clubs, and the normal bread ration in addition. Workers also receive a small payment, which is enough to purchase a food ration that is distributed once a fortnight.'

This fortnightly ration consisted of 600 grams of flour, 450 grams of sugar, 50 grams of oil, occasionally 50 grams of margarine, and, but only rarely, 200 grams of meat. In six months, 4,600 Jews died of starvation, furthering the aims of Wannsee that they should 'fall away through natural reduction'.

Towards the end of 1943 warnings were spread of a new large-scale deportation, but no such deportation took place. In January 1944 there were further rumours of an imminent expulsion of all

Children working in the clothing factory.

remaining children. But again nothing happened. Thus it was that the eye-witness could write, in the spring of 1944, with a confident air:

'There is a model cleanliness in the ghetto, work in the factories goes forward energetically and productively. The German committee which inspected the ghetto was full of praise for the productivity of the workers and the cleanliness which they found in the ghetto. This state of affairs saved the ghetto from final liquidation, which was about to take place according to the rumours current.'

In fact, the 76,701 Jews who were registered in the Lodz ghetto on 1 June 1944 were neither safe, nor saved. As, 800 miles to the west, the Allied armies were landing on the Normandy beaches, the Germans decided to destroy the Lodz ghetto altogether. On 4 August 1944 the workers of the ghetto were presented with Announcement No 418, headed 'Trans-shipment of the ghetto'. The announcement stated that all Jews still in Lodz would be leaving shortly for another destination. On 7 August a further notice, Announcement No 422, ordered everyone to prepare themselves for their imminent departure.

The Jews of Lodz sought to resist: surely safety lay in remaining where they were, despite the terrible hunger? Had they not survived this far, to the point where, from both east and west, the Allied armies were driving the Germans back towards the borders of the Reich? So it was that the workers went on strike. They refused to be taken elsewhere.

But the authorities were insistent, and on the afternoon of 7 August the workers were addressed by Hans Biebow, a graduate of a German school of business administration, now Chief of the Ghetto Administration. Bombs, he said, had

Awaiting deportation, another of the photographs taken by Mendel Grossman, a young professional photographer in Lodz. Grossman died during a march from a labour camp in Germany, aged thirty-two.

fallen near the city, and the Germans intended to evacuate it. Inside Germany, thousands of workers were being sent to the front line. New workers were needed. The munitions factories of the Reich must be fully manned. The Jews of the Lodz ghetto would go to factories in Germany. The journey would take between ten and sixteen hours. Food was already loaded on the trains. Everyone would be allowed to take with him 17 kilos of luggage. If they refused to go, force would be used, and there would be dead and wounded.

The workers of Lodz gave in. They would exchange one workshop for another. Hopefully, there might be more food further west. But it was not to be. The Germans had only one destination in mind: Auschwitz. On 15 August Wilhelm Max Burger, a former Chief of Administration of Auschwitz and now in charge of concentration camp administration at the SS Economic-Administration Main Office, reported to an official in the 'economic enterprises' section that only a small 'clean up' group of Jews would remain in Lodz. All the rest were on the way to Auschwitz.

By 1 September 1944 nearly all the surviving 60,000 Jews of Lodz had been murdered and a once thriving industrial centre had been destroyed.

One Jew, however, had been spared deportation by the Germans themselves: this was Rumkowski, who had served as Elder of the ghetto for more than four years. He and his family were told that they could remain in the ghetto. This offer they declined. Instead, they voluntarily joined that last transport for Auschwitz, where they too were murdered.

On the morning of 19 January 1945 Soviet troops, driving westwards towards Berlin, entered Lodz and liberated the ghetto. By nightfall all the surviving Jews had emerged from their hiding places. They totalled 870 starving beings, the sole survivors of 164,000 people.

7

'Nobody Came Back . . .'

Breakfast in the Jewish school in Gorlice, April 1942.

During 1942 and 1943 more than 600,000 Jews were taken, mostly from the former Polish province of Eastern Galicia, and murdered at Belzec. A German document, dated 17 March 1942, stated that the camp could 'handle' as many as five trains a day, each with 1,000 deportees, 'none of whom will ever return to the General Government'.

Like most of the sites chosen for the death camps, Belzec was a small, remote Polish village. In 1921 it had fewer than 2,000 inhabitants, of whom 124 were Jews. In May 1940 a labour camp had been established there, to which some 7,000 Jews from Lublin, Warsaw and Radom had been deported, and by August 1940 it held more than 11,000 labourers, all of whom were forced to dig anti-tank ditches, aimed at halting any future Soviet tank advances. By December 1940, when the ditches were completed, the camp was closed. So weakened were those who then returned to Warsaw, that many of them died soon after.

It was as a result of the decisions of the Wannsee Conference that Belzec was opened again in March 1942, and for more than nine months it served only as a killing centre. Jews were first brought to Belzec from Lublin, then from all the towns, villages and hamlets of Eastern Galicia, of which Lvov was the capital, and finally some from as far away as Germany, Czechoslovakia and Rumania. Only one person is known to have survived.

A young German engineer, Dr Kurt Gerstein,

Awaiting deportation from Eastern Galicia.

Lvov: four Jews awaiting deportation.

whom Eichmann employed as a poison gas expert, was so disgusted by what he saw at Belzec that while the camp was still 'operational' he passed on details of the exterminations to a Swedish diplomat and, as the war ended, typed out the full story which he then gave to a British and an American officer, to whom he surrendered. Imprisoned in Paris, Gerstein committed suicide on 7 July 1945.

As Gerstein recalled, the Belzec camp had a special compound for the SS, above the entrance of which was the sign: 'Entrance to the Jewish State.' From their compound, under the command of a former Stuttgart pohce officer, Christian Wirth, the SS men could actually see the entrance to the gas chamber, the doors to which had been draped with synagogue curtains bearing the Hebrew inscription: 'This is the gate of the Lord into which the righteous shall enter.' Gerstein also described the scene as each train was unloaded, and 1,000 people went forward to the gas chamber. As he remembered it:

'For a number of men there still flickers a lingering hope, sufficient to make them march without resistance to the death chambers. The majority know with certainty what is to be their fate. The horrible, all-pervading stench reveals the truth. Then they climb some small steps and behold the

Deported in open trains.

reality. Silent mothers hold their babies to their breasts, naked; there are many children of all ages. They hesitate, but nevertheless proceed toward the death chambers, most of them without a word, pushed by those behind, chased by the whips of the SS men.

'A woman of about forty curses the chief of the murderers, crying that the blood of her children will be on his head. Wirth, an SS officer, himself strikes her across the face with five lashes of the whip and she disappears into the gas chamber. Many pray. . . .

'The SS men squeeze people into the chambers. "Fill them up well", orders Wirth. The naked people stand on each other's feet. About seven to eight hundred people in an area of about a hundred square metres. The doors close, the rest of the transport stands waiting, naked. . . . In the winter, too, they stand waiting, naked. But the diesel engine is not functioning . . . fifty minutes pass by; seventy minutes. The people in the death chambers remain standing. Their weeping is heard. SS Sturmbannführer Professor Dr Pfannenstiel, lecturer in hygiene at Marburg University, remarks: "Just like in a synagogue.". . .

'Only after two hours and forty-nine minutes does the diesel finally begin to work. Twenty-five minutes pass by. Many have already died, as can be seen through the small window. Twenty-eight minutes later a few are still alive. After thirty-two minutes all are dead. . . . Jewish workers open the doors on the other side. . . . The dead, having nowhere to fall, stand like pillars of basalt. Even in death, families may be seen standing pressed together, clutching hands. It is only with difficulty that the bodies are separated in order to clear the place for the next load. The blue corpses, covered with sweat and urine . . . babies and bodies of children, are thrown out. But there is no time! A couple of workers are busy with the mouths of the dead, opening them with iron pegs; "With gold to the left – without gold to the right", is the order. Others search in the private parts of the bodies for gold and diamonds. . . . Wirth points to a full preserves tin and exclaims, "Lift it up, and see how much gold there is." '

Gerstein also recalled how, in order not to 'hamper' the smooth flow of people into the gas chamber, old people and invalids were taken away, as if to the hospital, but in fact to open pits, where they were then shot.

Kurt Gerstein had spent time actually inside Belzec. Thousands of other people passed by the camp, which was on the railway line between Lvov and Cholm, and which gave rise to considerable talk among the Germans who worked in the locality. The mass killings were no secret to those who worked in the region. On 30 August 1942 a German non-commissioned officer, Wilhelm Cornides, was in Rzeszow, on his way to Cholm by train. In his diary he recorded that a railway policeman in Rzeszow had told him that 'a marble plaque with golden letters will be erected on 1 September, because then the city will be free of Jews'. The policeman also told him that trains filled with Jews 'pass almost daily through the shunting yards, are dispatched immediately on their way, and return swept clean, most often the same evening'. Some 6,000 Jews from Jaroslaw, the policeman added, 'were recently killed in one day'.

Cornides then took the regular passenger train from Rzeszow to Cholm, reaching Rawa Ruska on 31 August, and recording in his diary, while staying in the 'German House' there:

'At ten minutes past noon I saw a transport train run into the station. On the roof and running boards sat guards with rifles. One could see from a distance that the cars were jammed full of people. I turned and walked along the whole train: it consisted of thirty-eight cattle cars and one passenger car.

'In each of the cars there were at least sixty Jews (in the case of enlisted men's or prisoner transports these wagons would hold forty men; however, the benches had been removed and one could see that those who were locked in here had to stand pressed together). Some of the doors were opened a crack, the windows criss-crossed with barbed wire. Among the locked-in people there were a few men and most of those were old; everything else was women, girls and children. Many children crowded at the windows and the narrow door openings. The youngest were surely not more than two years old.

'As soon as the train halted, the Jews attempted to pass out bottles in order to get water. The train, however, was surrounded by SS guards, so that no one could come near. At that moment a train arrived from the direction of Jaroslaw; the travellers streamed toward the exit without bothering about the transport. A few Jews who were busy loading a car for the armed forces waved their caps to the locked-in people.

'I talked to a policeman on duty at the railway station. Upon my question as to where the Jews actually came from, he answered: "Those are probably the last ones from Lvov. That has been going on now for five weeks uninterruptedly. In Jaroslaw they let remain only eight, no one knows why." I asked: "How far are they going?" Then he said: "To Belzec." "And then?" "Poison." I asked: "Gas?" He shrugged his shoulders. Then he said only: "At the beginning they always shot them, I believe."

'Here in the German House I just talked with two soldiers from front-line prisoner-of-war camp 325. They said that these transports had lately passed through every day, mostly at night. Yesterday a seventy-car one is supposed to have gone through.'

From Rawa Ruska, Cornides took the afternoon train to Cholm. The things he learned on this journey were so extraordinary that he made three separate entries in his diary within an hour, the first at 5.30 pm.

'When we boarded at 4.40 pm an empty transport had just arrived. I walked along the train twice and counted fifty-six cars. On the doors had been written in chalk: 60, 70, once 90, occasionally 40 – obviously the number of Jews that were carried inside.

'In my compartment I spoke with a railway policeman's wife who is currently visiting her husband here. She says these transports are now passing through daily, sometimes also with Ger-

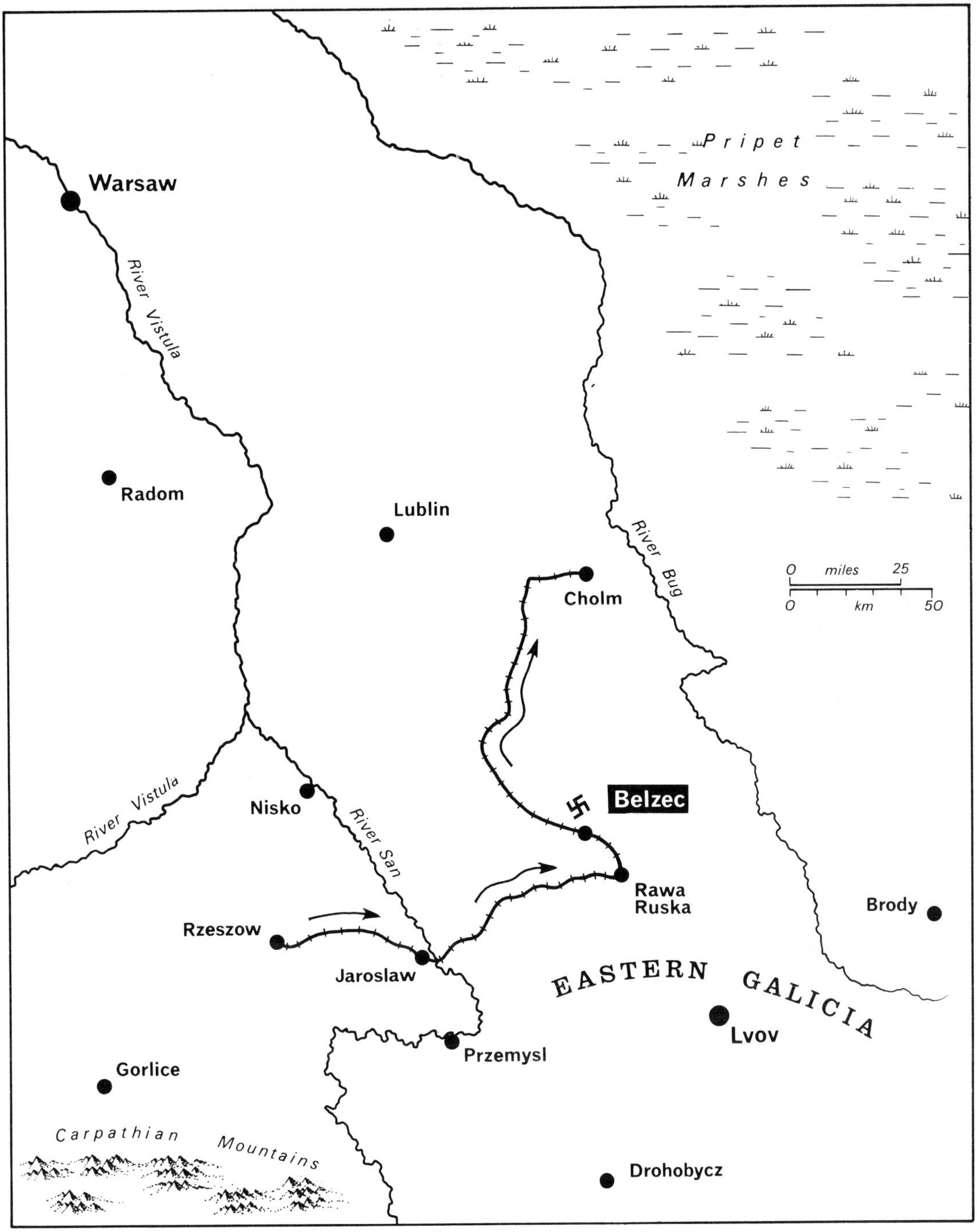

Wilhelm Cornides' journey.

man Jews. Yesterday six children's bodies were found along the track. The woman thinks that the Jews themselves had killed these children – but they must have succumbed during the trip.

'The railway policeman who comes along as train escort joined us in our compartment. He confirmed the woman's statements about the children's bodies which were found along the track yesterday. I asked: "Do the Jews know then what is happening with them?" The woman answered: "Those who come from far won't know anything, but here in the vicinity they know already. They attempt to run away then, if they notice that someone is coming for them. So, for example, most recently in Cholm where three were shot on the way through the city." "In the railway documents these trains run under the name of resettlement transports," remarked the railway policeman....

'Camp Belzec is supposed to be located right on the railway line and the woman promised to show it to me when we pass it.'

'5.40 pm. Short stop. Opposite us another transport. I talk to the policemen who ride on the passenger car in front. I ask: "Going back home to the Reich?" Grinning one of them says: "You know where we come from, don't you? Well, for us the work does not cease." Then the transport train continued – the cars were empty and swept clean; there were thirty-five. In all probability that was the train I saw at 1 pm on the station in Rawa Ruska.'

'6.20 pm. We passed camp Belzec. Before then, we travelled for some time through a tall pine forest. When the woman called, "Now it comes", one could see a high hedge of fir trees.

'A strong sweetish odour could be made out distinctly. "But they are stinking already", says the woman. "Oh nonsense, that is only the gas", the railway policeman said laughing. Meanwhile – we had gone on about 200 metres – the sweetish odour was transformed into a strong smell of something burning. "That is from the crematory",

Belzec death camp: the shoes of the victims, waiting to be sorted for despatch to Germany.

says the policeman. A short distance farther the fence stopped. In front of it, one could see a guard house with an SS post. A double track led into the camp. One track branched off from the main line, the other ran over a turntable from the camp to a row of sheds about 250 metres away.

'A freight car happened to stand on the table. Several Jews were busy turning the disc. SS guards, rifle under the arm, stood by. One of the sheds was open; one could distinctly see that it was filled with bundles of clothes to the ceiling. As we went on, I looked back one more time. The fence was too high to see anything at all. The woman says that sometimes, while going by, one can see smoke rising from the camp, but I could notice nothing of the sort. My estimate is that the camp measures about 800 by 400 metres.'

Wilhelm Cornides reached Cholm on 1 September 1942. In the beer hall there he had a long conversation with a German policeman, who told him, as he recorded in his diary:

'"The policemen who escort the Jewish trains are not allowed in the camp. The only ones who get in are the SS and the Ukrainian Special Service (a police formation of Ukrainian volunteers). But these people are doing a good business over there. Recently a Ukrainian visited us, and he had a whole stack of money in notes, and watches and gold and all kinds of things. They find all of that when they put together the clothing and load it." Upon the question as to how these Jews were actually being killed, the policeman answered: "They are told that they must get rid of their lice, and then they must take off their clothes, and then they come into a room, where first off they get a hot blast of air which is already mixed with a small dose of gas. That is enough to make them unconscious. The rest comes after. And then they are burned immediately."'

By the spring of 1943 almost all the Jews of Eastern Galicia had been deported to Belzec, and murdered. It was not only the local Germans, and railway travellers, who learned the truth. Details of the killings had even reached the Jews in the Warsaw ghetto during 1942. There, two years later, Yitzak Zuckerman, one of the leaders of the Jewish resistance in Warsaw, wrote in a letter which was sent secretly from Warsaw to London on 24 May 1944:

'The Jewish underground Press published detailed reports of this mass slaughter, but Warsaw refused to believe them! The human mind found it impossible to believe that tens and hundreds of Jews could be exterminated. It was claimed that the Jews were being conveyed to agricultural labour in the Russian territories occupied by the Germans.'

The Jewish Press, Zuckerman added, 'was condemned and accused of disseminating panic, although the descriptions of the population "Resettlement" activities were completely in accordance with the facts'.

8

The Warsaw Ghetto

On the outbreak of war in 1939 there were nearly 400,000 Jews living in Warsaw: one third of the city's population. Here, in the Polish capital, was one of the largest, most vibrant Jewish communities in the world, a centre of Yiddish culture and of Zionist enthusiasm, of Jewish family life and Hebrew culture.

An old community, its written records stretched back more than 500 years, showing the extent to which the Jews of Warsaw had survived several outbursts of persecution, repeated expulsions, and the intolerance of a succession of conquerors. It was under Tsarist rule from 1815 to 1915 that Warsaw Jewry had grown most rapidly, and flourished. In 1881, after the mob violence against Jews elsewhere in Russia, more than 150,000 Jews, many from Lithuania, White Russia and the Ukraine, had found permanent refuge in the city.

Jews from Warsaw participated, and led, in every area of Jewish life: as rabbinical scholars and teachers, as educationalists and doctors, as Socialists and Zionists. Above all, the Yiddish language bound together the 400,000, gave them a vigorous Press and a superb literature, poetry, songs, plays and a wealth of cultural expression. There was poverty too; and the strain of trying to earn a living at a time of both widespread economic distress and spasmodic outbursts of Polish anti-semitism, made life difficult for many, and harsh for some.

Both under the Tsars until the First World War, and under the independent Polish Republic after 1919, tens of thousands of Warsaw Jews sought a new life by emigration. The United States was the choice of the majority of those who left – they called it the 'Golden Realm'. Thousands more went to western Europe, to Britain, and to France in particular, hoping thereby to escape forever the anti-semitism which seemed to pursue them even in Warsaw, the city in which they were so much 'at home'.

Several thousand Warsaw Jews had gone to Palestine. But there were others, among those who remained in Warsaw, who had begun to assimilate, who spoke and wrote Polish in preference to Yiddish, and who saw their future bound up not in adhering to their Jewish culture, or in emigration, but in the Polish state itself, and in their own eventual acceptance as equals by the Poles.

With the German armies advancing across Poland, these hopes were shattered. On the very first day of the war, 1 September 1939, the Germans bombed Warsaw. Among the first dead of the war were several dozen children in a Jewish educational institution at Otwock, run by the children's welfare organization, 'Centos'. The newly appointed manager of the institution, Adolf Berman – who survived the war – later recalled what he saw when he reached the town:

'The scene that unfolded before my eyes was shocking. Houses were in ruins; blood and pieces of the murdered children's brains were splattered over the floors and the remains of the walls. The children who survived were overcome by fear and were on the verge of despair.'

The German conquest of Poland was swift; on 5 October 1939, only five weeks after the German troops had crossed the Polish border, Hitler himself took the salute at the German 'victory' parade

Hitler in Warsaw, October 1939, a photograph issued as a postcard by Hitler's own photographer, with the caption 'The "Supreme Commander" with His Troops in Warsaw'.

in Warsaw. A ten-year-old Polish Jewish schoolboy, Avraham Kochavi, too young to realize the implications of this scene, later recalled the parade to welcome Hitler: 'there was a German band playing. For me it was very nice. I was happy; I even remember that I clapped.'

Within a few weeks of Hitler's visit the atmosphere had changed completely. In the streets of Warsaw, where the sights and sounds of Jewish life had been for so long an integral part of the daily scene, Jews were attacked by groups of roving Nazis who made a sport of seizing those religious Jews with long beards and side-locks, kicking them, pushing them, cutting off their long hair, mocking at their religious observance, and treating them as objects of derision and 'sport'.

Life soon became particularly difficult for the Jews. Avraham Kochavi later recalled how, when food ran out in their home:

'... my mother, may her soul rest in peace, asked me to go down to the bakery and stand there the whole night in order to get a loaf of bread the next day so that there would be something to eat at home.

'I got up in the middle of the night and went down to get into line. When I arrived there were already masses and masses of people waiting in the line. At dawn, a Pole who was of German origin arrived with a rifle slung over his right shoulder, a band with a swastika on his left arm. He was, presumably, supposed to keep order so that everyone would receive bread.

'Among us there were little children – non-Jews, Poles – running around. They dragged that same Pole with a rifle over and pointed at each and every person – "That's a Jew – that's a Jew – that's a Jew – *das Jude – das Jude – das Jude*", so that these people would be taken out of line and not get bread.

'My turn came. I turned around and saw that the boy was a friend with whom I played. I said to him in Polish, "What are you doing?" His answer was "I'm not your friend – you are a Jew – I don't know you."

'That same German with the swastika armband was standing in front of me. I saw that he was a neighbour of ours. I spoke to him in Polish. He answered in German; he said "I don't know Polish. I don't know you." And then he forcibly took me out of the line where I was waiting for bread and slapped me.

'I burst into tears because I didn't know what had happened. My world had collapsed. My mother had asked me to stand in line so as to get some bread and a strange thing happens: the friend with whom I play, and also the German, two people whom I've known for so many years, suddenly turn on me; they don't want to know me; they deny knowing me, and hit me. They don't let me eat. I thought to myself "What will I bring home?".'

Looking back at this incident, typical of so many in those early days of the German occupation, Kochavi reflected on how this was 'the first time', as he put it, 'that somebody made me feel that I was different from other people; that I wasn't like all the Christian boys, the boys with whom I played'.

During the winter of 1939 and the spring of 1940 repressive measures followed with bewildering rapidity. By a special decree issued on 23 November 1939, every Jew was ordered to wear a white armband, on which was sewn or painted a blue Star of David. All Jewish-owned land was confiscated. Jews, denounced by the Nazis as having been 'responsible' for the war, were formed into labour gangs and made to clear away the rubble caused by the German bombing. By a decree of 11 December 1939, Jews could no longer change their residence, and were forbidden to leave their homes after nine at night or before five in the morning. Following a further decree on 26 January 1940, Jews could no longer travel by train without special permission.

Then, in order to try to terrorize the leaders of the community still further, the Gestapo arrested more than a hundred of the leading Jewish intellectuals in Warsaw: lawyers, doctors, scholars and public figures, including Brianski, the director of the children's welfare organization. All were taken to the Palmiry forest, and shot.

There were many petty harrassments also. No Jew was allowed to enter any shop owned by a German – even by one of the local Germans, or *Volksdeutsch*, who had for many years been their neighbours in the city. Whenever a Jew passed such a German, he was forced to raise his hat. If he failed to do so, he could find himself shouted at, spat at, punched or kicked – without redress. On 1 September 1940 a further decree transferred most of the Jewish-owned cafés to German hands. During the autumn of 1940 all Jewish chemist-shops were forcibly handed over to local Germans. Throughout Warsaw, Jews could be seized in the street at any time of the day, and taken off to forced labour. At night all Jews were obliged by the law of the curfew to remain indoors.

To ensure the carrying out of their orders, the Germans established special Jewish councils in almost every town in Poland, and made these councils responsible for Jewish obedience to the Nazi will. Jewish bureaucrats were to ensure that the Nazi edicts were carried out, helped by Jewish police.

In Warsaw, Adam Czerniakow was appointed Chairman of the Council. An engineer by profession, Polish- as opposed to Yiddish-speaking, Czerniakow was a well-known Jewish community leader, a man in his late fifties, who between the wars had been an active leader of the Jewish workers of Poland, who made up some 40 per cent of Polish Jewry.

Czerniakow had been appointed Chairman of the Council within a month of the German conquest of Poland. He and his council were soon faced with a Nazi demand that all Jews in Warsaw should be confined to a single part of the town, enclosed by a wall, forbidden to leave, and deprived of all contact with the outside world.

One of those who was determined to chronicle the fate of the Jews of Warsaw from day to day was the forty-year-old Chaim Kaplan, born in White Russia but a citizen of Warsaw since his early twenties. Kaplan was the founder, and Principal, of an elementary school in Warsaw in which the language of instruction was Hebrew, taught as a spoken language. He had twice travelled outside Poland, going in 1921 to the United States and in 1936 to Palestine. In 1937 he had published a volume of articles on the Hebrew language and Jewish education. He had written several text-books for children, including one on Jewish history and customs. Now, in his diary, he set down for posterity the story of the creation of the Warsaw ghetto, and of its fate.

The edict for the creation of the ghetto was announced just before sunset on 12 October 1941, towards the end of the most solemn day of the Jewish calendar, the Day of Atonement: all Jews living outside the walls must move inside them, and all Poles living inside the ghetto must leave it. 'A hundred and twenty thousand people', Chaim Kaplan noted in his diary that night, 'will be driven out of their homes and will have to find sanctuary and shelter within the walls. Where will we put this great mass of people?'

Streets in which Jews had lived for hundreds of years were excluded from the ghetto area. All those who were to be moved from these streets had to give up not only their homes, but also their shops and livelihood. 'In leaving their homes', Kaplan noted, 'they are also leaving their incomes.' The ghetto area was already crowded with Jewish refugees from the provincial towns, so that there was no way in which those who were being displaced could be housed adequately.

Yet at first there seemed a glimmer of hope, even about the ghetto. It was rumoured that it would be an 'open' ghetto, into which and out of which Jews could travel freely. 'Will it be a closed ghetto?', Chaim Kaplan asked in his diary on 24 October 1940. 'There are signs in both directions, and we hope for a miracle – which doesn't always happen in time of need.' Three days later, and still no decision had been made. Meanwhile, the 50,000 Jews of the Warsaw suburb of Praga, on the eastern bank of the Vistula, had been told that they too would have to move into the Warsaw ghetto. Kaplan noted in his diary:

'Although it has been administratively joined to Warsaw, Praga is actually a city in itself, and they were sure a separate ghetto would be created there. But there is no analysing the stupidity and evil of the Nazis. By 31 October Praga must be empty of its Jewish inhabitants, who were rooted in its soil for hundreds of years. Most of them are poor. They have no money to move their belongings. And where would they move them to? Many Poles drove the Praga Jews from their apartments in advance, before the fixed date.

'The scroll of agony which the rabbis of Praga unrolled before us touched our souls. Even the stout-hearted ones in the audience could not hold back their tears.'

The move to the ghetto was ordered to be completed on 31 October. But on that day there was a reprieve, until 15 November. The belief that it would be an 'open' ghetto revived; it was announced that President Roosevelt himself had obtained this concession from the Germans. But the rumour was false. The ghetto was to be a closed one. And in mid-November it came into being. Avraham Kochavi's family was one of those which had lived outside the area now set aside for the Jews. As he later recalled:

'I, together with father, made a small cart, and we began to move. Thousands and thousands, tens of thousands of people were walking, taking their belongings with them; some on their heads, some on their backs, some on their shoulders.

'There were children, old people, babies – all of them, like the exile of the peoples, the exile from Egypt.

'But it was also of interest to see the Aryan side, the Poles, the Christians, how they were watching; some of them, lots of them, clapped their hands, for they were happy about it. "Now we'll buy their flats; we'll take over; we'll have it good; all the furniture that the Jews have – we'll have everything." '

By December 1940 nearly half a million Jews were crowded into the Warsaw ghetto. Of these, more than 70,000 were refugees. Spasmodically, and without warning, the Germans would order a

Part of the wall which sealed the Jews inside the Warsaw ghetto.

reduction in the area of the already restricted ghetto zone, leaving overnight thousands of families without any shelter at all.

But there was no security even behind the ghetto walls for those who were now trapped inside them. 'A Jew does not dare make a sound of protest', Chaim Kaplan wrote on 6 December 1940:

'There have been cases where courageous Jews were shot in full view of their entire family and the murderers were not held responsible, because their excuse was that the filthy Jew cursed the Führer and it was their duty to avenge his honour.'

On 18 January 1941 Kaplan noted:

'All along the sidewalks, on days of cold so fierce as to be unendurable, entire families bundled up in rags wander about, not begging, but merely moaning with heart-rending voices. A father and a mother with their sick little children, crying and wailing, fill the street with the sound of their sobs.'

On 31 January 1941 the Germans forced a further 3,000 more Jews from the suburbs around Warsaw to move into the ghetto. Kaplan recorded in his diary:

'The exiles were driven out of their beds before dawn, and the Führer's minions did not let them take money, belongings or food, threatening all the while to shoot them. Before they left on their exile, a search was made of their pockets and of all the hidden places in their clothes and bodies. Without a penny in their pockets or a covering for the women, children, old people, and invalids – sometimes without shoes on their feet or staffs in their hands – they were forced to leave their homes and possessions and the graves of their ancestors, and go – whither? And in terrible, fierce, unbearable cold!'

In April 1941 a further 72,000 more Jews were driven from their homes in the Warsaw district and forced into the ghetto. Overcrowding increased, so much so that there were now an 'average' of thirteen people to a room, while thousands of others had no room at all: only corridors or yards in which to try to find some shelter.

Systematically, the Germans confiscated Jewish property, even inside the ghetto, placing individual houses under German 'plenipotentiaries' and selling Jewish property to fill their own coffers. Carefully kept German records show, month by

Jews expelled from the towns around Warsaw were driven into the ghetto, where the growing overcrowding forced whole groups to live in a single room.

month, the value of Jewish goods seized, and sold by the Germans; for the first four months of 1942, the total was equivalent to more than £2,000,000 or $4,000,000.

By the early months of 1942 life in the ghetto had become a cruel and losing battle against hunger and disease. So short was fuel, that in a survey of 780 dwellings in the winter of 1941–2, it was found that as many as 718 had no heat at all.

Food was desperately short, the food allocation allowed by the Germans being only 194 calories per Jew per day. Outside the ghetto walls, the Poles of Warsaw were allowed 634 calories and the Germans 2,310 calories. With such precise calculations did the Nazis ensure that tens of thousands of Jews, without any means of earning a living, unable to keep themselves warm in winter, died of starvation. The adults and older children

The Warsaw ghetto: at the window of the soup kitchen.

struggled as best they could to find food, to eke out their meagre rations, to subsist on 500 grams of sugar and 2 kilos of bread a month: even the bread was mixed with potato peel and sawdust. When there was no bread, there was no hope. Yet for the younger children, it seemed unreal. Avraham Kochavi recalled how his younger sister Adela would ask his mother repeatedly for something to eat:

'She always said "Bread, bread, bread." And mother had nothing to give her. I somehow understood the situation and accepted it. But my sister was three years younger – she was eight years old. She didn't want to accept this because she didn't understand it. She always shouted "Bread, bread, bread – food." And there was none.'

Hunger and disease were the curse of the ghetto. Old men and children, too weak to move any further, would lie down in the streets and die. In October 1941, in order to ensure that food could not be smuggled in from outside, the Germans announced that anyone leaving the ghetto without permission would be shot. By the early months of 1941 more than one person in ten had died: a total of 40,000 people, each slowly and deliberately starved to death, trapped behind a wall in a city under Nazi rule, in a conquered land, in a Europe which could do nothing against the German will.

Despite this terrible oppression, and isolation, the Jews of Warsaw struggled to maintain, amid starvation and sickness, a decent, civilized way of life. In each block of houses a charitable organization was set up to try to help those who were weakest. Musical evenings, lectures and reading groups were formed. Financial aid from Jews in America, which was still neutral, enabled soup kitchens to be maintained, giving small but free meals to the destitute. Illegal schools operated in

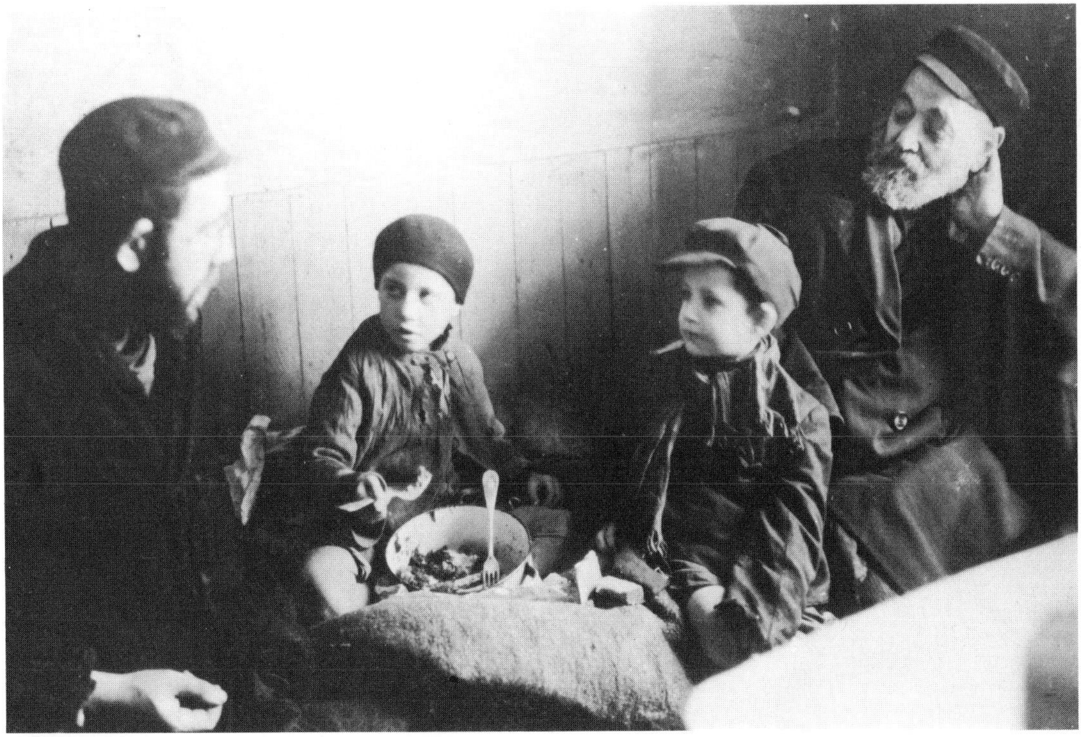

Above: **a meal in the ghetto.**
Left: **death in the ghetto.**

the guise of soup kitchens. A secret archive was formed, in which the records of the ghetto were carefully preserved. A group of doctors, refusing to accept that only evil could exist in such conditions, began a careful study of 'the disease of hunger', determined that at least future doctors in some more sane society would be able to benefit from the deliberate inhumanity of ghetto malnutrition. Religious seminaries worked in secret. Resistance groups were organized and, although they had no weapons, their determination not to surrender was unquenchable. Illegal magazines and pamphlets were published in Hebrew, Yiddish and Polish.

'This is our third winter under the Nazi regime', Chaim Kaplan noted on 10 November 1941, 'and our second within the ghetto. Contagious diseases and especially typhus continue to take their toll. There is not a family which has not lost one, or even several of its members.' Nine days later, Kaplan recorded in his diary:

'All over the ghetto groups of Jews stand in front of wall posters signed by the ghetto commissar, Auerswald, announcing that eight Jews caught leaving the ghetto without permission had been sentenced to death. The sentence was carried out on 17 November 1941. The eight martyrs were six young women and two men. These "criminals" had been caught making quick forays into Aryan territory in an attempt to smuggle food. They were murdered for breaking the law which forbade leaving the ghetto without the required pass. One of the victims, a young girl not quite eighteen, asked the Jewish policeman who was present at the execution to tell her family that she had been sent to a concentration camp and would not be seeing them for some time. Another young girl cried out to God imploring Him to accept her as the expiatory sacrifice for her people and to let her be the final victim.

'The representative of the Jewish jail on Zamenhof Street, Mr Lejkin, and several representatives of the Jewish police were present at the execution. Their task was to lead the victims to the execution spot and to bind their eyes and their hands. The men refused to have their eyes and hands bound. Their wish was granted. The execution squad was composed of Polish policemen. After carrying out their orders, they wept bitterly.'

On 7 December 1941 the Japanese attacked the United States at Pearl Harbor. Within a week the United States had declared war against Germany. Inside the Warsaw ghetto, those events seemed to portend both evil and good. 'Whatever aid we receive now from America', Chaim Kaplan noted in his diary on 12 December, 'will be stopped completely. The American philanthropic institutions here will be abandoned; the community leaders who had dealings with plutocratic America will be arrested; the soup kitchens will be shut down.' And yet, Kaplan added, 'We live with one hope: the Nazis are not strong enough to fight the entire world.'

As the war entered upon its new global phase, the daily suffering of the ghetto continued without respite. 15 December 1941 was the festival of *Hanukkah*, the feast of lights, celebrating a Jewish victory against oppression two thousand years before. That night Kaplan recorded in his diary:

'Our holiday has been turned into a day of mourning. The courtyard of the prison on Dzielna Street was turned into a slaughterhouse today. At ten o'clock this morning within earshot of thousands of people who were jammed around the fence encircling the jail, fifteen people were shot to death. They had been caught outside the ghetto limits. This murder, like the earlier ones, was carried out after a "trial" and "legal sentencing".

'Seventeen "criminals" had been brought to trial but one had committed suicide and another was sick in bed. The cries of the victims in the prison courtyard were heard by the throng outside. Rage and frustration turned into mass weeping. Other prisoners locked inside the prison began to shout and beat their heads against the walls. There is nothing more nerve-shattering than the concerted weeping of a great crowd. The wailing at this hour in history was an echo of the weeping and lamentation decreed upon the generations of the people of Israel. It was a protest against the loss of our human rights. The sentence was carried out by Polish policemen in the presence of rabbis and other representatives of the Jews. The Poles fired the shots – and they too wept. They had been given no choice either.'

Hope and despair alternated in the closed world of the Warsaw ghetto. On 19 December, six months after the German armies had begun their advance against Russia, the Jews of the ghetto rejoiced at the German failure to capture Moscow. According to rumours, it was said that the Germans were in full retreat. 'These rumours spread like wildfire', Kaplan noted in his diary, and he added bitterly: 'That's the way our people are – the bitter reality does not constrain their glowing imaginations.'

The year 1941 ended in the ghetto without celebration. A special Nazi decree issued on 26 December demanded that the Jews give up, within three days, and at the coldest time of the year, every piece of fur which they possessed, so that it could be sent to the freezing German soldiers on the eastern front. Coats, collars, cuffs, fur-lined boots, even loose scraps of fur, had all to be handed over, not for payment, but for a special

A street scene in the ghetto; a frame from a film taken by a German cameraman. The film was intended to be shown as propaganda, but proved so distressing that it was banned by Dr Goebbels.

written 'receipt', which itself would cost 2 zlotys. On 28 December, the last day for the handing over of fur, Chaim Kaplan wrote angrily in his diary:

'The biggest commotion of all is stirred up by a few Jews who are buying up furs at rock-bottom prices, not for themselves, but as agents for Aryan customers. The merchandise thus purchased is passed from hand to hand, quickly reaching the real buyer who has the cash for payment, and leaving the Jew with his agent's commission.'

A week later Kaplan wrote with even greater anger: 'Two kind of leeches suck our blood: the Nazi leeches who set up the machinery to annihilate us, and their offspring, the Jewish leeches, who thrive on smuggling and black-marketeering.'

These were harsh words; but in the terrible conditions of the ghetto, it was perhaps inevitable that all the human characteristics, vices as well as virtues, should find their expression. The reality was indeed terrible, without precedent in the lives of these starving people, for whom each day had become more full of foreboding than the day before. On 4 January 1942 Kaplan wrote:

'In the gutters, amidst the refuse, one can see almost naked and barefoot little children wailing pitifully. These are children who were orphaned when both parents died either in their wanderings or in the typhus epidemic. Yet there is no institution that will take them in and care for them and bring them up as human beings. Every morning you will see their little bodies frozen to death in the ghetto streets. . . .'

During the spring of 1942, horrific stories began to reach the inmates of the ghetto. Refugees from Lublin spoke of a Nazi massacre from which, apparently, almost no Jews had escaped. Tens of thousands had been slaughtered. The sick, the aged and the orphans had been the very first to be shot. In his diary on 18 April Chaim Kaplan, after noting the grim details, went on to ask: 'Why should Warsaw fare better than Lublin?', and four days later he reported what was becoming a typical incident:

'Today a German automobile travelled up Okopowa Street and stopped beside a ditch. A Nazi officer jumped out followed by a Jewish youth. The German pointed to the spot where the Jew was to stand. The youth obeyed. The officer then drew his pistol and put a bullet into the Jew's heart. The German got back into the car and drove off as if nothing had happened.'

'The sound of shots', Kaplan added, 'continued through the day and into the night.'

Night after night the Nazis moved through the ghetto, shooting people as if it were a pastime. 'Last night', Chaim Kaplan recorded on 27 June, 'fourteen people were shot to death on the streets of the ghetto. In the morning their naked corpses were found near the gates of the houses. Yes, naked; for the Nazis strip their victims. All the possessions of those killed by the regime are forfeit.' Two of those killed, Kaplan added, 'fell victim right before the window of my house.'

When, in the first week of July, two Jewish porters dared to try to fight back, with their bare

Nazi 'sport'.

hands, against two Nazis who were about to shoot them, 110 Jews were murdered in the ghetto as a reprisal. And yet the desperate porters, for all their efforts, had themselves been shot before they could kill their executioners. The reprisal was intended to warn the Jews against even hopeless resistance.

In the second and third weeks of July news reached the ghetto from the rest of Poland of the shooting of hundreds of thousands. No one knew what had become of friends and relatives elsewhere, in eastern Poland, in Lithuania and in the Ukraine. Rumour followed rumour, each one more horrific than the last. On 11 July Kaplan noted, in a diary that had become more pessimistic with every day:

'Death is hard; harder still are the moments before death; and even hardest of all is being condemned to a death which is inevitable, but whose time has not been set. . . . Everyone must wait until his turn comes. That is when life becomes too hard to bear. The desire to live grows stronger at just that point. On the very eve of their death, the masses in the ghetto worry about their routine affairs as though they still had a long life ahead of them. But the intelligent and perceptive walk around like mourners.'

On 19 July the Warsaw ghetto was filled with rumours that the Jews were about to be deported. Many people argued that the rumours were part of a Nazi hoax, designed to extort from the Jews what little money they had left. On 20 July these rumours of imminent deportations were officially denied by the Jewish Council; the Gestapo went so far as to say that anyone spreading such rumours would be shot.

The rumours, however, were true. On 20 July the Jewish Council had been ordered by the Gestapo to prepare for the 'resettlement' of the ghetto, beginning on 22 July. The railway administration had been instructed to prepare enough goods wagons to transport 10,000 people

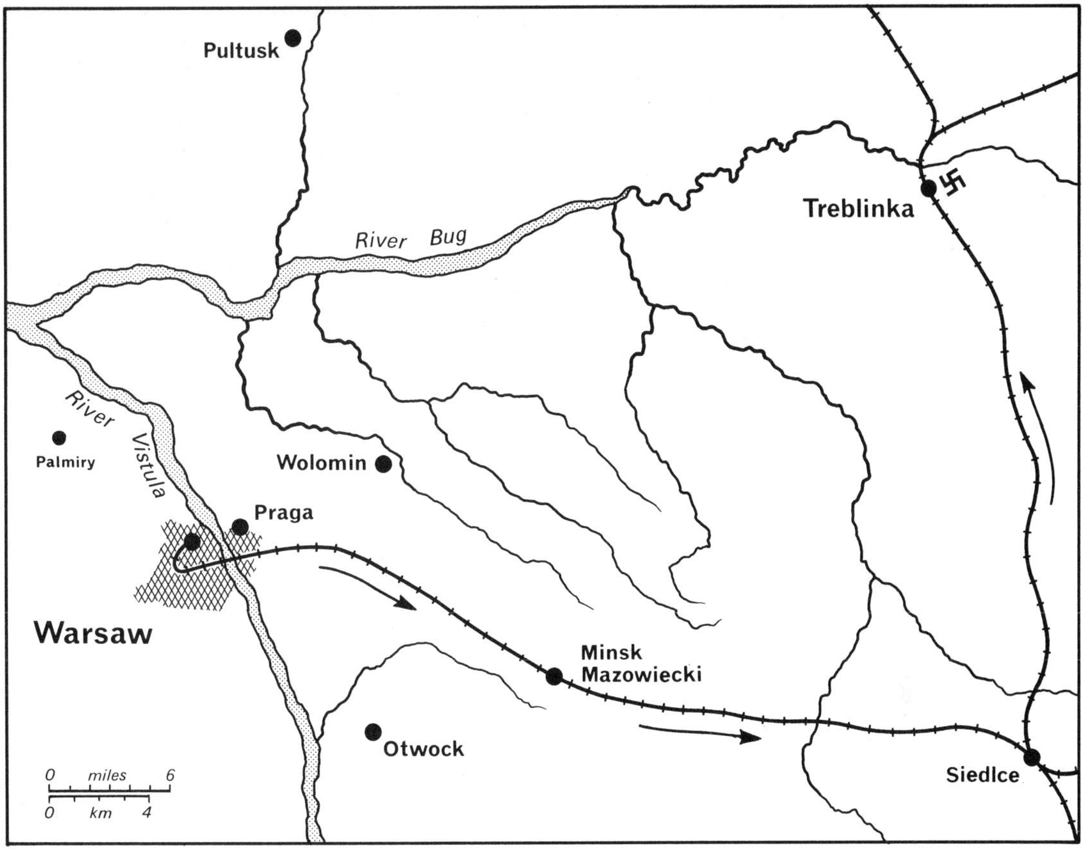

The route of the deportations from Warsaw to Treblinka.

each day, to take the Jews of Warsaw eastwards to the death camp at Treblinka. The Jews themselves were to assemble 'voluntarily' at a railway siding just outside the ghetto wall. On 22 July, at four in the afternoon, the notices were posted up in the ghetto.

That same afternoon the Jewish ghetto police began rounding up the street children – the starving waifs and strays for whom there had not even been the shelter of a desperately overcrowded room. Adolf Berman, of the children's welfare organization 'Centos', recalled how 'Shocking scenes took place in the streets. The children sensed the death threatening them and resisted the police, struggled with them and tried to escape. The streets echoed with the heart-rending screams and crying of children.' By nightfall, hundreds of these 'street urchins' had been caught, loaded into lorries, and taken to the railway sidings at the *Umschlagplatz*, immediately outside the ghetto wall.

On the morning of 23 July it was the turn of the poorest dwelling houses of the ghetto. As Berman recalled, 'Thousands of children from these "Death houses", so called because the majority of their inhabitants had already died as a result of deprivation and hunger, were deported.'

Also on 23 July, the police took away to the railway sidings the 250 children from two of the city's orphan homes, the large home for refugee children at 3 Dzika Street and the shelter for 'street urchins' at 6 Gesia Street. This deportation was contrary to an agreement between 'Centos' and the police.

After frantic protests by the 'Centos' management, the deportation order from the two homes was rescinded. But it was too late. The children had already reached the railway sidings, and had been loaded on to the cattle trucks.

It fell to the head of the Jewish Council, Adam Czerniakow, to ensure that the deportation orders were carried out. For twenty-four hours he tried to persuade the Nazis to rescind them. Asked to sign the deportation orders for children, he refused:

and then, on the evening of 23 July, he committed suicide. 'I am powerless', he had written in his diary before swallowing the poison. 'My heart trembles in sorrow and compassion. I can no longer bear this.' And in a note which was found near his body, he wrote: 'They are demanding ten thousand for tomorrow. . . .'

Within a week of Czerniakow's suicide, more than 59,000 men, women and children had been deported from Warsaw to Treblinka, and murdered. Those left behind in Warsaw had no idea where their friends and relatives had gone. People puzzled over the fact that no letters, or even postcards, had arrived from the deportees. Individuals disappeared, leaving no record. Nor did the Gestapo take the trouble, as they were doing each day in Paris, to record the names of those being deported. 'Everyone is but a step away from deportation', Chaim Kaplan noted in his diary on 27 July. 'People are being hunted down in the streets like animals in the forest.'

The Nazis tried many tricks to lure the Jews to their deaths. Thus Chaim Kaplan noted on 30 July:

'Besides the blockading of houses and hunting in the street, there is still a third method of expulsion – premiums. Large posters have been put up in many courtyards to say that all those who voluntarily come to the transfer point will receive 3 kilos of bread and 1 kilo of marmalade to take with them in their wanderings. They are given until 31 July.'

On 1 August a proclamation was posted in the ghetto, headed 'To the inhabitants of the Jewish District'. It read:

'In accordance with official instructions of 22 July 1942 all persons not employed in institutions or enterprises will definitely be resettled.

'Forcible removals are being continued uninterruptedly. I call once more on all members of the population subject to resettlement to report voluntarily at the railway siding, and will extend for three days, including 2, 3 and 4 August 1942, the distribution of 3 kilos of bread and 1 kilo of marmalade to every person who reports voluntarily.

'Families presenting themselves voluntarily will not be separated.

'Assembly point for volunteers: Dzika 3-Stawki 27. The Director of the Order Service.'

Many people could not resist the chance of some food. Among them was Abraham Kochavi's father. Kochavi himself was now nearly thirteen years old. Asked after the war whether he did not fear the destination, he replied:

'Wherever it would be, we imagined that it couldn't be a worse place. It couldn't be worse. Everyone who volunteered, that is came of his own free will to be sent out of the ghetto wherever it might be, got bread; he also got a little margarine and drink, and also some jam. We decided to show up of our free will.'

But once at the railway sidings, conditions quickly became unbearable. Up to 6,000 people were to travel on a single train, 100 forced into each wagon:

'The minute we got in, the minute they closed it on us with a bolt – terrible cries began inside, in Polish, Yiddish, German; pleading requests, "There is no air, and we are suffocating . . ."

'The first to faint were children, women, old men and women. They all fell down like flies, exactly like flies. Father was standing next to me. All of a sudden I see that he is falling, he's collapsed. I cried "Father, father". He no longer heard me, he'd fainted and I, with all my strength, as much strength as I had, tried to lift him up, bring him to, but I didn't succeed.

'Then I found a piece of wood on the floor of the wagon. I got up and began to beat with the piece of wood – it was a club or something – I began to beat the people who were standing round me in the wagon so that they'd make room for father – so that father could get up.

'I remember that I didn't care about the suffering of others, their cries, their threats – only that father should get up, so I shouldn't be left alone.'

Kochavi was one of the few Jews who survived the Warsaw ghetto deportations. As each train disappeared eastwards across the Vistula, those who remained behind could only speculate on its fate, fighting in their minds against what many suspected must be the truth. On 1 August Chaim Kaplan wrote in his diary, in desperation: 'We have no information about the fate of those who have been expelled. When one falls into the hands of the Nazis one falls into the abyss. The very fact that the deportees make no contact with their families by letters bodes evil.' Two days later Kaplan began hiding away his library, 'the joy of my life and the delight of my soul', and on the evening of 4 August he noted in his diary: 'I have not yet been caught... my building has not yet been confiscated. But only a step separates me from all these misfortunes.'

On each day of the deportations, the Gestapo came to a different street. As Chaim Kaplan had noted on 1 August:

'A command is suddenly given to evacuate an entire block of apartment houses within a single hour. This starts an uproar, a turmoil that Dante could not have envisioned. It is the Nazis' intention that every decree come as a complete surprise. Hundreds of families hurt by this decree become frantic from the enormity of the misfortune. Where will you go? What can you save? What first? What last? They begin to pack bundles in haste and fear, with trembling hands and feet which refuse to do their bidding, and to take their belongings outside, for they no longer have a home. Hundreds of women and swollen infants rend the heavens with their cries. The sick are taken outside in their beds, babies in their cradles, old men and women half-naked and barefoot.'

That day, 10,000 more Jews were taken to the railway sidings, and disappeared.

In the Warsaw ghetto there were more than 100,000 children under the age of fifteen. Like Avraham Kochavi, they were seized, together with their parents, and deported. But one group of children, the orphans, were thought by the Jewish community to have immunity from deportation. Since the creation of the ghetto in November 1940 there had grown up in Warsaw a network of 100 children's homes, in which lived 25,000 Jewish children, a quarter of the city's child population. In these homes they were given shelter, such food as could be found for them, education, and the devoted care of more than 1,000 adults. The orphanages were scattered throughout the ghetto, their work co-ordinated by the children's welfare organization.

In the first week of August the Nazis decided to deport all 25,000 orphans and instructed the Jewish ghetto police to carry out the 'action'. The Jewish police, however, were a reluctant, and therefore an unsatisfactory instrument for this task, which was at once handed over to the Gestapo themselves, helped by Ukrainian and Lithuanian units. These men began their work by killing orphans at the orphanage doors. The children in the medical-educational institute at Otwock, which had suffered from the air raid on the first day of the war, were seized by Ukrainian troops and shot in the grounds of the institute. As Adolf Berman wrote:

'The barbarous system of "hunting out" victims – flushing them out of the houses and then shooting them instantly had fatal consequences for the orphanages and children's houses. The Nazis made no allowances for the tender age of their victims, nor revealed any manifestations of conscience in carrying out their criminal tasks. They murdered hundreds of children. Both children and teachers were overcome by utter desperation.'

The fate of the remaining children was no longer in doubt, for, as Berman recalled, it had quickly become known that, during the first week of the deportations,

'the large majority of the children and old people had not been taken from the "transfer station" to the deportation wagons, but had been brought directly to the Jewish cemetery in Gesia Street where they were shot to death and buried. Some groups of children were shot at another spot, outside Warsaw, and the wagons, piled high with their corpses, were sent to the Jewish cemetery. Some policemen and even grave-diggers described these death wagons with horror.'

Each day during the first two weeks of August the Gestapo ordered the deportation of a street, or group of streets, and with them, in almost every instance, of a different orphanage. One of the first to be deported was a small home for children of refugees at 29 Ogrodowa Street, from which all fifty children were marched away. Another orphanage to be raided was that of Dr Janusz Korczak, the sixty-four-year-old educator and social welfare worker whose writings were known throughout the world. Korczak, whose first book, published in 1901, had been a moving description of the plight of homeless orphans in large cities, had become head of a new Jewish orphanage in Warsaw in 1911, and for the next thirty-one years this orphanage had been the centre of his activities. During the inter-war years he had been a frequent broadcaster on children's topics, he had persuaded the local authorities to set up a non-Jewish orphanage near Warsaw, along the lines of his own, and he had written many popular children's stories. Twice, in 1934 and 1936, Korczak had visited Palestine, where he found many of his former orphans, who had become farmers in the collective villages, the kibbutzim. Attracted by its communal life and creative philosophy, Korczak seriously thought of settling on a kibbutz himself, but having decided that his orphans in Warsaw must come first, he returned to Poland in 1936.

In the first week of August 1942, Korczak was told that all the children in his orphanage must go at once to the railway sidings. Adolf Berman has recalled how:

'All the staff, with Dr Korczak and his faithful assistant Stefa Wilczynska at their head, accompanied the children. The authorities offered to release Dr Korczak on the spot, but he adamantly refused. He was worried that the children would become ill since, due to the suddenness of the deportation, they had not had time to take their belongings with them and many were wearing summer shirts. Wilczynska, with a smile on her lips, tried to calm the small children, telling them that they were going on a trip, that at long last they would be seeing forests, fields and trees. The Jewish police, bewildered by these actions, tried to help Korczak and the children in some manner. They arranged for them to have extra wagons so that the journey would be more comfortable. Usually 120 to 130 persons were crammed into one wagon, but in this case 50 to 60 children were put into each one. After a long wait, Korczak left the transfer station with the children.'

Korczak and his assistant were not alone in insisting that they accompany their orphans. On the same day that all those in Korczak's orphanage was deported, the children of the model home at 7 Twarda Street, and the girls in the home at 28 Sliska Street, were also led away through the streets of the ghetto to the sidings. They too were accompanied on their final journey by the principals and staffs. Then, a few days later, as Berman recalled:

'... the hardest blow was delivered. During the round-up on Wolnocz and Dzielna Streets, many of the largest children's homes were destroyed simultaneously and nearly 2,000 children were deported. The large "Beit Hayeled" institution at 14 Wolnocz Street was destroyed. The director of the institution, Shimanski, a man of excellent qualities, went to his death together with the children. Before leaving the building he gave poison to his aged mother to save her unnecessary suffering, and he himself together with most of his staff members joined the children in their tragic journey. The inmates of the "welfare station" for street urchins at 16 Wolnocz Street were also deported then and its director, Goldkorn, also accompanied the children. The marvellous institution for orphans and abandoned children "Dowra Wolla", at 61 Dzielno Street, was also destroyed on the same day.'

Together with the children, more than a thousand children's doctors, nurses, social workers, teachers and psychologists were shot, or deported.

The Gestapo devised every possible stratagem to try to prevent the survival of the children of Warsaw. Policemen were offered 100 zlotys for each person they brought to the sidings, together with a 'bonus'– a loaf of bread. As Adolf Berman recalled, 'repulsive scenes took place. The ghetto police turned into veritable dog-catchers, hunting human beasts. Obviously the first to be captured were women and children. . . .' As the daily searches continued, Berman recalled:

'. . . thousands of persons lived as "cave dwellers". Children especially, were hidden for weeks on end in numerous hiding places and secret refuges. They were hunted down by particularly zealous policemen, or they were forced to come out by the shots of the SS men during the round-ups which became more and more frequent. The cruelty reached such a degree that if the Nazis and their Ukrainian aides found children inside the houses at the time the round-up was taking place, they would toss them through windows or crush their skulls with the butts of their rifles.'

By 15 September, when the deportations halted, the Nazis were able to record, with their usual precision, that the incredible total of 310,322 Jews had been 'deported', most of them to the death camp at Treblinka. Those 70,000 people who remained behind, weakened by hunger and wracked by mental uncertainty, did not know what to think, or what to do.

One of the survivors, the historian Emmanuel Ringelblum, pieced together an archive of the ghetto, and of its fate. It was he who had urged Chaim Kaplan to keep a diary, but, as he now noted, the whole of Kaplan's manuscript had been 'lost' when Kaplan himself had been taken to the railway siding. Actually, Kaplan's diary survived; but Kaplan and his wife were among hundreds of thousands who perished. With incredible tenacity, Ringelblum persevered with his records, noting down the stories told by those few survivors who had witnessed the massacres to the east. He recorded yet another German action, the rounding up of several thousand Jews in the ghetto on 10 November. According to the Germans, Jews were needed as tailors in the Lublin ghetto; such was the pretext, and indeed, shortly after their deportation, letters had reached Warsaw from some of the deportees, sending greetings and assurances. But this was nothing more than yet another Nazi subterfuge. All the deportees had been murdered.

The Jews who remained in Warsaw were not without courage. Ringelblum recorded the details of the efforts being made within the ghetto to challenge the Nazi power. On 20 October 1942 the various resistance groups had banded together to form a single, tightly-knit group, the 'Jewish Fighting Organization', and on 2 December 1942 it issued its charter; it would arm itself with whatever weapons it could obtain, guns smuggled in from Polish groups outside the ghetto, axes, knives, and even brass knuckles; it would organize fighting cells, prepare a plan of action in each area, embark on sabotage missions, and engage in a propaganda campaign 'to move the community to resistance and struggle'.

The Jewish Fighting Organization, led by a twenty-four-year-old Zionist, Mordechai Anielewicz, was determined not only to maintain the unity of all Jewish resistance groups, but to create among the remnant of Warsaw Jewry a spirit of defiance. On the day after it issued its charter, it issued an appeal to all Jews. One paragraph read:

'Jews, residents of the Warsaw ghetto, watch out: don't believe one word or trust one deed of the SS bandits; death lurks. Remember the latest "campaign"– snatching "labour" details for Lublin. They needed "tailors" and grabbed old people and children. They needed people for "labour" and just took persons as they were: bare and naked. The story repeats itself – greetings and letters arrive from persons sent to Lublin. We are reminded of the "letters", the "reliable" greetings manufactured by the Germans from Brest, Minsk and Bialystok. We are reminded that in Lublin there is a Belzec where tens of thousands of Jews were murdered à la Treblinka.'

Secretly, bunkers were built, linked in places to

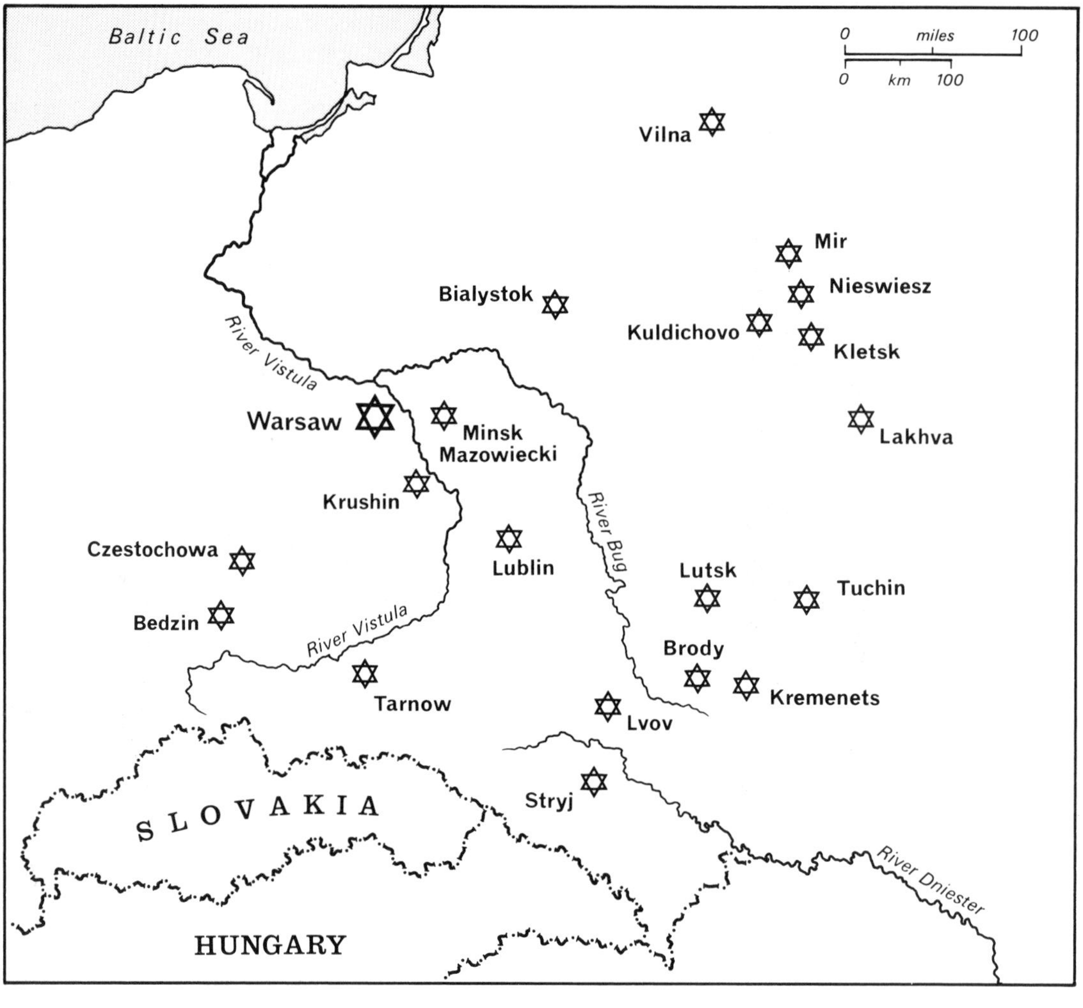

Ghetto uprisings in German-occupied Poland.

the city's sewerage system. Arms were sought from Polish resistance groups, and several hundred pistols were bought. Then, in January, without warning, the Nazis entered the ghetto and seized another 6,500 Jews. There was a brief attempt at resistance, and a German police captain was shot in the stomach. Himmler himself was enraged, and on 16 February 1943 he ordered the ghetto to be destroyed. No single Jew must remain. Even the buildings must be levelled.

Himmler's orders were to be carried out by the newly appointed German SS and Police leader in Warsaw, Brigadier Stroop. While it was still dark, at three o'clock in the morning of 19 April 1943, Stroop's forces surrounded the ghetto. At dawn they entered it, their assault led by a tank. The Jewish Fighting Organization now put its plan into action. The tank was immobilized by a 'Molotov cocktail', and the SS troops driven off by rifle fire.

For nearly a month the Jews resisted, fighting with outstanding bravery, their efforts forming a part of the extraordinary saga of Jewish ghetto revolts throughout Nazi-dominated Poland. Among the uprisings were those of Bialystok, Vilna, Lublin and Czestochowa.

The Warsaw ghetto uprising: German artillery in action as the ghetto burns.

German officers interrogate a Jew captured during the Warsaw uprising.

The Jews of Warsaw could muster in their defence about 1,500 men, two or three light machine guns, about a hundred rifles, a few hundred revolvers and pistols, and a few thousand hand grenades. Against them were nearly 3,000 men, far more heavily armed, with three anti-aircraft guns, one medium howitzer, flame-throwers, heavy as well as light machine guns, submachine guns, rifles, pistols, grenades and substantial amounts of explosive charges.

Steadily, the Germans advanced into the ghetto, blowing up the sewers and dugouts as they went. After eight days the Jewish powers of resistance had been almost totally crushed. Brigadier Stroop recorded from day to day his savage progress. On 22 April he learned, from Jews who had been captured, that many of those in the dugouts had become 'insane from the heat, the smoke and the explosives'.

On 8 May Anielewicz was killed, and by 15 May the Jewish resistance had been overcome. Brigadier Stroop prepared an official report, the title of which was: 'The Warsaw Ghetto is No More.' More than 55,000 Jews, many of them women and children, had surrendered to the advancing forces. More than 7,000 were shot immediately after they had surrendered. Another 7,000 were deported to Treblinka, and a further 15,000 to Majdanek, the death camp just outside Lublin. The rest were sent to slave labour camps.

After the Warsaw uprising: Jews on their way to the ghetto railway siding for the journey to Treblinka. They were allowed to take with them whatever they could carry, but no more.

In the year that followed, the Germans levelled the ghetto to the ground: more than 190 hectares of buildings being totally demolished. To remove the rubble, the railway administration laid down 17 kilometres of narrow gauge railway. The great Jewish community of Warsaw was no more. At most, at the time of the creation of the ghetto, some 12,000 Jews had remained hidden in the Polish part of the city. They were joined after the rising by several hundred individual Jews who managed to flee from the ruins of the ghetto.

The historian Ringelblum was among a group of Jews who found refuge together in an underground bunker in Polish Warsaw. For ten months, confined to his hiding place, he continued with his work of collecting evidence, and writing several books, including a history of Polish-Jewish relations during the Second World War. Then, on 7 March 1944, Ringelblum was betrayed to the Gestapo, and all those hiding with him were arrested. For three days Ringelblum was interrogated and tortured, pressed to reveal what he knew of the tiny resistance group that had managed to survive and in which he himself was a leading figure. But he revealed nothing. Then, a few days later, together with his wife and thirteen-year-old son Uri, he was taken back to the ruins of the ghetto, forced to watch the murder of his two loved ones, and with the thirty-five others who had been captured with him, he was shot.

9

The Treblinka Death Camp

In August 1942 a young Austrian infantryman was transferred with his company from Vienna to the eastern front. His name was Hubert Pfoch, and he was a member of the illegal Austrian Socialist Youth Organization.

Pfoch's Company travelled by train – from Vienna to Moravska Ostrava, then to Katowice, Radom, Lukow and Siedlce. The train arrived at Siedlce in the early evening of 21 August, where the soldiers were to have an overnight stop.

Pfoch was a diligent and brave young man. He had a camera and he kept a diary. What he saw, he both photographed and recorded. 'We arrive in the evening', he wrote, 'and are given soup.' It was a typical diary entry: but its sequel made him a witness to one of the main deportation journeys, the journey to the death camp at Treblinka. As Pfoch recorded:

'From time to time we can hear shooting, and when I got out to see what was happening, I saw, a little distance from our track, a loading platform with a huge crowd of people – I estimated about 7,000 men, women and children.

'All of them were squatting or lying on the ground and whenever anyone tried to get up, the guards began shooting.'

Pfoch had no idea who these 7,000 people were. The night itself, he noted, was a sultry one, and the soldiers slept badly. But early the next morning, 22 August, the soldiers' train was shunted to another track,and they found themselves alongside the station's loading platform. It was there, Pfoch wrote, 'that we heard the rumour that these people were a Jewish transport'. His diary continued:

'They call out to us that they have been travelling without food or water for two days. And then, when they are being loaded into cattle trucks, we become witnesses of the most ghastly scenes. The corpses of those killed the night before were thrown by Jewish auxiliary police on to a lorry that came and went four times.

'The guards – Ukrainian volunteer SS – some of them drunk – cram 180 people into each car, parents into one, children into another, they didn't care how they separated families. They scream at them, shoot and hit them so viciously that some of their rifle-butts break.

'When all of them are finally loaded there are cries from all cars – "Water" they pleaded, "my gold ring for water." Others offered us 5,000 zlotys for a cup of water.

'When some of them manage to climb out through the ventilating holes, they are shot the moment they reach the ground – a massacre that made us sick to our souls, a blood-bath such as I never dreamed of.

'A mother jumps down with her baby and calmly looks into a pointing gun-barrel – a moment later we hear the guard who shot them boast to his fellows that he managed to "do" them both with one shot through both their heads.'

At last the time came for the soldiers to continue their journey eastwards to the frontline. 'When at last the train leaves the station', Pfoch wrote, 'at least fifty dead, women, men, and children, some of them totally naked, lie along the track.'

Eventually the soldiers' train was routed behind the Jewish train. Both were going in the same direction, the soldiers to the war zone, the Jews to Treblinka. As the soldiers' train followed the deportation train, Pfoch noted:

'... we continued to see corpses on both sides of the track – children and others. They say Treblinka is a "delousing camp". When we reach Treblinka station the train is next to us again – there is such an awful smell of decomposing corpses in the station, some of us vomit. The begging for water intensifies, the indiscriminate shooting by the guards continues.'

Hubert Pfoch's journey from Vienna towards the eastern front; and the deportations to Treblinka from western Europe, Macedonia and Thrace.

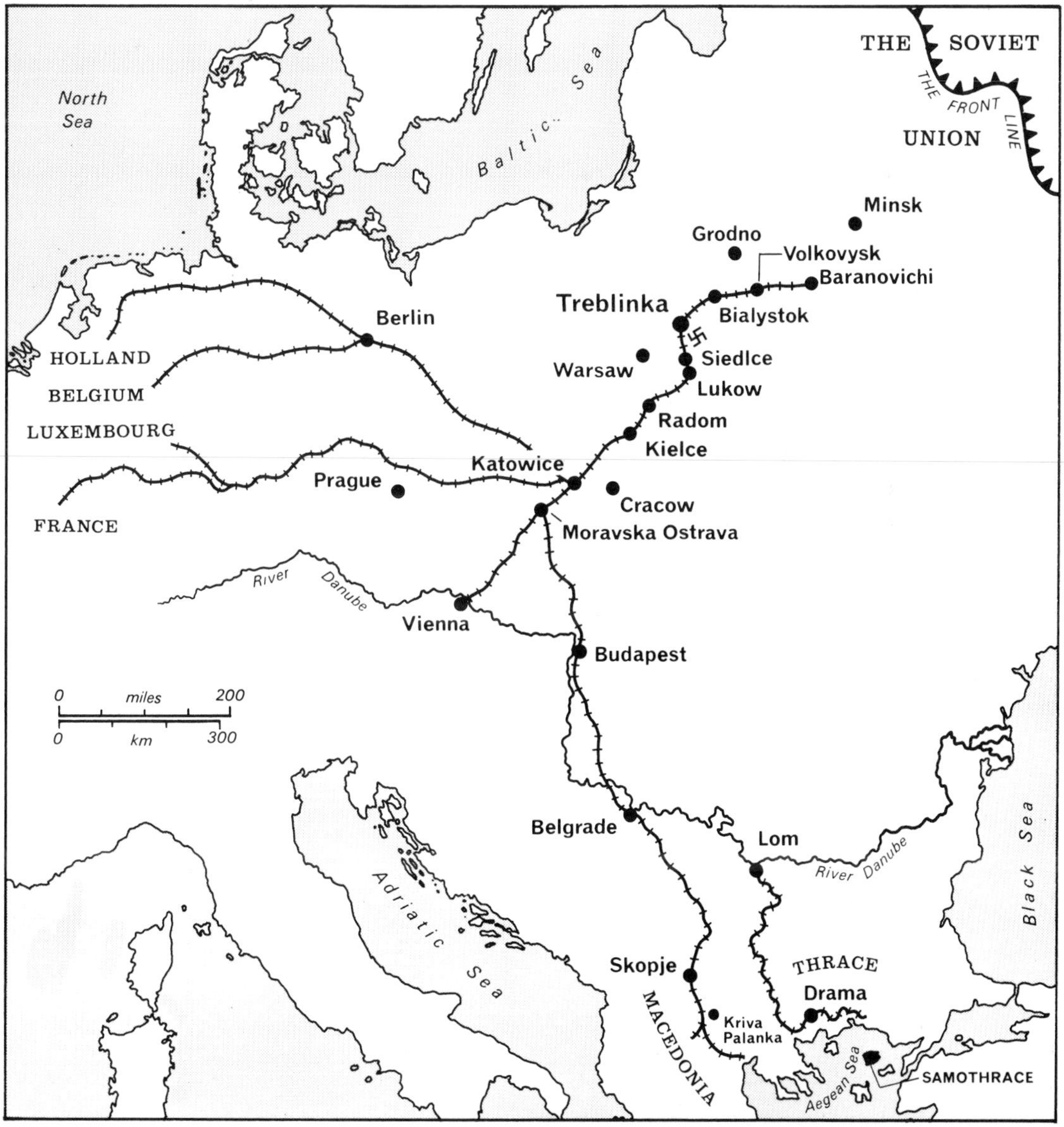

Two of Hubert Pfoch's photographs: the bodies of two Jews who died during the journey to Treblinka; after the train had continued on its way to the death camp, the bodies were loaded on to a lorry.

One of Hubert Pfoch's photographs of Jews boarding the railway trucks to Treblinka. Shortly after taking this photograph, Pfoch saw the guard (on the right) kill a Jew with a single blow of his rifle butt.

Did Pfoch and his fellow soldiers know of the ultimate fate of those whose terrible journey they had glimpsed such awful moments? It was only August 1942, and yet in his diary he was able to write, tersely and accurately: 'Three hundred thousand have been assembled here. Every day ten or fifteen thousand are gassed and burned.' He added: 'Any comment is totally superfluous.'

How was it that so many people could be shunted so efficiently, and at times so brutally, to their deaths? How was it that a 'standard' deportation to an unknown destination could turn within a few hours into the ultimate horror? This was the question asked by Vassili Grossman, one of the first outsiders to reach the site of the camp in 1944. By talking to the local Polish peasants, he was able to give his answer.

Most of the Jews who were brought to Treblinka had been so weakened by the terrible conditions of the journey that all their strength had gone. Broken in body and in spirit: shattered by the jolting, starving and afraid.

Many of the deportees had been told that they were being deported to the Ukraine, to work on farms. After the confinement and hunger of the ghetto this seemed to hold out at least a possible hope of survival. A few train loads actually arrived, from distant communities, having been told that they were being taken out of Nazi-occupied Europe altogether, to neutral countries, and freedom: the passengers on these trains had paid huge sums to the Germans for exit visas and foreign passports. One train of the many hundreds that came to Treblinka even arrived with sleeping cars and a dining car: its 'passengers' bringing with them heavy suitcases and large food supplies for their longer journey to emigration, freedom and a new world.

Those who had actually been made to pay for their tickets had been told that their destination was a specific station in the Ukraine, 'Ober Maidan'. No such station existed. But on arriving at Treblinka there were children who would ask their parents – 'is *this* Ober Maidan?'

To try to lull the arrivals at the station into a calmer frame of mind was yet another 'bluff' – a mock railway station with the sign: 'Station for *changing* trains.' Everywhere the deportees looked were signs with arrows which announced, in the style of a true railway junction:

TRAINS FOR BIALYSTOK →
TRAINS FOR BARANOVICHI →
TRAINS FOR VOLKOVYSK →

Next to the arrival platform were signs of a bustling local railway station: a uniformed ticket collector for those trains where passengers had tickets, the façade of a station restaurant, the entrance to a left-luggage room, and even a station clock. But those who were being hustled forward into the station square did not have time to notice that it was a clock not only with painted numerals but also with painted, motionless hands. Vassili Grossman noted of the next stage for those on one of the trains that had arrived (and up to five trains arrived each day):

'Three to four thousand people, laden with sacks and suitcases supporting the old and the sick, came out. Mothers held their young children in their arms; older children clung to their parents.

'The people began to notice rapidly the disquieting trifles – the swept ground on which there were dropped objects: a little bundle of clothing, open suitcases, shaving brushes, enamel saucepans. How did they get here? And why does the railroad track end immediately after the station platform? Where is the track to Bialystok, Siedlce, Warsaw, Volkovysk?

'And why did the new guards grin so strangely at the men who are straightening their ties, at the neatly dressed old women, at the boys in sailor jackets, at the thin girls who had somehow managed to retain a neat appearance on the trip, and at the young mothers who are lovingly adjusting the blankets around their babies?'

As soon as the last 'passenger' is off the train, an SS corporal begins to give orders. They must leave all their belongings in the square, and go to the public baths; here was the so-called 'delousing' of which Hubert Pfoch had heard tell. 'Take only your personal documents, valuables, soap and towels', the orders rang out.

'Move! Quickly! Move quickly!'

The 'passengers' move along the road towards the 'baths'. As they walk along, constantly urged to hurry by SS men, and guarded by armed Ukrainian volunteers, yet more deceptions greet them. Painted on a large board is the name of a street – 'Street of the deportees' – and near it is another sign: 'To the Railway Station →', underneath which is a painted panel representing a group of Jews, with beards and glasses, carrying their baggage to yet another mythical station. Further on, a second painted panel shows a young shepherd boy watching farm animals. On one side of the street, false shop fronts display the decorative signs of several crafts: scissors for the barber's shop, an ear of corn for the bakery, a tooth for the dentist. All this masquerade has been nicknamed by the Nazis: *Juden Staat* – the Jewish State.

The Jews hurry on, past a little zoo, set out around an ornamental pond, in the centre of which is a stone frog, spouting water through its mouth. There are rustic benches by the edge of the pond, and cages housing the zoo's birds and squirrels.

A final street sign announces: TO THE GHETTO → It is in fact the road to the gas chamber. The Germans have nicknamed this road *Himmelstrasse* – the road to Heaven – and its final stages *Himmelfahrt* – the Ascension.

The Jews reach the 'baths'. Orders snap out, more ferociously now. 'Men remain here! Women and children undress in the barracks on the left.' For some, the dreadful truth begins to dawn. Terrible doubts well up. But, as Grossman noted:

'It is at such moments that people's minds must be confused again; they must again be filled with hope, with rules of death given out as if they were rules of life. And the same voice shot out each word distinctly: "Women and children are to take their shoes off at the entrance to the barracks. The stockings are to be put into the shoes. The childrens socks are to be put into the sandals, in the little shoes and slippers. Be neat."

'And then again: "When going to the baths, take along your money, documents, valuables, a towel and soap. . . . We repeat . . ."

'Inside the women's barracks there was a barber's shop. The naked women were given haircuts, and the wigs were taken from the old women. This death haircut – according to the testimony of the barbers – convinced the women that they were being taken to the baths. Young girls felt their heads and asked: "Over here it is not straight, please cut it a little more!" Usually, after the hair-cutting, the women were calmer, though some of the young ones wept for their beautiful hair.'

For the German war machine, even the hair of those about to be killed was of military utility: used by the army for stuffing mattresses and by the navy for weaving rope and cable. Many of the clothes were likewise – if suitable – packed up and sent to Germany. Back in the station square, 200 Jewish forced labourers – the inhabitants of the camp – were busy at work scattering the contents of the suitcases and bundles over the ground, sorting out the things to be sent to Germany, and the things to be burned. For burning were all the personal belongings of those who are already naked at the 'baths'– bundles of letters, family photographs, prayer shawls, and children's school books.

Meanwhile, the naked people were taken to a small booth in which a 'cashier', guarded by SS men and Ukrainians, demanded all valuables: paper money to be thrown into one box; coins into another; earrings, bracelets, jewellery and watches into a third. Now the truth was clear, for as Grossman relates:

'Here at the cashier's booth things came to a head – here ended the torture through lies, which kept people under the hypnosis of ignorance, in a fever which tossed them in a few minutes from hope to despair, from visions of life to visions of death.

'This torture through lies was one of the attributes of the conveyor execution block – it helped the SS men in their work. At the last stage of the process of robbing living corpses, the Germans drastically changed their manner of treating their victims. . . .

'The road from the cashier's booth to the place of execution took six to seven minutes. The people, driven by blows and deafened by noise, came to the third square and stopped there for a moment, completely stunned.'

The sight for stupefaction was the final bizzare 'deception' of that journey from the railway station. In front of the naked, frightened people was an elegant stone building, in the style of an ancient temple, with wide ornamental doors, and all around flowers and potted plants. Above the doors was written, in German, Polish and Yiddish, the single word: BATHHOUSE. Beyond these doors was the gas chamber: and all around, armed guards, ferocious dogs, pitiless SS men, driving human beings forward to their death.

Now there was no way to turn back. Naked and vulnerable, 1,000 people were driven brutally into the gas chamber. Yet even at the last moment desperate hope did not die, and young mothers would try to cover, with their own naked bodies, their tiny infants.

More than 700,000 Jews were murdered in Treblinka between the spring of 1942 and the autumn of 1943. On each train as it arrived was chalked up the place from which it had come: Warsaw, Prague, Budapest, Paris, Bialystok, Minsk . . . an almost endless list.

In addition to the Jews, tens of thousands of Poles, and tens of thousands of Gipsies, were brought to Treblinka to be killed. On a 'busy' day, five trains, each with up to 6,000 Jews, would arrive at the 'station', and by nightfall all 30,000 people from those trains would have been murdered. Their belongings had meanwhile been sorted and packed for despatch to the Reich, and – as another investigator, Polanker, reported in 1944 – after Soviet troops had reached the site of the camp, all corpses were inspected by 'seven dentists with pincers' who extracted the gold and silver teeth.

After this final pillage, the bodies were thrown into two enormous pits covered with iron bars: the furnaces of Treblinka. According to Polanker's account:

'The pyres of dead bodies burned by day and night. The smoke that rose from the chimneys of dozens of crematoria could be seen over the entire district. Human dust was sifted down on the entire area, and the death factory never ceased its work even for a single day.'

The sadism in Treblinka was horrific, even in

Jews from Bialystok being rounded up before deportation to Treblinka, August 1943.

the few brief hours that passed between arrival and death. Polanker's account told of one of the Nazis in the camp, Wanhaufen, who lived in the camp together with his family:

'It was this man's habit to murder a few Jews before his meals, otherwise he could not sit down at table. The Untersturmführer Meuter and Scharführer Fast used to amuse themselves by setting dogs on Jewish children.

'One of the particular methods of tormenting their victims was the staging of Jewish weddings. They would bring a young fellow, a girl and an old Jew to the spot. They dressed the old Jew in the clothes of a rabbi, and to the strains of "joyful" music, the rabbi would conduct the Jewish wedding ceremony. The Jews were compelled to dance after this. Immediately after the "wedding" the Jews were taken off to the "bathhouse".'

The first Commandant of the camp, SS Hauptsturmführer von Eupen, a keen horseman, delighted in trampling the prisoners to death while on horseback. Another of the SS men in the camp, Hans Heinbuck, was a German university graduate: he once supervised a Ukrainian volunteer SS man in killing thirty children from the Warsaw Ghetto with an axe. Another German, Kurt Franz, known as 'Doll', had a large dog, 'Bari', who would tear at the flesh of the naked victims in their final moments on the way to the gas chambers.

The murder process was an unending one. Even the local peasants could not remain ignorant of what was happening beyond the wire. As Polanker wrote in his account of the camp:

'The cries of the victims and the weeping of the children could be heard in the neighbouring villages. In order to prevent them from being heard, the Germans brought the most famous musicians in the world from the Warsaw ghetto. They brought Professor Gomolka, Professor Kohn and the musician Gold.

'These musicians were compelled to play when

Rumanian Gipsy girls photographed by a German soldier in front of their house. Many Gipsies had become town dwellers. The Nazis sought to kill them all.

the transports arrived. This "music" instilled terror throughout the entire neighbourhood.'

The largest single group of Jews brought to Treblinka were those from the Warsaw ghetto. During the summer of 1942, 310,000 of the Jews of Warsaw, Europe's largest single Jewish community, perished. All of those who were taken to Treblinka were murdered within a few hours of their arrival in camp. But the spirit of resistance could not always be crushed; even after the terrible journeys and privations, several acts of individual bravery have been recorded, by a Polish peasant woman, and by some of the very few inmates to survive.

On 26 August 1942 – four days after Hubert Pfoch and his fellow soldiers had passed through Treblinka station – a young Jew who had been brought by train from Kielce, armed only with a penknife, attacked the Ukrainian guard who had prevented him from saying goodbye to his mother. As a result of this act, all the men who had arrived on this same transport were shot at once. Two weeks later, on 10 September 1942, a Jew from the Argentine who had been visiting his parents in Warsaw when war broke out, and who had been deported despite his Argentinian citizenship, killed an SS man, Max Biel, with a knife.

These two brave acts of despair could not halt the daily arrival, and daily murder, of tens of thousands of Jews: but they are a testimony to the courage of the human spirit. So too was the act of a tall young girl who, while already walking naked along the final road, seized a gun from one of the guards and opened fire on a dozen SS men, who shot her down in a barrage of fire. Her name is not known, but her deed is indestructable.

At the end of 1942 there was a brief halt in the deportations: and on 5 December 1942 police leader Friedrich-Wilhelm Kruger wrote to Himmler to warn him that, as a result of sabotage on the railway lines in the Bialystok district, 'our master plan for Jewish settlement is severely jeopardized'. Himmler took action at the highest official level, writing to Dr Theodor Ganzenmuller, the State Secretary at the Ministry of Transport, on 20 January 1943, that it was the Jews who were responsible for the railway sabotage, the sooner they were all 'cleared out' of eastern Europe, the sooner the sabotage would end. Indeed, he argued, unless extra trains were made available to transport Jews from elsewhere in Europe, sabotage would break out there as well.

The deportations started up again. Citizens of more than thirty countries met their deaths at Treblinka, including Gipsies from all over Europe. German, Austrian, Slovakian, Dutch and Belgian Jews were among those brought across Europe by train. Even the few Jews of Luxembourg were deported to this distant railway station, and killed.

The records of these deportations are copious, formal and precise. Thus, on 22 February 1943, the Bulgarians agreed to allow the Germans to deport all the Jews both from Thrace, which Bulgaria had seized from Greece, and from Macedonia, which she had seized from Yugoslavia. The agreement was detailed. Negotiated in Bulgaria by Eichmann's representative, Theodor Dannecker, it allocated twenty-six trains for the deportations. The trains were to be sent to six stations, to which were brought the Jews of twenty-three communities, many of them dating back more than two thousand years, to the days of ancient Greece. Among those brought to the railheads were the three Jews living on the Aegean island of Samothrace, the 589 Jews of the ancient town of Drama, five Jews from the remote Macedonian village of Kriva Palanka, and 3,351 Jews from the city of Skopje: the largest city in southern Yugoslavia.

In all, 11,000 Jews were mentioned in Dannecker's agreement with the Bulgarians, and that precise number was assembled as planned. 'The German Reich', the agreement stated, 'is ready to accept these Jews in their eastern regions.' Once on their journey, there was a change of trains for some on account of a change of gauge. At these stations, the Germans gave priority in changing trains to 'invalids on stretchers' and 'women who were ready for childbirth'.

Conditions inside the goods wagons were horrific: terrible overcrowding, no sanitary arrangements, virtually no food and hardly any water. Each morning the trains would stop in the open countryside, and the bodies of those who had died during the night were thrown out on to the track. For more than 6,000 of the deportees there was an added horror: transfer at the Bulgarian town of Lom, from the train to a river barge, for the journey up the Danube. Here too, the con-

ditions were appalling: so much so that several hundred sick people, old people and children died before reaching Treblinka.

Before the Jews were deported from Thrace and Macedonia, all their property had been confiscated and sold. A receipt was provided for the money raised by the sale. But added to the receipt was a deduction for the so-called 'cost' of the journey to Treblinka. The deportees having already left, the money itself was deposited in banks. But the deposit statements were meticulously sent on to their owners, reaching Treblinka only after the 'recipients' had been murdered.

Three months later there was a further influx of Jews to Treblinka: more Jews from Warsaw, survivors of those who had been driven to challenge the full power of the German army.

As the deportations continued, so also did the sabotage of the railway lines. Jewish partisans were extremely active in the area east of the river Bug. Even inside Treblinka itself, despite the ferocity of the guards and the utter wretchedness and weakness of those who were pushed into the gas chambers, the 'permanent' inmates organized a revolt.

Thus it was that on the afternoon of 2 August 1943, against overwhelming odds, a group of 700 brave men challenged the Nazi power, killing one of the Nazi chief executioners, Kuetner, and setting fire to the barracks. Many of the rebels were machine-gunned by Ukrainian guards, whose guard turret dominated a large area of the camp. Nevertheless, more than 150 of the 700 prisoners escaped. Many of them were killed in the weeks to come during a massive manhunt. When the Soviet troops reached the area, only twelve of the rebels were still alive.

Meanwhile, the camp itself had disappeared: in September 1943, a month after the revolt, the Germans had set about burning the remaining bodies, and a month later they blew up all the buildings, ploughed the land and planted an innocent crop of potatoes.

'Somebody', Polanker recorded, 'tried to dig in the field, and found countless numbers of hats, sweaters, utensils, children's clothes, and toys. . . .'

The Germans deport the Jews of Thrace: a sequence of four photographs. The wagons bear the initials of the Bulgarian railways.

10

France: Convoy No 1

The 'final solution' was to affect Jewish communities throughout Nazi-occupied Europe. Some of these communities were more ancient in their origins than Germany itself. One of these was the Jewish community in France.

Six years after the death of Jesus, the Emperor Augustus had banished one of the leading Jews of Judaea, Archelaus, to the Rhone valley. Archelaus was the first Jew of whom there is evidence that he actually lived on the soil of France. Thirty years later, his younger brother, Herod Antipas, was also exiled to France, by the Emperor Caligula, and in AD 70, after their conquest of Jerusalem, the Romans sent three boatloads of Jewish captives to Bordeaux, Arles and Lyons.

During the Roman period there were small Jewish communities in Metz, Poitiers and Avignon, and by AD 590 there were synagogues in Paris and Orléans. By AD 600 Jewish communities were to be found throughout France, from Brittany to the Pyrenees, their numbers continually swelled by Jewish refugees fleeing from persecution in Italy and Spain.

For the Jews of France there followed more than a thousand years of alternating persecution and prosperity, of massacre and of acceptance, of struggle, and of scholarship, until, at the time of the French Revolution, there were some 40,000 Jews living in France.

During the nineteenth century the Jews of France not only flourished, despite recurrent outbreaks of anti-semitism, but took an effective lead in organizing help for persecuted Jews elsewhere, especially those in North Africa and the Near East. As Frenchmen, they were active in commerce and the arts, in civic life and in the sciences. They were among the pioneers of Jewish self-help, and also of a self-effacing assimilation.

It was the anti-semitic violence in Russia between 1881 and 1914 that brought more than 25,000 Jewish immigrants to France, several thousand from Warsaw alone. Thousands more Jews came to France from the Ottoman Empire after the Young Turk revolution of 1908.

During the First World War French Jews fought on all fronts: at the Dardanelles, on the Somme, in northern Italy and in the Balkans. Then, when the war was over, France once more provided a haven for Jews, especially those from eastern Poland and the Ukraine where anti-semitic violence had flared up again; and from the cities of western Turkey where the war between Greeks and Turks had led to repeated bloodshed and destruction.

By 1939, of the 180,000 Jews living in Paris, as many as 120,000 had been born outside France, and Yiddish was heard more frequently than French in the streets of the Jewish areas.

The Jews of France participated in French cultural life. As painters, musicians, actors, writers and philosophers, they were accepted by their fellow Frenchmen, and made their contribution to the quality of life. The names of Marcel Proust and André Maurois, Camille Pissaro and Marc Chagall, Amedeo Modigliani and Sarah Bernhardt, were an integral part of France.

Nevertheless, anti-semitism was strong in certain circles inside France and successful Jewish politicians such as Léon Blum, Prime Minister from 1936 to 1938, and Georges Mandel, Minister of the Colonies in 1939, aroused among such circles a strong and at times vicious dislike.

Since 1924 the United States had, by its Quota

Act, effectively closed its borders to all but a small percentage of Jews seeking to escape the uncertainties and anti-semitic violence of eastern Europe, and between Hitler's coming to power in January 1933 and his conquest of Poland in September 1939, tens of thousands of German, Austrian, Czechoslovak and Polish Jews, who might otherwise have found their way to the United States, were given refuge in France. For these people there was to be only a short respite.

On 10 May 1940 the German armies invaded France. Many thousands of Jews, both French-born and refugees, fought in the ranks of the French army. But the German attack was swift and strong; Paris was occupied on 14 June, and an armistice was signed with Germany nine days later. About 300,000 Jews were now under Nazi rule in France, in two zones, one occupied by the Germans, the other ruled by Marshal Pétain from the provincial town of Vichy.

Slowly but methodically the German occupation forces moved to isolate and weaken the Jews. An ordinance of 27 September 1940 ordered a special census of all Jews, while a second ordinance of 18 October 1940 required all Jewish businesses to identify themselves and to accept a non-Jewish 'administrator'. A third ordinance, of 26 April 1941, extended the category of 'Jew' to all people of Jewish origin who were baptized or practising Catholics or Protestants.

As 1941 progressed, a further series of ordinances isolated the Jewish communities of France

Foreign-born Jews arrested in Paris in May 1941, and sent to Drancy detention camp.

Below: **Jews arrested in Paris on 16 and 17 July 1942 were brought to a sports stadium where the men and women were separated before being taken to Drancy.**

Bordeaux, 28 March 1942: the entrance to an exhibition 'The Jews and France', portraying the Jews as an evil influence.

Inside the exhibition: the grasping hand is meant to represent a Jew ordered to take all that he can from non-Jews.

still further. On 14 May the Gestapo arrested several thousand Parisian Jews who were not French nationals, collected them together at the Velodrôme d'Hiver sports stadium, and then interned them in a large suburban complex at Drancy, a suburb of Paris. Two weeks later, on 28 May, it was made illegal to deal in Jewish-owned capital, and on 13 August all wireless sets in Jewish possession were confiscated. On 15 August more than 7,000 foreign-born Jews were arrested by the Vichy authorities in 'unoccupied' France. They too were interned, while on 20 August several thousand more foreign-born Jews were taken from their homes in Paris by the Gestapo and interned at Drancy. A month later, on 28 September, Jews were forbidden to make use of the financial proceeds of the forced sale of their own property. In this way, by a succession of orders and arrests, the Jews were slowly but steadily cut off from the world around them.

Since March 1941 the Vichy Government had conducted its relations with the Jews of the 'unoccupied' zone through the Commissariat for Jewish Affairs, headed by a well-known anti-semite, Xavier Vallat. On 31 July 1941 a leading French Jew, Jacob Kaplan, writing on behalf of the Chief Rabbi of France, protested to Vallat against the Vichy Government's own anti-semitic measures. Surely, Kaplan wrote, it was illogical for a Christian to defame Judaism, which was both the 'mother' of Christianity and the source of the Ten Commandments. Surely, in addition, the impressive record of French Jews in the First World War was proof of their love of France and of their willingness to sacrifice their lives for the French nation. As for the Jewish war effort in 1940, Kaplan added, 'when the final story is written, it will reveal that the Jews have done their duty like all other French citizens'.

On 5 August Xavier Vallat replied to this appeal through his deputy, Jarnieu. There would not have been any anti-Jewish legislation at all, Jarnieu asserted, 'if there had not been, during the last few years, an invasion of our territory by a host of Jews having no ties with our civilization'. As for the Jews who had died fighting for France, that, he wrote evasively, 'is a matter which deserves too much respect to become the object of a controversy'. In the Government's policy, Jarnieu wrote, 'there is no anti-semitism,

Some of the huts at Rivesaltes detention camp: a photograph taken in 1977.

simply the application of reasons of state'.

The Jews of France were not without courage and, despite the risks involved, many of them responded eagerly to the call to resistance. Indeed, it was as resistance fighters that the initiative and heroism of Jewish groups and individuals was conspicuous. Not only did Jews, both French and foreign-born, take a main part in the different French groups that had begun to emerge, ranging from the right wing to the Communist, but specifically Jewish groups also took up the cause of resistance.

On 20 October 1941 Eichmann's representative in Paris, Captain Theodor Dannecker – who was later to go to Bulgaria – sent the Foreign Ministry in Berlin a letter with certain statistics about the state of French Jewry. In the German-occupied region, Dannecker estimated, there were 165,000 Jews, of whom as many as 148,000 were living in Paris. In the territory controlled by the Vichy Government there were a further 145,000 Jews.

Dannecker also reported that 7,443 foreign-born Jews, most of whom had been taken from their homes in the 'actions' of May and August 1941, were still being held in internment camps in the German-occupied zone of France, the majority at Drancy, others at Pithiviers and Beaune-la-Rolande. On 1 November 1941 the German Secretary of State, Ernst von Weizsäcker, noted, in Berlin, that the German Government had no objection to the continued detention of all Jews arrested in France with foreign nationality, with the exception of those who were United States citizens, who should be released.

Measures designed to isolate and weaken the Jewish community still further were announced on 29 November 1941, when the Vichy Government decreed that all Jewish organizations be dissolved and their property handed over to a special council, the General Union of Israelites in France.

One source of help had remained open for the Jews of Vichy France since the capitulation in June 1940 – money sent from Jewish charitable organizations in the United States. For eighteen months this had proved a major source of relief and support. But when, on 10 December 1941, the United States entered the war against Germany, the Jews of France no longer could have funds from America.

Some of the towns and detention camps in France from which Jews were deported to the death camps in the east.

Meanwhile, the Vichy Government had itself continued to arrest foreign-born Jews and by December 1941 had interned a total of 20,000 Jews, mostly recent refugees from Germany, Austria, Czechoslovakia and Poland. These unfortunate people were held in a number of camps, mostly near the Pyrennees, chief among them Gurs, Rivesaltes, Noé, Récébedou, Le Vernet and Les Milles. Among the Jews held at Gurs were many who had been expelled by the Germans in October 1940 from the towns and villages of southern Germany and the Rhineland.

In the second week of December 1941 a member of the French resistance shot at, and slightly wounded, a major in the German air force. Seizing upon this incident as its excuse, the German military authorities took immediate action. A collective 'fine' of a billion francs was imposed on the

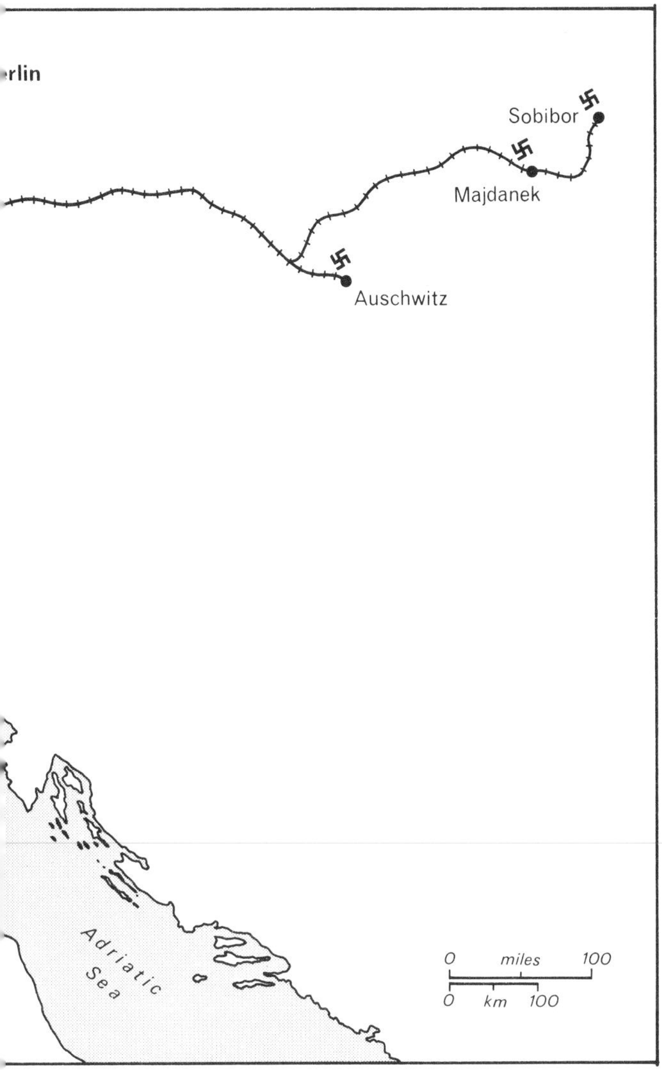

The station at Les Milles from which several hundred deportees were sent to the death camps in the east: a photograph taken in 1977.

Jews of Paris while, as a further reprisal, the Gestapo arrested several hundred French Communists and more than 750 Jews. This 'action' took place in Paris on 12 December and at the same time a further 300 Jews were taken from the internment camp at Drancy to join those who had been arrested.

The German military authorities had no desire to keep the hostages in camps in France and asked their superiors in Berlin if they could be deported. On 27 December, however, the Army Command in Berlin telegraphed to Paris that, on account of transport difficulties, no Jews could be transferred to the east until February or March and that meanwhile all those arrested in the 'action' of 12 December must be held in barracks at Compiègne.

In charge of the camp at Compiègne, and of all

the other internment camps in France, was a thirty-two-year-old German, Kurt Lischka, once a law student in Breslau. Three years earlier Lischka had led the operation for the arrest of the Jews during the Night of Broken Glass. Since then, he had been steadily promoted in the ranks of the Gestapo and by 1941 he had risen to the position of Chief of the Nazi Police in Paris.

Now Lischka, having been given command of the internment camps in German-occupied France, saw as his principal aim the deportation of as many Jews as possible to the east, to the forced labour camps which he knew were being prepared to receive them.

When it was suggested that those Jews over fifty-five, who were clearly too old to work as forced labourers, should be released, Lischka protested and, in a letter of 15 February 1942 to the German military authorities in Paris, he warned that if any Jews at all were released from internment, they would conduct 'an intense anti-German campaign'.

Lishka's protest was successful. The 1,000 Jews remained interned at Compiègne. They were not without friends, however, and there was pressure for their release. Lischka took alarm and on 26 February 1942 he sent a telegram to Adolf Eichmann in which he declared that, in view of the 'innumerable requests' for the release of the internees, it had now become a matter of urgency to deport the 1,000 Jews 'as quickly as possible'. Lischka went on to warn Eichmann that the failure to carry out the deportation so far 'is interpreted by the French as an example of German weakness'.

Lischka's telegram led to a flurry of activity in Berlin. On 1 March Eichmann was able to report to the Security Police Commander in Paris, SS Colonel Helmut Knochen, that discussions were already taking place with the railway authorities to fix the timetable of the deportation train; and within a month the train was ready.

Thus it was that on 27 March 1942 the first train was made ready to leave France for Auschwitz. Marked out for that journey were 1,112 men, all Jews, drawn from every corner of Europe. Several hundred had been born in France, both in Paris and in the provinces. Several hundred more had been born in the Polish provinces of the then Russian Empire, at least eighty-four of them in Warsaw. Among the birthplaces listed in the tally were many towns outside Europe altogether. More than a hundred of those deported had been born in Turkey and were from Smyrna, Constantinople and Bursa. The fifty-year-old Ignatz Baum had been born in Haifa, when that town too had been a part of the Turkish Empire. Several dozen of the deportees were from North Africa, from Tunis, Algiers, Oran, Marrakesh, Bizerta and Alexandria. The twenty-six-year-old Henry Eckstein had been born in London. The forty-two-year-old Moses Schneider had been born in Auschwitz itself when it had been part of the Austro-Hungarian Empire.

Among those Jews in the detention camp at Compiègne who witnessed the preparation of Convoy No 1 was Professor Georges Wellers. He had been arrested during the round-up of 12 December and was to remain a prisoner at Compiègne until his own deportation to Auschwitz two-and-a-half years later. He was one of the few deportees who survived the war. Ten years after the departure of Convoy No 1, he recalled the atmosphere of the weeks leading up to that day:

'The weather was good, the sun spring-like, and during the day it was almost warm. It was, indeed, delightful not to feel any more, without respite, the endless wet cold, mortifying and demoralizing. Even our hunger now felt less sharp, and our spirits rose. Even the Germans seemed to be less fierce; having imposed on us total isolation from the outside world for three months, they had just given us permission to write to our families and to ask for the clothing and medicine which we so cruelly lacked.

'And yet, a few days later, the Germans ordered every one of us to have hair, beard and moustache close-cut, and if anyone showed the least reluctance, he became the target of much mockery.

'Then, even while the haircutting was still in progress, an insolent blow of the whistle summoned everyone to the yard. It was two o'clock in the afternoon. Complaining and joking, we got into line, curious to know what it was about, slightly uneasy, but calm.

'Hardly had we lined up in our usual order than the camp commandant, Kuntze, appeared, carrying a green file, and accompanied by several other German officials. Without any explanation, Kuntze began to call out names. Each person who was called had to leave his place, and go to the left of the parade.

'As the calling out of the names continued, it became more and more rapid, while the Germans, in the effort to organize those who had been called out, began to show increasing irritation and indeed brutality. Suddenly, literally from one minute to the next, the atmosphere became more dramatic, heavier and more sinister.

'What was happening, we asked ourselves, but despite the new atmosphere, we did not allow ourselves to give in either to nervousness or to despair.

'Two hours later, 550 men were assembled to the left of us, surrounded by armed German soldiers. Some eighty of us remained uncalled. Then the 550 men were told that they had fifteen minutes to collect all their personal belongings, and so, in the greatest rush imaginable, in the chaos, and in a state of nerves, hundreds of weak, emaciated and sick men ran across to the huts to get hold of an already tattered or shapeless shirt, shoes, a blanket and a handful of worn clothing.

'The 550 men were put into two huts, guarded by Germans with fixed bayonets. No one was able to sleep. Some spent the night trying to put together as best they could their meagre belongings, repairing a strap, making up satchels. No one had the least idea where they were to be sent, or why. Every conceivable possibility was discussed; the most absurd destinations suggested, except the real one....

'In the morning the atmosphere was one of comradeship, of concern for the sick, and of toleration and goodwill towards those who, during the past three months, had shown themselves to be either selfish or apathetic.

'Then at two in the afternoon, all were once more summoned outside. It was a hot afternoon. The sun burned down, and everyone felt ill at ease in their accumulated clothes. The bundles and bags seemed terribly heavy.

'Roll-call began, its aim being to line everyone up in lines of five, in alphabetical order. This the Germans did in a savage manner, striking people in the mouth with their fists and even with their rifle butts.

'Cries of pain filled the air, as the Germans themselves became more agitated, counting and recounting the 550, as each time the totals did not seem to tally. For two hours the process continued, under a sun now amazingly hot, the men perspiring and covered in dust, their faces disfigured by fear and hunger, yet remaining silent and stoical.

'Water was brought and given out, and then, at about five in the afternoon, the 550 men were led off, weakened by their long detention and the constant blows, in a long column across the parade ground and out of the camp in which they had suffered so much since the previous December.

'The 550 deportees were led through the streets of Compiègne, watched in silence by many of the local Frenchmen who, sombre and preoccupied, managed to give at least a few desperate signs of sympathy and encouragement. Some of the deportees looked so thin and wretched, their faces so ashen, that those who watched them pass were themselves quite terrified. People were not yet used to such sights.

'Near the station the deportees caught a glimpse of a large number of women, a miracle it seemed, for it was a group of wives who, having heard somehow of the deportation, had come from Paris to say farewell. But the German soldiers refused to allow them to come anywhere near the column of deportees and such farewells as could be made were made at a distance.'

The 550 deportees had one more wait in store for them, for the arrival of a further 550 or so deportees from Drancy. Once these men too had reached Compiègne station, Convoy No 1 steamed slowly eastward.

Of the 1,112 men deported on 27 March 1942 from Drancy and Compiègne, only nineteen survived the war.

11

France: The Deportations Continue

The Nazi campaign against the Jews of France began in earnest in the second week of May 1942, six weeks after the Compiègne deportation. On 12 May the Army Command in Berlin, in a secret order to the military authorities of Greater Paris, laid down that in all instructions issued to the public on the subject of deportation, the words 'to the east' must not be used, in order to prevent critical comments about the German-occupied regions in the east. In addition, the word 'deportation' must likewise be avoided, because in Tsarist times it had suggested evacuation towards Siberia. In all ordinances and in all correspondence the expression to use, the Army Command insisted, was 'consignment to forced labour'.

At 11.00 in the morning of 13 May the deportation plans took yet another step towards completion when Captain Dannecker, now 'Chief of the Anti-Jewish Section' of the Gestapo in Paris, took up the question of providing a substantial number of goods wagons for the deportees. After a long discussion with the head of railway transport in German-occupied France, Lieutenant-General Kohl, Dannecker – who had just celebrated his twenty-ninth birthday – was able to inform his Gestapo colleagues Knochen and Lischka that General Kohl 'approves 100 per cent of a final solution of the Jewish question, with the aim of annihilating the enemy to the very end'. The General had gone on to say how pleased he was to be working with the Gestapo in this matter, and added: 'If you tell me – "I wish to transport 10,000 or 20,000 Jews to the east" – you can count on it that for each request I will put at your disposal whatever rolling stock and railway engines you need.'

Lischka was delighted with Dannecker's report, writing to Eichmann two days later: 'We have succeeded in establishing good relations with Lieutenant-General Kohl, the head of the railway transport department. Kohl, who is an outright enemy of the Jews, has given us an assurance that he will give us all the rolling stock and locomotives we need. . . .' As a result of Kohl's help, Lischka added, 'It will soon be possible for ten trains a month to leave France.'

The Gestapo officials now began to put in motion the machinery that would enable these massive deportations to take place. Two weeks later, on 29 May, all Jews over the age of six were ordered to wear a special sign, the yellow star, with the word *Juif* – Jew – written over it. This order applied not only to French-born Jews but to all Jews living in France who were still citizens of Germany, Poland, Holland, Belgium, Croatia, Slovakia and Rumania.

Even before the yellow star decree was put into effect, the second of the Auschwitz trains was being prepared. Consisting entirely of men, the train was made up of a further 751 internees from Drancy and a further 182 from two other internment camps, Beaune-la-Rolande and Pithiviers. All 933 were taken to Compiègne to await their special train. The youngest of them was eighteen, the oldest, fifty-four.

In preparation for the journey to Auschwitz, the camp administration at Compiègne prepared an alphabetical list of those about to be deported. The largest single group were those born in Poland, 571 in all. A further 95 had been born in Russia, 90 in Rumania, and 79 in France. Among the other nationalities represented were 15

German-born Jews, 10 from Turkey, 5 from Czechoslovakia, 3 from Austria, 2 from Holland, 2 from Belgium and 2 from Egypt. Single Jews were included from Bulgaria, Hungary, Greece, Luxembourg and Switzerland. There were also 3 who had been born in Britain – including the thirty-eight-year-old Erich Riemany.

One of the deportees on Convoy No 2, Zeeb Yevnine, had been born in Palestine in 1894, in the town of Safed, one of the holy cities of Judaism. Another of the deportees, Jonas Silber, had been born in San Francisco in 1905.

An elderly Jew in Paris during the German occupation.

On 5 June 1942 Captain Dannecker telegraphed to Eichmann in Berlin, and to Camp Commandant Hoess at Auschwitz, that 'Convoy DA301', containing 1,000 Jews, had left Compiègne station at 9.30 that morning, destination Auschwitz.

The train reached Auschwitz two days later, on 7 June, when each of the deportees had a number burned into his forearm. The Auschwitz records show that numbers 38,117 to 39,116 were allocated to these new deportees. Within ten weeks, 783 of them were dead. And by the end of the war, only 32 were still alive.

It was on 7 June, the day on which Convoy No 2 reached Auschwitz, that the yellow star decree came into effect throughout France. At first the decree caused a certain confusion, and indeed derision. Some Jews decided not to wear it, or to wear it upside down, or to wear several stars instead of one. With much courage, there were also non-Jews who insisted on wearing the star as a protest against the measure. But such protests were to no avail, and on 26 June the official German newspaper in Paris, the *Pariser Zeitung*, reported that both the Jewish offenders and their non-Jewish supporters had been arrested and interned.

Meanwhile, in Berlin, Eichmann was completing his plans for the speeding up and systematization of the 'final solution'. On 11 June he called together his Gestapo experts from Paris, Brussels and The Hague, to work out the statistical aspects of the deportations. Captain Dannecker represented the Gestapo in France. The conference of 11 June set a 'target' figure of 100,000 for the total number of Jews to be deported from France. The deportees were to consist of both men and women, between the ages of sixteen and forty. A 'transportation fee' was to be charged for each deportee, 700 Reichsmark, to be paid by the French State.

On 16 June a hitch presented itself to the Gestapo planners. It took the form of a message from General Kohl, to the effect that the German spring offensive against Russia had led to the sudden transfer of rolling stock from occupied

Drancy detention camp: four photographs taken by the Germans in 1942, at the time of the first deportations to Auschwitz.

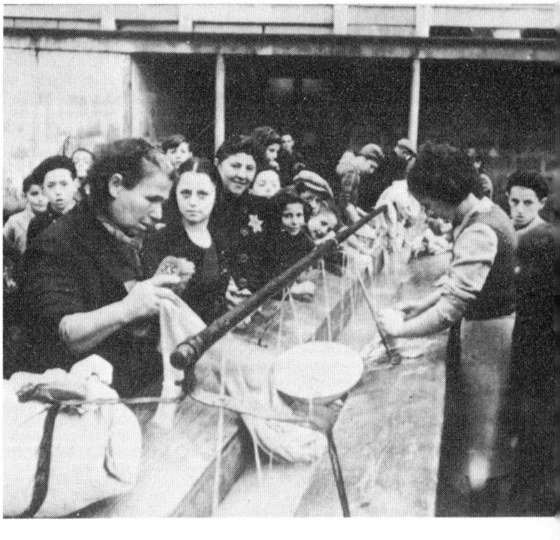

France to the eastern front. In all, 800 passenger wagons, 37,000 goods wagons, and 1,000 railway engines had been despatched to the east. So urgent was the need for them, that it had been necessary to send them off empty.

Such news made no difference to the Gestapo. On that very same day, 16 June, the commandant at Drancy was told to prepare for the 'departure' of a further 1,000 Jews, and within twenty-four hours some 583 internees, each of them judged 'capable of work', had been listed by the commandant for Convoy No 3.

On 18 June Eichmann telegraphed from Berlin to the Chief of the Security Services in German-occupied France, Colonel Knochen, that Convoy No 3 was to leave direct from the nearest railway station to Drancy, at 8.55 am.

Not only the precise time of departure but the exact transit times through France were carefully prepared in advance, typed out, signed and circulated to the Gestapo and railway administration personnel involved. The timetable for Convoy No 3 gave exact times of arrival and departure from Paris to the German border:

Le Bourget	8.55
Bobigny	9.20
Noisy-le-Sec	9.30
Epernay	*arr* 13.14
	dep 13.47
Châlons-sur-Marne	*arr* 14.36
	dep 14.42
Bar-le-Duc	*arr* 17.05
	dep 17.15
Lerinville	*arr* 18.39
	dep 18.44
Neuberg (Mosel)	*arr* 19.57
	dep 20.20

This timetable was ready on 18 June. Two days later, Captain Dannecker arrived at Drancy to arrange the details of the convoy's departure. As a result of Dannecker's specific instructions, a total of 934 Jews were taken from their staircases during Saturday 20 June and Sunday 21 June and held in isolation from the rest of the camp.

At 5.45 on the morning of 22 June the Jews of

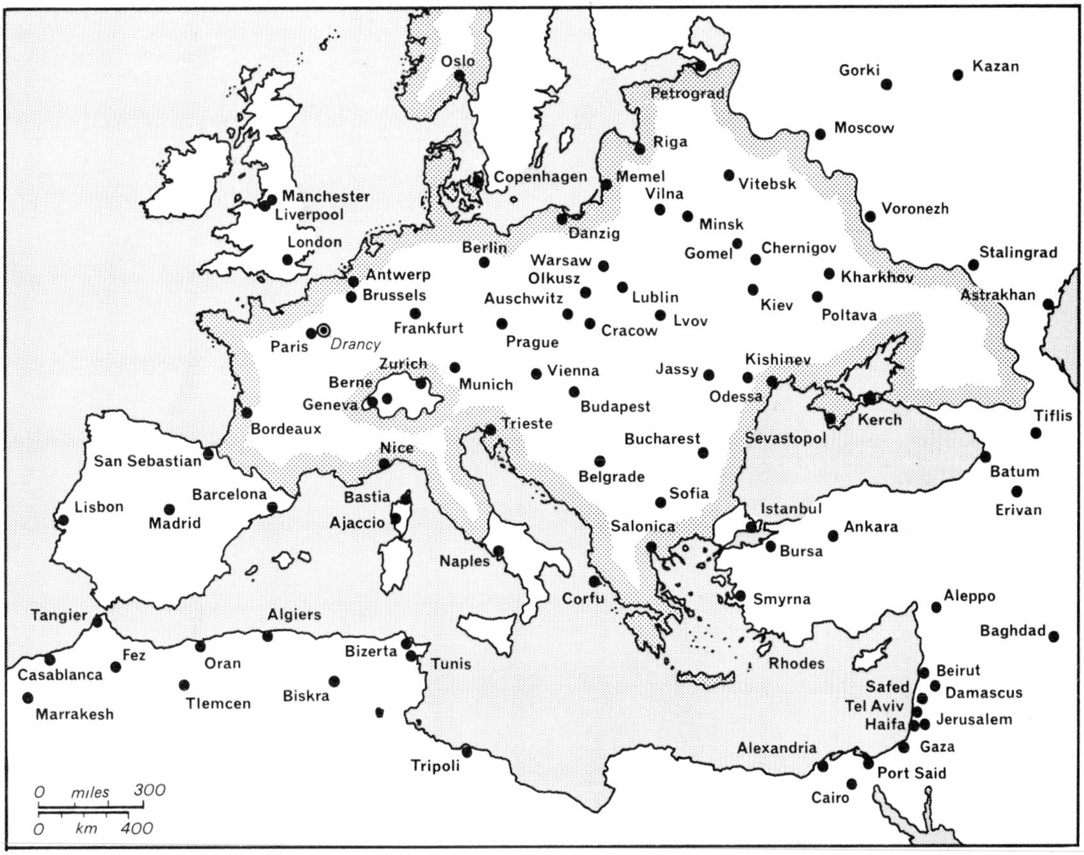

Some of the towns both inside and outside the boundaries of Nazi-occupied Europe, the birthplaces of Jews who were living or working in France at the outbreak of war and who were subsequently deported to the death camps in the east.

The Paris suburban station of Le Bourget-Drancy, from which Convoy No 3 and more than seventy subsequent trains, took the deportees to Auschwitz.

Convoy No 3 were assembled in the great courtyard of Drancy. They included 435 French Jews, 211 Polish Jews, 59 Russian Jews, 56 Rumanian Jews and 27 Turkish Jews. There were also Jews from Czechoslovakia, Lithuania, Latvia, Germany, Greece, Belgium and Austria.

More than 100 of these new deportees were Jews who had fought in the French army in 1940, at the time of the German invasion. Fourteen of them were veterans of the First World War. One of them, the fifty-four-year-old René Bloch, had been decorated with the *Légion d'Honneur*. Learning that Bloch was among the deportees, the camp commandant at Drancy asked for him to be allowed to remain behind, but Dannecker insisted that Bloch continue with the convoy.

For two hours the deportees were loaded into buses, for transfer to the railway station. During the loading four of them were taken ill and had to be helped aboard the bus. One of them, who had collapsed, was put on a stretcher. The camp commandant suggested that this man should also be allowed to stay behind. But once more Dannecker insisted that he be taken aboard the bus.

Convoy No 3 was the first to contain women, sixty-six in all, from a special women's camp at

Les Tourelles. Among them was Annette Zelman, a twenty-year-old Jewess who had been born in Nancy, in eastern France. She had been arrested a month before. Her so-called 'crime' was to have become engaged to a non-Jew. Even a written declaration by herself and her fiancé that they were prepared to give up all thought of marriage could not save her.

The departure of the sixty-six women from Les Tourelles was witnessed by a non-Jew, Alice Courouble, who had herself been interned at the camp for having insisted on wearing the yellow star, in defiance of the occupation laws. After the war she recalled how, on the morning of 19 June:

'We were having breakfast in our dining room when the curt order came: "Everyone outside". Under the chestnut trees we saw three German officers. Another order was shouted: "All Jewesses between eighteen and forty-two years old, line up!" and then, a moment later, "Turn around, facing the courtyard! You others, return to your dormitories!"'

Alice Courouble returned to her dormitory with her fellow non-Jews. Some while later one of the camp gendarmes came in. 'The Jewesses are going to come through this dormitory', he told them. 'It is ordered, not a cry, not a word, not a sign, not a movement. Each of you stay by your bed. The first one who moves will join them, and will *go with* them. Understood?'

As the Jewesses filed through the dormitory, Alice Courouble recalled:

'Our silence was like a wall. All of us were calm. There were Sonia and Raya; there was Helen, so blonde; there was a mother, there a daughter. We wept, stifling our sobs; we did not even dare to wipe away our tears. The door closed behind them. The gendarme remained in front of it.'

For three days and nights the sixty-six Jewesses were forced to remain in isolation, in the most unsanitary conditions, locked in with nothing but large pails for relieving themselves, and pitchers of water. Mothers of the girls, and their non-Jewish friends, had tried to take them some food but, despite their pleas, the gendarme refused to allow any food at all to be passed in to them. In her account of those three days Alice Courouble recalled how, for one brief moment, the door had been partly opened by the gendarme as a result of the wild pleas of a desperate mother, and how:

'In the narrow chink of light, appeared a host of faces; dark hair and light; mouths open, crying, appealing; hands outstretched, imploring. It was impossible to tell which face belonged to which hand. A human tangle, a choir of begging cries:

Two Jews being deported to Auschwitz, photographed at Le Bourget-Drancy station.

"Water! Bring my mother! Tell Ginette to come! Pass me my handbag, quickly! Oh, be quick!" The gendarme, worried, rushed to close the door, and the Dantesque vision vanished.'

On Saturday, 21 June, before the sixty-six Jewesses were taken from Les Tourelles, Alice Courouble and the other non-Jewish internees were locked in their dormitories:

'We heard an enormous key turn in the lock, and heavy bars lowered against the door. We had been sealed in. The cursed beasts were about to pass.

They would find no single compassionate soul on their journey. This refusal to allow us to see them, it was for us as if they were already dead. Early on Sunday morning, at five o'clock while it was still dark, the noise of engines woke us up. My friends ran to the windows. It was the buses about to set off on the first stage – to Drancy. The headlamps of the buses swept across our ceiling, momentarily lighting us up. I didn't go to look, I was miserable. All of a sudden, from outside, two or three women's voices started to sing the *Marseillaise*. One by one, other voices took it up. In our room, sobs answered the music.'

The sixty-six women from Les Tourelles reached Drancy in time to meet Eichmann's carefully prepared schedule, departure at 8.55 am on that same morning of 22 June. Thus it was that Convoy No 3 travelled eastwards from Le Bourget, reaching the German frontier that evening and Auschwitz two days later, on 24 June. Once more, the records of Auschwitz itself show that the deportees were branded with a number, the men from 40,681 to 41,613 and the women from 7,961 to 8,026. Three weeks later, by 15 August, half of those who had set out from Paris had been murdered. Of the total convoy of 1,000, only 19 of the men and 5 of the women survived the war.

No amount of books could tell the full story of those who were deported from France to Auschwitz between the summer of 1942 and the autumn of 1944. The list of their names alone fills a substantial volume, and if a single page were to be devoted to the story of each individual sent to his or her death from France alone, it would need nearly *four hundred* books the size of this one to tell the tale.

The first three convoys had been sent according to the careful preparations of the Gestapo. A further eighty trains were yet to be despatched, each taking up to 1,000 Jews to their deaths. The amount of preparation involved was substantial, and several hundred telegrams survive, plotting in almost pedantic detail the despatch of each train, according to precisely calculated timetables and copiously prepared lists.

Each train had a different story to tell. Convoy No 4 of 25 June 1942 took 999 men to Auschwitz from the internment camp at Pithiviers, where they had been held since the round-ups of May and August 1941. All but sixty of them were Polish-born. Three days later, Convoy No 5 took 1,038 Jews to Auschwitz from the internment camp at Beaune-la-Rolande, among them thirty-four women. Against one name in the typed list, that of Adolphe Ziffer, a painter, born in Poland thirty-eight years before, a German official noted: 'Killed while trying to escape'. The two youngest deportees on this convoy had been born in Paris, Maurice Cytrynowiec, a schoolboy, and Jeannine Stickgold, a schoolgirl, both fifteen years old.

It was not only the able-bodied and the teenagers who were now marked out for death. On 20 July 1942 Captain Dannecker had been telephoned from Berlin by Eichmann himself, and by the Gestapo's transport expert, Franz Novak, who promised to make available to the Paris section 'at the end of August or early September, six trains for the General Government of Poland, to contain Jews of all types, including Jews who were unfit for work, and old Jews'.

From mid-July to mid-August the trains continued to steam eastwards, taking to Auschwitz over a period of less than thirty days more than 14,000 Jews who had been interned in Pithiviers, Drancy, Beaune-la-Rolande, Noé, Récébedou, Le Vernet and Gurs.

The list of deportees, the rate at which they were sent east, and the number of known survivors, gives a terrifying glimpse of the efficiency of the Nazi machine. Of the 1,015 Jews in Convoy No 19, which left France on 14 August 1942, there were 100 children under the age of sixteen. From this particular convoy, only one person is known to have survived, the fifteen-year-old Nathan Seroka. His father Jacob, his mother Ida, and his seventeen-year-old brother Baruch, were with him on the journey but were killed at Auschwitz.

In addition to those Jews who had been interned, one convoy in July was made up of French and foreign-born Jews living in the provincial towns, who had hitherto been left unmolested in their own homes, but who were now ordered to

A young man being deported from Le Bourget-Drancy station.

report to their local railway stations. These Jews formed Convoy No 8, which was made up almost entirely of those living in the provincial towns of Angers, Poitiers, Saumur, Nantes, Le Mans, Tours, Saint-Nazaire and Rennes. One of those taken by the Gestapo for this train was a girl of thirteen. Three others were over ninety.

Convoy No 8 left Angers station on the evening of 20 July. Only 14 of the 430 women and 394 men who were on the train are known to have survived the war, among them Dr André Lettich, whose wife, herself a doctor, and whose five-year-old son, Johnny, were both murdered at Auschwitz. Dr Lettich, one of the few people to have survived almost three years at Auschwitz, has told the story of his family's departure from Tours:

'. . . the German handed me a piece of paper, on which I read that I must go to work in Germany, that I must bring my work-clothes with me, a change of shoes, linen, food for five days, and money. The policeman turned to my wife; "You too, madam. You are also going."

' "But, sir, how is that possible? We have a young son, and cannot possibly leave him."

' "That's of no importance, you can bring him with you, he'll be fine with you."

'These gentlemen made us hurry and ten minutes later we had been taken to a truck that was parked outside our door. Inside it we found several of our friends who had been arrested before us. And the truck then continued on its way from house to house, collecting up the rest of our co-religionists in the same rough way. Finally the truck came to some huts on the outskirts of town, where the men were separated from the women and children. All night the truck unloaded its human cargo.

'That night we were forced to wait one hour, even two hours, in order to go to the lavatory. Even then, we were accompanied the 500 metres by a guard armed with a machine gun. People went almost mad, as the need to go to the lavatory became increasingly urgent, an intolerable pressure on the bladder. That night was nothing but one long nightmare, broken by cries and groans.'

On the following morning, all those who had been rounded up were taken to Tours railway station. There, a courageous Frenchwoman, a Christian, who had managed to find out where the deportees had been taken, brought Dr Lettich a suitcase filled with various foods, condensed milk, chocolate and fruit, each packet labelled by a friend or neighbour: 'For little Johnny from . . .' But the doctor had no idea where his wife and son had been taken and, in fact, was never to see them again. His account continued:

'We were taken from Tours to Angers in a passenger train. Once at Angers, we were stripped of all our valuables, and indeed of all souvenirs of our dearest ones, and were crammed like sheep in the small rooms of a convent, 25 and 30 of us to a room, and then locked in. In the morning we were let out, and forced into buses which took us to the station, where we were pushed into cattle trucks, 75 to 85 men to a wagon. All the windows and doors of the wagons were hermetically sealed.

'During the journey, crushed one against the other, we suffered terribly from thirst and we had, in addition, to give up one corner of the wagon as a space in which to relieve ourselves.

'After travelling like this for *six days* the train stopped, and we heard violent blows as the wagons were unlocked. With fierce cries, the SS made it clear that everyone had to get out of the wagon, together with our bags. They then ordered us to form up in lines of five.

'It was raining. We were standing up to our knees in mud. Up to now, we had still some hope of being considered as human beings. Here we quickly saw that this was no longer so. To those, for example, who tried to find their raincoat, or their hat, to protect themselves from the rain, it was quickly indicated, by blows on the head, that these objects no longer belonged to them.

'At last we were taken towards the camp. I could just make out, in the distance, the women, who were being led in a different direction. . . .'

The women of Convoy No 8, including those with children, were being taken straight to the gas chambers.

12

The Children's Convoys

In his telephone conversation with Captain Dannecker on 20 July 1942, Eichmann had told the Paris section of the Gestapo that he had decided 'that as soon as the deportations to the east could begin again, trainloads *of children* could begin to roll'.

On 28 July, only eight days after Eichmann's telephone call, Dannecker's successor as head of the anti-Jewish section of the Gestapo, Heinz Roethke, discussed the 'forthcoming programme' of Jewish deportations with Jean Leguay, the Secretary-General of the French Police in the German-occupied region of France. After their meeting a typed summary set out their decisions, one of which was that four new convoys, beginning on 19 August, should specifically be made up of 'those Jewish children who had been interned in Paris on 16 and 17 July 1943, and for whom the decision of the Reich Security Office likewise authorized that they should be transported'.

On 3 August Jean Leguay was able to send a detailed account of his progress in arranging the train timetable to his superior, Louis Darquier de Pellepoix. The trains being prepared for 19, 21, 24 and 26 August, he reported, 'will consist in the main of the children of those families who have been interned at Pithiviers and at Beaune-la-Rolande'.

On 13 August, at a meeting with Captain Dannecker, Leguay explained his plan. Jewish adults from Vichy France would be brought north to Drancy, where they would be 'mixed' with the Jewish children from Pithiviers and Beaune-la-Rolande in the proportion of 500 to 700 adults for each group of 300 to 500 children. In this way, it would be assumed by any chance onlooker that the adults were the parents of the children. In fact, the children's parents had already been deported in the July convoys; most of their mothers had already been gassed and their fathers put to work in the slave-labour battalions from whose ranks few were to survive.

Leguay also told Dannecker 'that during the month of September, thirteen trains would be despatched from Drancy, and that Jewish children could also be drawn from the non-occupied zone'. Thus, the Vichy Government not only co-operated with the Gestapo, but widened the base of Gestapo operations and speeded up its plans.

Three days after this meeting between the Gestapo and Vichy officials, the first group of children were brought by bus from Beaune-la-Rolande and Pithiviers to Paris. All of them were under twelve years old and all of them were without their parents. In two days more than 500 children were brought to Drancy. Georges Wellers was among those already interned at Drancy who saw them arrive. As he later recalled:

'They were all aged between two and twelve. They were let out of the buses in the middle of the yard, like tiny insects. Each bus arrived with a guard on the platform....

'The children got down from the buses and at once the largest among them took the smallest by the hand, and did not let them go during the short journey to their dormitories. On reaching the staircases, the oldest carried the little ones in their arms and, breathless, carried them up to the fourth floor. There, they stood one against the other, like a frightened flock of lambs, nervous of

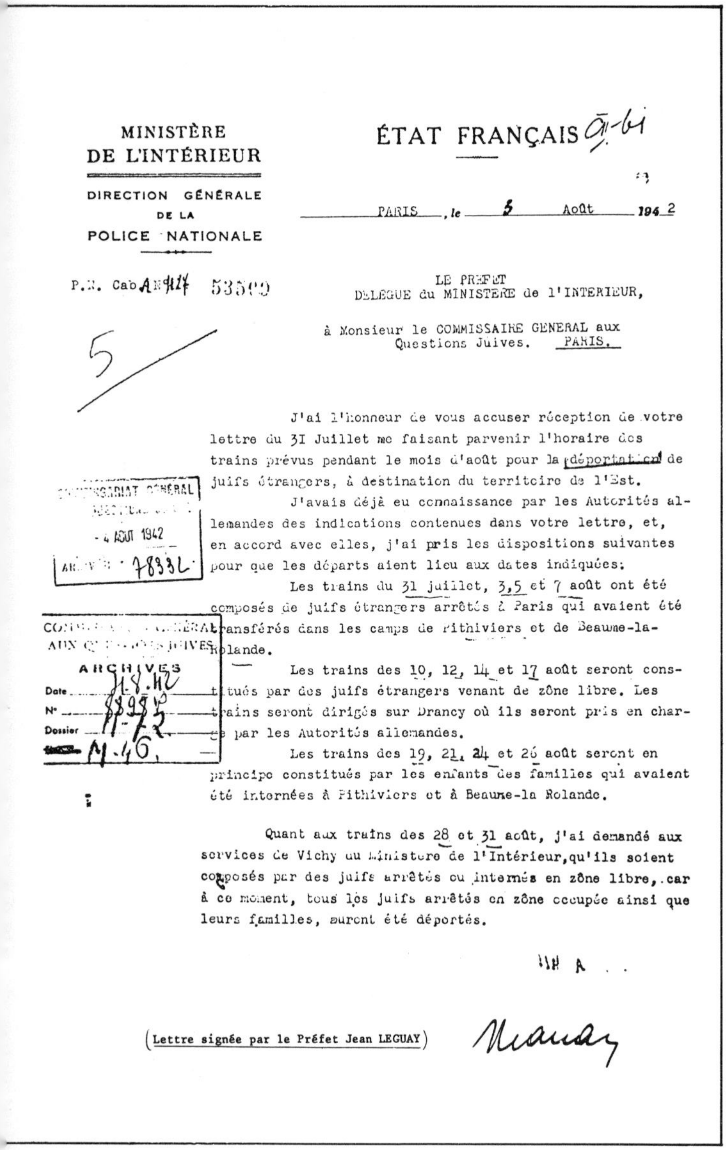

MINISTÈRE
DE L'INTÉRIEUR

DIRECTION GÉNÉRALE
DE LA
POLICE NATIONALE

P.N. Cab A 53509

ÉTAT FRANÇAIS

PARIS, le 3 Août 1942

LE PREFET
DELEGUE du MINISTERE de l'INTERIEUR,

à Monsieur le COMMISSAIRE GENERAL aux
Questions Juives. PARIS.

J'ai l'honneur de vous accuser réception de votre lettre du 31 Juillet me faisant parvenir l'horaire des trains prévus pendant le mois d'août pour la déportation de juifs étrangers, à destination du territoire de l'Est.

J'avais déjà eu connaissance par les Autorités allemandes des indications contenues dans votre lettre, et, en accord avec elles, j'ai pris les dispositions suivantes pour que les départs aient lieu aux dates indiquées:

Les trains du 31 juillet, 3,5 et 7 août ont été composés de juifs étrangers arrêtés à Paris qui avaient été transférés dans les camps de Pithiviers et de Beaune-la-Rolande.

Les trains des 10, 12, 14 et 17 août seront constitués par des juifs étrangers venant de zône libre. Les trains seront dirigés sur Drancy où ils seront pris en charge par les Autorités allemandes.

Les trains des 19, 21, 24 et 26 août seront en principe constitués par les enfants des familles qui avaient été internées à Pithiviers et à Beaune-la Rolande.

Quant aux trains des 28 et 31 août, j'ai demandé aux services de Vichy du Ministere de l'Intérieur, qu'ils soient composés par des juifs arrêtés ou internés en zône libre, car à ce moment, tous les juifs arrêtés en zône occupée ainsi que leurs familles, auront été déportés.

(Lettre signée par le Préfet Jean LEGUAY)

A letter from Jean Leguay, dated 3 August 1942, setting out details of fourteen deportation trains, including four which would be made up of children.

sitting down on the repulsively filthy mattresses.

'Most of the children had no idea what had happened to their belongings. The few who had had the presence of mind to take them down with them off the bus stood there, encumbered by their shapeless bundles. Meanwhile, the other bundles had been dumped in the yard and, when this was finished, the children came downstairs to the yard to look for their own. These little packets, without names, were extremely hard to recognize, and for a long while children of four, five and six years old wandered about among the bundles, hoping at any moment to retrieve theirs. After many vain searches, these little children gave up the search and stood in the yard not knowing what to do.

'Those little children who wanted to return to their dormitories were often unable to remember which room to go to. Very politely, in a quiet plaintive voice, they would ask us: "Excuse me, sir, I don't know which room my little sister is in. Perhaps she is afraid of staying all alone." So we would take the older ones by the hand, the tired ones in our arms, and take them into each of the dormitories which ran off those separate stairways, until one found the little sister or the little brother. Then there were reunions of a tenderness whose secret is known only to unhappy children.

'There were 100 children in each dormitory. Buckets were put on the landing for them to go to the lavatory. The little ones, unable to go by themselves, waited in despair for the help of a volunteer woman helper or of another child.

'It was the "era" of cabbage soup at Drancy. Almost at once, the children were suffering from violent diarrhoea. They dirtied not only their clothes – which they could not change – but also the mattresses on which they had to lie both at night and in the day time.

'Each night we adults, on the other side of the camp, could hear the endless sobs of frightened children and, from time to time, the anguished cries of little ones who could not restrain themselves.'

The 500 children who were brought to Drancy on 15 and 16 August were taken to Le Bourget railway station on the morning of 17 August. The now well-tested timetables followed the hour and route which had been laid down with such precision for the previous nineteen convoys, with departure from Le Bourget set exactly at 8.55 am.

Convoy No 20 contained some 300 adults, most of them German-born, who had been brought to

Identity documents of six children deported from Drancy to Auschwitz.

Drancy from the detention camp at Les Milles, near Marseilles, in the 'unoccupied zone' of France. These were the adults who were expected to make the sight of deported children look less unusual.

But it was a train which had, above all, been designed for the 530 children, among whom were six under the age of two – three boys and three girls; 184 of the girls and 154 of the boys were under ten.

Also in Convoy No 20 was the thirty-three-year-old London-born Gertle Klar, whose nationality was given as British, and the sixteen-year-old Myriam Perel, who had been born in Tel Aviv during the early years of the British Mandate. Also born in London was Jane Sztrausberg, aged forty-one.

At Le Bourget station the children and adults were loaded into fifteen goods wagons. The Gestapo lists show that a few of the children, mostly those from large families, were accompanied by their mothers. In Wagon Four was the fifty-six-year-old Lea Frandji, who had been born in Constantinople (Istanbul); with her were her three daughters – all born in Paris – Suzanne aged sixteen, Fanny aged fifteen and Marie aged twelve. Wagon Four also contained two families of children who were without their parents, Mina Monica aged eleven, her sister Hélène aged six, and their brother Joseph aged four; together with them was Esther Piotek aged fifteen, her sister Suzanne aged thirteen and their brother Jacques aged ten.

In Wagon Five were the five Jakubovitch children, deported without their parents; the oldest, Samuel was only nine years old, his sister Anna was seven, Rebecca six, Armand four, and Marguerite only two years old.

In Wagon Nine was the twenty-seven-year-old Pauline Poznanski with her three children, Esther aged six, Berthe aged four and Albert aged three; and in this same wagon was her neighbour from the same block of flats in Paris, the thirty-six-year-old Bajla Biglajzer, with her four children, Bernard aged seventeen, Lucienne aged nine, Paul aged seven and Claude aged three.

Wagon by wagon the same story was repeated. Mothers with their small children; brothers and sisters without their parents; babies all alone.

Each wagon was made to hold sixty children, with nowhere to sit and nowhere to rest their heads but the filthy wooden floor. Each truck was allowed a single pitcher of drinking water. Each was padlocked on the outside. Each had two or three adults to try to do what they could to calm the children during the hot, jolting journey, made more terrible by the stench and darkness.

A non-Jew, Georges Harden, who was deported to Auschwitz from Paris two years later, recalled

A fragment of the deportation list of Convoy No 20 from Drancy; the thirty-three children listed here who were born after 17 August 1932, including Lea Frandji's three daughters, were all under ten years old.

FRANDJI	SUZANNE	04.11.25
FRANDJI	FANNY	27.06.27
FRANDJI	MARIE	06.03.30
FRANDJI	LEA	11.04.96
FRANKEL	ROSETTE	10.01.39
FRANKEL	SARAH	01.02.32
FREUND	HANS	06.08.90
FREY	MARIA	09.02.92
FREY	LAZAR	28.07.87
FREYMANN	DAVID	18.10.10
FRIDKOWSKI	SERGE	24.02.37
FRIDKOWSKI	HENRI	18.12.32
FRINSZTEIN	SUZANNE	19.06.28
FRYDMAN	SURA	93
FRYDMAN	CLARA	01.05.34
FRYS	RACHEL	20.04.29
FUSS	WILHELM	31.02.02
FUSS	LEOPOLD	09.11.97
FUTERMAN	MADELEINE	19.03.32
GABEL	DENISE	31.05.31
GABOWICZ	LILIANE	25.07.36
GABOWICZ	SOLANGE	22.02.14
GAGER	LOUISE	21.08.27
GAGER	MARCEL	09.03.29
GANDELMAN	MARCEL	14.03.30
GARCARG	BERNARD	27.06.32
GARNGARD	BLANCHE	10.03.35
GELBERT	SUZANNE	08.12.26
GELBERT	PAULETTE	25.10.32
GELBERT	SIMONE	14.10.35
GETLICHERMAN	HELENE	10.10.34
GLADKEVIZER	GINETTE	34
GLADKEVIZER	JACQUELINE	40
GLATMAN	ERSDA	22.09.10
GLAJTMAN	SABINE	14.10.12
GLEICHER	HELENE	19.09.32
GLEKSZTAJN	JEANNETTE	27.01.35
GLOWINSKI	MICHELLE	20.01.39
GOLBERG	MAURICE	37
GOLCER	PIERRE	12.09.32
GOLCER	FANNY	28.05.34
GOLDBERG		99
GOLDCYMER	ABRAHAM	04.11.37
GOLDCYMER	SABINE	10.08.32
GOLDCYMER	ADELE	10.03.34
GOLDBERG	MARIE	07.03.36
GOLDENCWAJG	BERNARD	15.05.37
GOLDENCWAJC	ALTA	17.01.98
GOLDFAGER	MICHEL	21.10.32
GOLDFINGER	ANNA	20.01.30
GOLDFINGER	GILBERTE	05.10.32
GOLDFINGER	MARCEL	13.05.31
GOLDFINGER	SUZANNE	29.06.34
GOLDHAMER	SARA	11.09.33
GOLDHAMER	ROSA	02.01.28
GOLDHAMER	YVETTE	08.04.29
GOLDLIST	MAURICE	02.08.32
GOLDLIST	MARCEL	17.11.38
GOLDSCHMIDT	REBECCA	01.08.34
GOLDSZTAJN	MORDKA	06
GOLDSTEIN	BERNARD	24.05.35
GOLDSTEIN	SIMON	22.01.40
GOLDSTEIN	GEORGES	31.12.33
GOLSZTEIN	LUCIENNE	26.02.34
GONTARSKI	DORA	23.08.33
GONTARSKI	HELENE	28.05.37
GORFINKIEL	JAKE	10.06.08
GOTAINER	JEANINE	12.07.34
GOTAINER	HENRI	07.04.31
GOTFRIED	LILIANE	17.09.26
GOTLIB	RACHLA	22.03.08
GOTLIB	SIMONE	08.06.39

Immediately on reaching Auschwitz, the women and children were led off to the gas chambers.

the moment of arrival, when the deportees were ordered out of the trains:

'We walked forward slowly. An SS man stood a few dozen metres in front of us. As we passed in front of him, he made a sign with his stick, to some to go to the left, and to others to go to the right.

'To the left he directed all the old people, all the women with children, and all the children who were without parents. Sometimes he directed a mother to the right and her child to the left; if the mother refused to leave her child, both of them were sent to the left.'

To the left was the road to the gas chambers.

Convoy No 20 had reached Auschwitz on 19 August. There sixty-four of the men and thirty-four of the women had been selected for slave-labour. Of these, only three were to survive the war. The remaining 350 adults were taken straight to the gas chambers, together with all 530 children. By nightfall on 19 August every child was dead.

The systematic murder of young children took place throughout Nazi-occupied Europe. In all, more than a million Jewish children were murdered between 1941 and 1945.

The Nazi plans to try to wipe out the new generation of Jews, and thus to bring to an end altogether two thousand years of European Jewish life, pressed forward without respite or hesitation. On 19 August, the very day on which the 530 children of Convoy No 20 were being gassed at Auschwitz, a further 410 children were being put into the wagons of Convoy No 21, ready to leave Le Bourget. Once more they were on the 8.55, together with more than 400 adults. Once more, the Gestapo bureaucracy went to the trouble of listing the names and ages of the children, wagon by wagon. In Wagon Four the three-year-old Robert Goldberg was all alone.

Without respite the children's convoys continued on their terrible journeys: 543 children under the age of fourteen on 21 August; 553 children under seventeen on 24 August, of whom a quarter were under the age of six; 400 children under the age of twelve on 26 August; more than 250 children under the age of sixteen on 28 August. Each one of these children was gassed on arrival at Auschwitz. So too were those few mothers who managed to be with them.

One of the eight survivors of the convoy of 28 August – out of 250 children and 730 adults – was the twenty-two-year-old Albert Hollender. Born in Poland, living in Belgium between the wars, fleeing as a refugee to France in 1940, interned in

Jewish women and children at Auschwitz, before being taken to the gas chambers.

the unoccupied zone, deported with his father, mother and brother from the unoccupied zone to Drancy, he alone of his family survived. After the war he recalled the forty-eight hours which ensued after Convoy No 25 drew out of Le Bourget:

'Packed into cattle trucks, unable either to crouch or move about, stuck so close to each other that one could hardly breathe, crushed by every movement of the people nearby, it was already Hell. During the day the heat was unbearable, the wagon filled with a nauseating stench.

'After several days and nights the doors were opened. We had arrived at Auschwitz exhausted, dehydrated, sick.

'A newly-born child, torn out of the arms of its young mother, was thrown on to the platform. Its mother, maddened with grief, tried to rush across to be with it. But the SS man stopped her, striking her with a series of extremely violent blows on the head with his rifle butt. Her eyes were wild, her cries terrible, her beautiful hair spattered with blood. She was killed with a bullet in her head.'

In Paris, Ernst Heinrichsohn, the twenty-two-year-old deputy-head of the Jewish Affairs Section of the Gestapo, noted, after a discussion with his French opposite number: 'On Thursday 28 August 1942 the 25,000th Jew will be deported'.

At Auschwitz itself a senior SS doctor Johann Kremer wrote in his diary for 2 September 1942: 'At three o'clock this morning I was present during a "special action". Compared with what I saw, Dante's inferno seems to one a quasi-comedy. It is not without reason that Auschwitz is called an extermination camp!'

By the end of 1942, the trains from Drancy had taken to their deaths 2,464 children between the ages of thirteen and seventeen, a further 2,557 children between the ages of six and twelve, and 1,032 children under the age of six.

France: The Final Convoys

As the deportations from Drancy continued, the consciences of thousands of Frenchmen were stirred. On 28 August both the Papal Nuncio and the Catholic Church in France protested against the deportations. When the deportations spread throughout the 'unoccupied' zone, the Archbishop of Toulouse raised his voice in strong protest. Many Frenchmen hid individual Jews, and convents took in hundreds of Jewish children. In an attempt to stop these acts of mercy, the Germans ordered the arrest of all priests who gave shelter to Jews, and on 2 September the authorities in Vichy France seized a Jesuit priest who had hidden eighty Jewish children destined for deportation.

On 9 November 1942 the deputy head of the Anti-Jewish Section of the Paris Gestapo, Ernst Heinrichsohn, visited the Rothschild Hospice in Paris. At the hospice were a number of sick and infirm Jews, all of them in their seventies and eighties. The director of the hospice, Dr Salomon,

Women and children, having been taken from the railway siding at Auschwitz, wait in a wood near the gas chambers, before being ordered to undress.

later recalled how Heinrichsohn 'was very polite. He went up to each of those in the hospice, even asked a sick German if he wanted to return home. In the end he selected thirty-five old people. . . .'

It was Heinrichsohn himself who, two days later, on 11 November 1942, sent the customary telegram to Eichmann in Berlin, informing him that yet another convoy – the forty-fifth from France – had left Le Bourget station on its way to Auschwitz. In the sealed wagons were 745 Jews, of whom sixty-three were children under twelve.

The Gestapo lists show that the birthplaces of those deported spanned almost the whole diaspora of European Jewry. Among those on the train were Rachel Avigdor, born on the Greek Island of Corfu fifty-five years before. She was one of more than 1,000 Jews, all born in Greece, who had been arrested by the French police in Paris six days before. The forty-three-year-old Leon Bourlas had been born in Constantinople – still part of neutral Turkey. The fifty-eight-year-old Maria Briol was from Bucharest. The fifty-six-year-old Elisabeth Tschounsky had been born in Leningrad – the city which even then, cut off by the German armies from the rest of Russia, was maintaining a siege against all odds, and in which more than 800,000 Soviet civilians were to be starved to death or murdered in the incessant bombardment.

In addition, as the telegram stated, there were on this train '35 inmates of the Rothschild Hospice, selected by Mr Heinrichsohn', who had been brought to Le Bourget railway station on the morning of 11 November. Twenty of those whom Heinrichsohn had chosen were in their seventies, six were in their eighties. The oldest, Hélène Haas, was eighty-two. Deported with her was her

HOSPICE DE ROTHSCHILD, 76 rue Picpus, PARIS

LISTE DES PENSIONNAIRES DESIGNES PAR MONSIEUR HEINRICHSOHN

le 6 novembre 1942 et quittant l'établissement le 11 novembre 1942

NOMS ET PRENOMS	DATES DE NAISSANCE	NATIONALITES
CHAJGENBAUM Curtla	18.7.1868	Polonaise
FRIDMANN Moïse	I868	Réf. russe
GOUROVITZ Cypa	20.4.1867	Russe
GRINSPAN Rose	II.3.1877	Roumaine
HAAS Moritz	20.5.1862	Allemande
HAAS Hélène	31.7.I860	Allemande
JACOB Arthur	I8.5.I870	Allemande
JACOB Rosalie	I7.4.I87I	Allemande
LIN Chaya	I866	Polonaise
LIOUBAROFF Malka	I87I	Réf. russe
SACHENBERG Chya	I86I	Polonaise
SAMUEL Ida	5.5.I868	Allemande
SILBERBLATT Eugénie	27.I2.I877	Russe
SILBERBUSCH Cécile	27.IO.I866	Allemande
SOSONSKA Durojia	IO.2.I876	Polonaise
[illegible]INITZ Délia	26.6.I88I	Allemande
[illegible]INSKI Abraham	I867	Réf. russe
WEINGARTEN Caroline	2.2.I86I	Allemande
ZILBERSTEIN Sprintza	25.8.I862	Réf. russe
HOLMAN Freida	29.7.I863	Polonaise

IV J - SA 225a
He./Ne.

Paris, den 5. November 1942

An das

Reichssicherheitshauptamt
Amt IV - IV B 4 -
z.Hdn. von SS-Obersturmbannführer Eichmann o.V.i.A.

B e r l i n .

Betr.: Abtransport von Juden nach Auschwitz

Vorg.: Laufend.

Am 5.11.1942 wurden in Paris 1100 Juden griechischer Staatsangehörigkeit festgenommen. Infolgedessen wird es notwendig, dass noch ein vierter Transport am Mittwoch, den 11.11.1942 nach Auschwitz abgeht. Ich bitte, das Lager Auschwitz von der Ankunft des Transportes zu verständigen und für die Gestellung des Schutzpolizeikommandos in Neuburg Sorge tragen zu wollen. Ankunftszeit in Neuburg wie üblich 20,20 Uhr.

I.A.: H

husband Moritz. Both had been born in Germany in 1860, ten years before the creation of the German Empire. When the train reached Châlons-sur-Marne, at eight o'clock on the evening of 11 November, one young man of nineteen, Rudolf Herskovitz, managed to jump from the train. Both his legs were broken and he was forced to rejoin the train. He, all the children, and all the old people were gassed on arrival at Auschwitz, among them the two-year-old Mina Kantorowicz, deported with her mother, her two brothers and her three sisters. Mina Kantorowicz had been born in Paris on 22 November 1940 and, but for the Nazis, she would have been thirty-nine years old in 1979, still able to look forward to twenty or thirty years of active life.

No deportations took place in December 1942 or January 1943. All the goods wagons and cattle trucks that could be spared were needed to transport supplies and munitions to the eastern front, where still the German army was unable to capture either Moscow, Leningrad or Stalingrad, and where the gathering strength of the Red Army boded ill for the Nazi regime. Elsewhere, the course of the war was also turning slowly but decisively against Hitler and his generals. On the night of 7 November 1942 British and American troops had landed, successfully, in North Africa, and on the following evening Algiers surrendered to the Allies, followed by Oran on 10 November. Then, on 11 November, as Convoy No 45 was on its way from Drancy to the German frontier, German troops entered the 'unoccupied zone', taking possession of the principal towns of Vichy France, including Vichy itself.

In the east, on 22 November, the Russians launched a massive counter-offensive at Stalingrad, driving the Germans back as much as eighty kilometres from their former front line, capturing 24,000 prisoners by nightfall on 23 November, and a further 39,000 by 26 November.

Over Germany itself the Allied bombing raids now gathered a fierce momentum, with Frankfurt, Karlsruhe, Duisburg and Munich being bombed in December. In January 1943 Berlin was bombed twice, on the nights of 16 and 19 January, with 388 aircraft taking part in the attack. On 18 January the Russians raised the siege of Leningrad, forcing a sixteen-kilometre-wide corridor into the city. At the Casablanca Conference, Churchill and Roosevelt announced that they would fight on until Germany's unconditional surrender. On 25 January the Russians recaptured the important town of Voronezh, taking over 50,000 more Axis prisoners.

These dramatic preludes to the defeat of Germany did not affect the Nazi determination to search out and destroy the Jews of Europe. On 25 January, the day on which German forces abandoned Voronezh, Colonel Knochen of the Paris Gestapo, learned through Eichmann's office in Berlin that the German Ministry of Transport had given the 'green light', as far as the provision of goods wagons was concerned, to the renewal of deportations from Drancy to Auschwitz. On the following day, 26 January, Knochen sent a telegram to each of the regional Gestapo headquarters, ordering them to arrest Jews still at liberty and to send them at once to Drancy.

The local Gestapo officers acted as instructed on receipt of Knochen's telegram. On 28 January, 170 Jews were arrested in Bordeaux. On 29 January, in Orléans, seventy-six Jews, including four children, were arrested. In Poitiers twenty-two and in Dijon seventy Jews were likewise taken from their homes and held in detention, awaiting future orders from Paris.

The deportations were ready to be started again. On 3 February Heinz Roethke telegraphed from Paris to Eichmann in Berlin that two trains, each with 1,000 Jews on board, would be made ready to leave for Auschwitz within a week. Two days later he sent a further telegram to the provincial Gestapo, instructing them to transfer the Jews whom they had arrested to Drancy. On 9 February

***Top:* the first page of the list of old people deported on 11 November 1942 from the Hospice de Rothschild, Paris. The oldest, Hélène Haas, had been born in Germany eighty-two years before.**
***Below:* a Gestapo report from Paris, sent to Eichmann in Berlin, about the forthcoming arrest of 1,100 Greek-born Jews and their deportation from Paris to Auschwitz.**

the first of the new convoys – the forty-sixth to leave France – was ready. Among the deportees was the forty-three-year-old Chaja Zausznica, with her eight children, Chana aged twenty-one, Malka aged nineteen, Fajga aged sixteen, Brana aged fourteen, Tema aged ten, Irma aged nine, Samy aged six and Alain aged three.

Convoy No 46 reached Auschwitz on 11 February. Of its 1,000 deportees, only twenty-one survived the war. More than 800 of the deportees, including all the children, were gassed that same day.

Thus the Nazis continued their war against the Jewish people. On Convoy No 47, which left Paris on 11 February, were several hundred Jewish inmates of hospitals, lunatic asylums, old peoples' homes and orphanages. Among the old people was Githel Mendelevitch, born in Kishinev two years before the Crimean War, and who had celebrated her ninety-first birthday the previous May.

On 11 February, while Convoy No 47 was crossing eastern France, a major search was in progress throughout Paris for any further old people who might have been overlooked. By nightfall the Gestapo agents reported on their success: the arrest of four people over ninety, fifty-eight people in their eighties, 447 in their seventies and 689 in their sixties. Georges Wellers, who was still at Drancy, recalled the arrival there of the old people:

'Many of these unfortunate ones were not strong enough to carry their own bags, to climb to the fourth or even the third floor, to set off to the kitchen in search of soup, to clamber into the upper bunk of the bunk-beds. Their rooms looked like some terrible old people's asylum put together by some theatre director with a sick mind.'

On 12 February the old people were ordered to prepare for the journey. Then they were stopped, and told that the deportation order had been annulled. A few weeks later they were deported.

In July 1943 the Gestapo themselves had sent thirty Jewish children to an orphanage at La Rose, a small village outside Marseilles, having

The Bompard camp in Marseilles: soup distribution, and *(opposite)* Jewish children at table, shortly before their deportation.

deported their parents to Auschwitz. For four months the orphans were left unmolested. Then, on 20 October, they were taken to Drancy. In order to prevent local protests, the Germans took sixty hostages for the duration of the deportation. The woman in charge of the orphanage, Alice Şalomon, was the only person from the orphanage who was excluded from deportation. She insisted, however, on joining the transport, not wanting the children, as she put it, 'to face death alone'. There remained in the orphanage only the staff, and some thirty old people. Two months later they too were deported.

As the Paris convoys continued throughout the winter of 1943 and the spring of 1944, Eichmann himself made sure that no one was allowed to slip through the net. On learning that a certain Max Gollub was about to be given 'national' status by a country in South America, he telegraphed to Paris, ordering Gollub's immediate arrest and

deportation. When the Rumanian Government asked that a seventy-one-year-old Rumanian-born lawyer, Rosenthal, should be allowed to stay in Paris, Eichmann turned down the request. In January 1944 Heinz Roethke, Eichmann's own agent in Paris, suggested making an exception for the Polish-born Jew, Abraham Weiss, aged forty-three, the inventor of a light which, being invisible from above, was of enormous value in the black-out. Eichmann replied, however, that 'as the patent of the Jew Weiss has already been transferred to the Reich Patent Office, there is no further interest in the affair and he should be dealt with in accordance with the general measures'. Roethke wrote at once to Drancy, to tell the camp authorities that Weiss must be deported. A note on Weiss's file states: 'Leaves with the next transport.'

Weiss was deported on Convoy No 66, which left Drancy on 20 January 1944 taking to Auschwitz 632 men, 515 women and 221 children under the age of eighteen. There were further convoys on 3 and 10 February, 7 and 27 March, 13 and 29 April, and on 15, 20 and 30 May.

The course of the war itself now changed dramatically, for on 6 June 1944 the Allied armies landed on the Normandy beaches. In the east the Red Army advance was gaining a massive momentum. On 27 June Soviet troops surrounded the German forces near Vitebsk, killing 20,000 and taking 10,000 prisoner. On 29 June the Russians defeated the German forces at Bobruisk, killing 16,000 and taking 18,000 prisoners. In France itself, the resistance movement was harassing German military installations and activities; many Jews were among the resistance groups.

The deportations from France continued. Not even the imminent arrival of the Allied forces in Paris could halt the now two-year-old process, and thus it was that on 30 June, more than three weeks after the D-Day landings, Convoy No 76 was sent to the east: another train with more than 1,000 people locked into its cattle trucks, among them 162 children.

The net for this convoy had been cast widely. Many of those deported had been born in French North Africa. Others were from towns all over France, including Avignon, Orléans, Pau, Nancy and Toulouse. The seventy-three-year-old Sadie Leon had been born in San Francisco. Esther and Joaquin Yahia had been born in Beirut just before the turn of the century, when it was still part of the Ottoman Empire. Maurice Vidas, aged ten and deported alone, had been born in Sofia. Others were from Warsaw, Vienna, Moscow and Budapest. The twenty-six-year-old Benjamin Rabinsky had been born in London. So too had the twenty-nine-year-old Fanny Mittelstein, whose Parisian husband Simon was deported with her, as were their four children, Serge aged eight, Marcel aged seven, Jean aged five and Nicole aged eighteen months; Nicole had been born on Christmas Day 1942.

Marc Bloch, a distinguished French historian and a Jew. A resistance leader, he was captured by the Gestapo, tortured, and shot near Lyons on 16 June 1944.

Also on Convoy No 76 was Georges Wellers, who was among more than a hundred men and women who tried to escape from the deportation. But, he wrote:

'This attempt was discovered by the Germans, and sixty of us were stripped naked and, in this state, put into an empty truck. These sixty men, wracked with thirst, sitting one on top of the other on the filthy floor of the wagon, were a highly grotesque, piteous and revolting sight.'

Throughout July the Allies advanced through German-occupied Europe, from east, west and south. On 3 July the Red Army liberated Minsk, on 13 July, Vilna, and on 24 July, Lublin. On 27 July United States troops broke through the Normandy bridgehead. But in Paris the Anti-Jewish Section of the Gestapo continued to carry out its task, led now by the thirty-two-year-old Alois Brünner, who in 1943 had been in charge of sending the 80,000 Jews of Salonica to the gas chambers. In July 1943 Brünner had been put in charge of a special Anti-Jewish 'commando', which had seized thousands of Jews who had found refuge in the former Italian zone of France, around Nice. This done, he had become camp commandant at Drancy, from where, on 20 July 1944, he gave the order for the arrest of all the remaining Jewish children, no matter how young, who were in homes and orphanages in the Paris region. Beyond Paris and its suburbs he could no longer reach; the Allied air forces were systematically destroying road and rail bridges, and railway junctions, as they slowly advanced on Paris.

Beginning on the night of 20 July, Brünner sent his SS helpers in buses to every Jewish children's home and nursery. For three nights the buses drove out in search of their victims, and by nightfall on 24 July Brünner had succeeded in bringing to Drancy 300 children between the ages of one and fifteen. Most of them were orphans, whose guardians and nurses insisted on travelling with them. The old, the sick and the feeble were likewise seized from their asylums and rest homes. So it was that on 31 July 1944 the last mass deportation took place from Paris: 1,000 adults and 300 children. Among those who were put into the wagons was an old man, terribly ill, on a stretcher; and a baby, Maiu Blumberg, born only fourteen days earlier, carried by her elder brother in a little wooden box.

Once more, for this final convoy, the Gestapo prepared their lists. Alice Levy, aged seventy, had been born in Zurich, in neutral Switzerland. Milly Pomerance had been born in London in 1893.

On the walls of one of the rooms at Drancy some of the deportees of this final convoy scrawled their farewell messages. Among the writers were Moise Chetovy, born in Constantinople fifty years earlier, and his eighteen-year-old son, Marcel. 'Arrived on the 1st', they wrote, with triple underlinings and capital letters: 'departed on the 31st

A postcard from Drancy. 'We are both *very brave*', the message reads, 'and we hope to *come back soon*'.

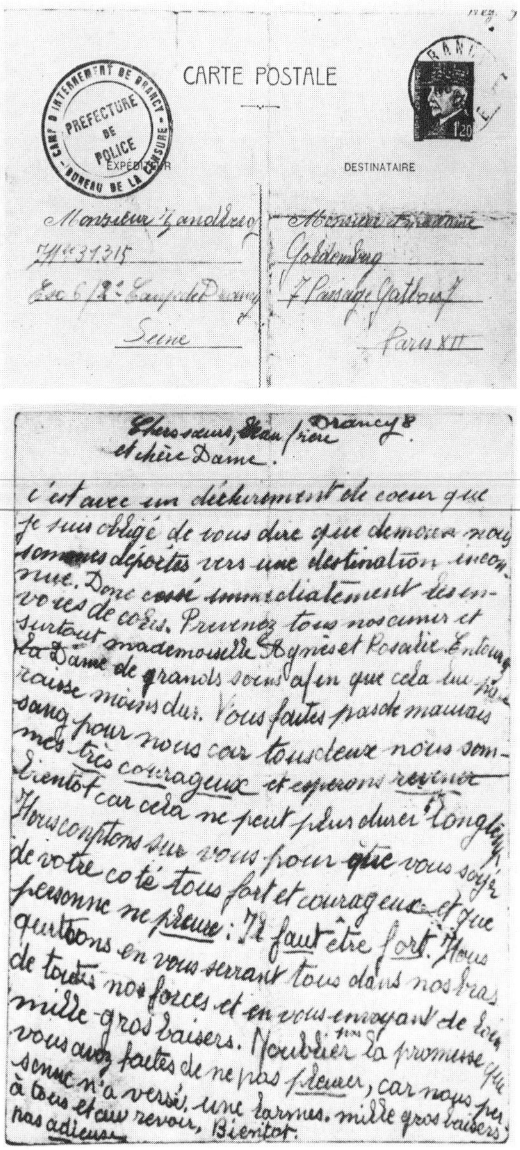

Drancy 8
Chers amis, Mon frère
et chère Dame.
c'est avec un déchirement de coeur que
je suis obligé de vous dire que demain nous
sommes déportés vers une destination incon-
nue. Donc cessé immédiatement les en-
vois de colis. Prévenez tous nos amis et
surtout mademoiselle Agnès et Rosalie. Entourez
la Dame de grands soins afin que cela lui pa-
raisse moins dur. Vous faites pas de mauvais
sang pour nous car tous deux nous sommes très courageux et espérons revenir
bientôt car cela ne peut plus durer longtemps.
Nous comptons sur vous pour que vous soyez
de votre côté tous fort et courageux et que
personne ne pleure: Il faut être fort. Nous
quittons en vous serrant tous dans nos bras
de toutes nos forces et en vous envoyant de loin
mille gros baisers. N'oubliez pas la promesse que
vous avez faites de ne pas pleurer, car nous personne n'a versé une larmes. mille gros baisers
à tous et au revoir, Bientôt.
pas adieu

July, in *very very* GOOD SPIRITS, and in the hope of coming back soon'. Neither of them were, in fact, to survive. Another of the messages was written by Lucie Fuantes, a young Parisian woman, and her mother, the forty-six-year-old Fortunée Fuantes, also born in Constantinople. Unlike her mother, Lucie survived the war; she was one of more than 160 of the deportees who managed, in the growing chaos of the war, to escape from the train while it was still in France. But of the 1,300 who set out on this last convoy, only 209 survived the war.

As the Allied armies approached the suburbs of Paris, the city prepared itself for the day of liberation. Resistance groups mustered their forces, determined to make their contribution to the day when the Germans would be driven from the streets. On 10 August Nantes and Angers fell to the advancing American troops, and by 17 August these same troops had liberated Chartres and Orléans, while an American armoured column had reached Dreux, only eighty kilometres west of the capital.

In Paris itself, Alois Brünner prepared to leave. Ahead of him, in German-occupied Hungary, lay a task on an even larger scale than that which he had completed in France: the deportation of several hundred thousand Jews from the provinces of Hungary to the gas chambers of Auschwitz.

As he organized his own departure from Paris, Brünner decided to take as many Jews as possible with him. On 17 August, with the American forces only eighty kilometres away, he managed to arrange for three railway wagons to be attached to the train of an artillery unit, obtaining the wagons in return for a supply of pork – live pigs in fact – and permission to attach himself to the artillerymen's train.

Brünner and his Gestapo colleagues filled two of the wagons. The third they reserved for as many Jews as they could find, fifty-one in all, including several Jewish members of the French resistance who had fallen into German hands.

The train with the fifty-one deportees left Paris on 17 August. Progress to the east was slow, as the Allied bombardment of railway junctions and bridges continued. On the night of 20 August they were still only 160 kilometres east of Paris. Then, in the night, the deportees tried to break out. Fifteen of them succeeded, and survived. The remaining thirty-six remained and were shunted northwards to Belgium, then eastwards to Buchenwald concentration camp. Of those who reached Buchenwald, twenty survived the war, sixteen did not.

This last Paris convoy reached Buchenwald on 25 August. That same day, the German forces were driven from Paris, and Charles de Gaulle walked in triumph down the Champs Elysées.

The 80,000 Jews who went to their deaths from Drancy have several memorials, some in fine stone in the city of Paris. Their most comprehensive tribute is the memorial volume, published in 1978, by Serge Klarsfeld, whose father was among those who were murdered at Auschwitz. Klarsfeld's volume, stark in its simplicity and overwhelming in its impact, had made it possible to recount in these pages many precise details of the story of the Drancy deportations.

What of the men who organized the deportations, who arrested the deportees, who arranged the train timetables and supervised the loading and despatch of their human cargo? Their fate, too, has been in part recorded. Theodor Dannecker committed suicide in an American military prison in December 1945. Alois Brünner disappeared at the time of the German surrender and has not been seen since: condemned to death in his absence by a Paris military court in 1954, he is believed to have found refuge somewhere in the Middle East. Kurt Lischka, condemned in his absence to life imprisonment with hard labour by a Paris military court, but never arrested, worked in a German import-export business dealing in grain: now he lives in retirement in Cologne. Dr Helmut Knochen was condemned to death by a Paris court in 1954, pardoned in 1958 and released in 1962; after his release he became an insurance agent in the town of Offenbach, where he still works. Ernst Heinrichsohn was condemned to death in his absence by a Paris court in 1956; but he was never arrested and is now a lawyer in a small town in Bavaria.

14

The Jews of Holland

The Jews of Holland trace their ancestry back to the time of the Roman Legions. Sometimes protected, sometimes persecuted, they clung tenaciously to their small communities throughout the Middle Ages. Reinforced by merchants expelled from Spain and Portugal, they took a leading part in the spread of British trade to southern Africa, to the Americas, to India and to the Far East. Their cultural life also flourished: the work of the Jewish book printers of Amsterdam, begun in 1626, was of the highest standard of its time.

The seventeenth century saw a great influx of eastern Jews, from Germany, Poland and Lithuania: Yiddish speakers, escaping the persecutions and privation of the east. By 1830 there were more than 45,000 Jews in Holland; by 1930 over 110,000. Their part in public life was considerable: as lawyers, industrialists, doctors, writers, musicians and teachers. After the First World War, more Jews came to Holland from eastern Europe, to train as pioneers for life in Palestine. The study of modern Hebrew spread and there were several Zionist newspapers.

By 1939 more than 30,000 German Jews had fled across the German border into Holland. The Dutch Government, reluctant to try to absorb so many refugees, set up a camp for illegal immigrants at Westerbork, near the German border. Then, on 10 May 1940, the German army invaded Holland and four days later the Dutch Government was in exile, its land conquered, its people subjected to all the rigours of Nazi rule.

For the Jews, the persecutions began slowly, but without respite. In September 1940 Jews were forbidden to enter certain residential areas and were refused entry into a number of professions. At the same time all Jewish newspapers were banned. A month later all Jewish teachers and civil servants were dismissed from their posts, and in January 1941 all Jews were issued with special identity cards.

'Jews not wanted': a notice on a tree in Holland.

What was to be the fate of Dutch Jewry? A year later, in February 1942, a Dutchman, once a chauffeur from Arnhem, who was serving with the *Waffen SS* on the Russian front, wrote from German-occupied Russia to his friends in the Arnhem stormtroop:

'How are things with your Jews? This place is crawling with them, though I don't think many will be left by the time the war is over, for there's

Seized in their homes, men and women were brought to the railway sidings in Amsterdam, to be deported to the east.

been a lot of clearing up, and I myself have shot down a whole plague of them, for what that lot has done over here defies all description....

'I only hope to get the chance of leading a group of comrades when we start rooting out the Jew vermin back home: they just won't know what's hit them....'

This letter did not reach Jewish eyes. Nor did a tale that reached Holland three months later, in mid-May 1942, brought by two Dutchmen who had come back from Auschwitz itself. They had reached Holland shattered by the mass killings, by gas, of Jews and of tens and thousands of Russian prisoners of war. Driven almost insane by their knowledge, they told their tale to the Church authorities, but it seemed so wild, so incredible, so absurd, that not only the Church authorities but even their own friends refused to believe them.

During 1941 the Jews of Holland had been relatively unmolested. On 12 February 1941 a German order set up a Jewish Council, headed by two Jewish 'Presidents', with authority over all Jewish institutions. Did this bode well or ill for the Jews of Holland? By the autumn of 1941 all Jewish children had been forced to leave school and to go instead to special schools under the supervision of the Council. That August, the Germans confiscated all Jewish funds and property: 20 per cent of their value was given to the Jewish Council, the rest kept by the Germans as booty. At the same time all Jewish businesses were seized and more than 5,000 Jewish men were sent to forced labour camps throughout Holland. On 2 May 1942 every Jew was forced to wear the yellow badge as a symbol both of isolation and degradation.

What did these measures portend? On 15 June 1942, six months after the Wannsee Conference, the senior German political adviser in Holland, *Generalkommissar* Schmidt, told an audience of German and Dutch Nazis that the destruction of Jewry 'will continue'– as he declared –'until the last Jew has disappeared'. His Nazi audience applauded loudly.

A month later, on 14 July 1942, Jews were

A Jewish family being deported from Amsterdam. They were allowed to take only what they could carry.

arrested all over Amsterdam. Suddenly a new German slogan burst upon the harrassed, bewildered community: 'Work in the east.' The new German aim, so it was declared, was to make the whole of Holland *'Judenrein'* – clean of Jews. Their method, so it was claimed: deportation to labour camps far away.

Several hundred Jewish families were arrested during the night of 14 July 1942. All of them were taken, without time to gather up more than a few possessions to be carried by hand, first to Westerbork camp, and then by train 'to the east'. What was the meaning of this phrase, 'to the east'? Early in June the Communist underground newspaper, *De Waarheid*, which was read 'illegally' by thousands of Dutchmen, reported that in areas like the Ukraine, the homeland of millions of Jews, 'not a single one has survived. Men, women, children and old people have been exterminated one and all.' On 26 June, two weeks before the first deportation of Dutch Jewry, the official Dutch Broadcasting service from London, *Radio Oranje*, had likewise given news of the murder, in the east, of more than 700,000 Polish Jews: details of which it had received from the Polish authorities in exile. A month later, on 29 July, while the Dutch deportations were in full spate, *Radio Oranje* had mentioned the existence of gas chambers in which tens of thousands of Jews were being exterminated.

But these warnings, heard by those very few with secret radios, was contradicted by the assurances and statements of the Germans themselves. Indeed, on 2 August *Generalkommissar* Schmidt, in a speech published on the following day in all the Dutch newspapers, stated specifically that the Jewish deportees would be put to work 'making a start', as he phrased it, 'with clearing the rubble in the empty towns of the devastated east'.

Whatever the destination of the deportees, there was a further raid in Amsterdam four days later, on the night of 6 August, when several hundred more Jews were seized, and sent to the east. But the Germans were still not satisfied with the numbers they had taken. Henceforth, night after night, helped by Dutch policemen, parties of Germans broke into Jewish homes throughout Amsterdam, dragged all those they could find to the Jewish Theatre, and then transferred them to Westerbork, and beyond. In all, in those first three weeks, 15,760 Dutch Jews were transported to the east.

It was only on 13 August that the Jewish Council heard the first news of the destination of the deportees, for on that day they received the first packet of letters from those who had been sent away – fifty-two letters in all. The route of these deportees was still not known, for the letters all came from a place that the Council could not find on the map, Birkenau. For five days the Council members searched the maps at their disposal, before finding Birkenau in eastern Silesia. It was, in fact, just outside Auschwitz. But the name of Auschwitz was as yet unknown to the Council.

These fifty-two letters were all alike, each one written at the Gestapo's instigation. In them, the work at the camp was described as 'hard' but 'tolerable', the food in the camp as 'adequate', the sleeping accommodation 'good', the hygienic conditions 'satisfactory' and the general treatment 'correct'.

Such were the letters: fifty-two in all, from a total of nearly 16,000 deportees. What had happened to those who had not written? And why did a whole month pass without any further letters? As the days went by the relatives of the deportees became more and more alarmed. Could the few letters that had arrived really have been telling the truth?

Meanwhile, the deportations continued. From 28 August to 14 September six more trains left Westerbork for the east, carrying in their stifling sealed wagons a further 4,588 men, women and children.

The Jewish Council met again in Amsterdam on 18 September. Its minutes recorded, briefly, and with a wrong spelling born of unfamiliarity: 'the first report of a case of death in Auswitz is received by the meeting'.

The facts were very different. Of the 4,588 men, women and children deported between 28 August and 14 September, about 940 men and boys had been taken off the train before it reached Birkenau, for work camps in Silesia. On arriving at Birkenau, the Nazi records show that a total of 79 men and 132 women had been registered in the camp. Using the Nazi's precise 'accounting' methods, this left 3,437 men, women and children unaccounted for. They had, in fact, been taken straight from the wagons to the gas chambers: murdered within a few hours of their arrival.

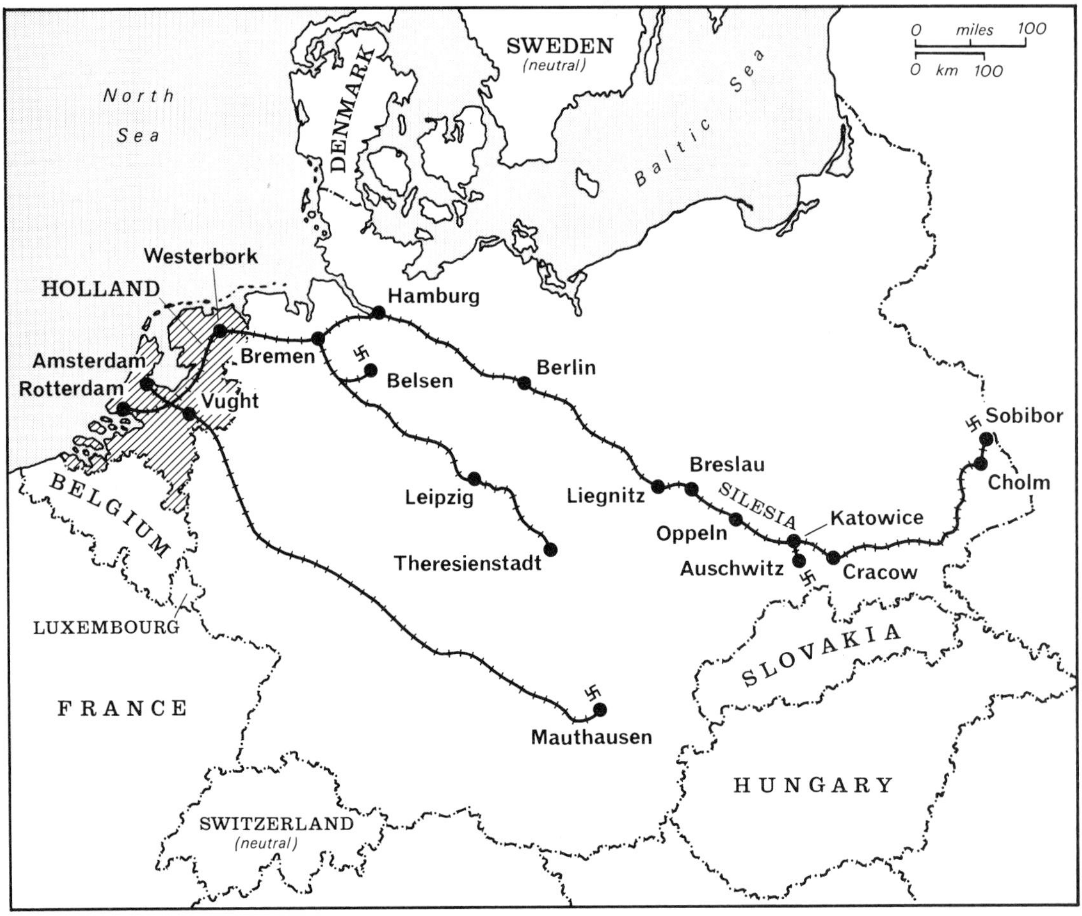

The deportation routes from Holland to the east.

Jewish detainees at Westerbork camp, building the branch railway from the main line to the camp, before being deported along the same line. These photographs were among those found in the album of the camp commandant.

Such had also been the fate of the earlier deportees: the 16,000 whose fifty-two letters had reported such apparent normality. At least 10,000 had been gassed, or murdered, by the third week of September.

For another year, until September 1943, the deportations from Holland continued. But for those who remained, the truth seemed impossible to believe. The BBC, heard in secret, broadcast the Allied declaration of 17 December 1942, in which it told of 'hundreds of thousands' of Polish Jews put to death by barbaric means. But even such news could be discounted, so much so that one of the two Presidents of the Jewish Council, A. Asscher, could state, emphatically: 'As far as I am concerned, the reports are nothing but English propaganda, with the sole intention of inciting the world against Germany.' The other President of the Council, Professor D. Cohen, later recalled:

'The fact that the Germans had perpetrated atrocities against Polish Jews was no reason for thinking that they behaved in the same way towards Dutch Jews, firstly because the Germans had always held Polish Jews in disrepute, and secondly because in the Netherlands, unlike Poland, they had to sit up and take notice of public opinion.'

The German massacres in the east had many witnesses. At Christmas 1942 a member of the Dutch Nazi Party, a nurseryman, returned on holiday leave from the Ukraine where he had been working for the previous eight months for an Austrian firm. Over Christmas he told several other Party members something of what he had seen and heard of the mass murder of Russian Jewry. Some believed him and some did not. Returning to the Ukraine in January 1943, he met a fellow Dutch Nazi, from Leyden, who was opposed to the killings on religious grounds. These two decided to take action, and the nurseryman, a man of courage, wrote a letter direct to the leader of the Dutch Nazi Party, A. A. Mussert. In Russia, he wrote, the Germans were carrying out 'the systematic and total extermination of Jewry, down to the smallest child'. The letter continued:

Jewish children: three photographs taken in Holland during the occupation, shortly before the children and babies were deported to the death camps in the east.

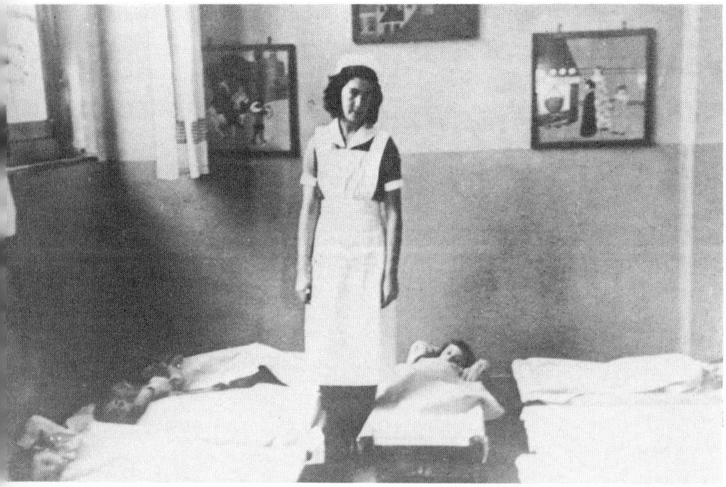

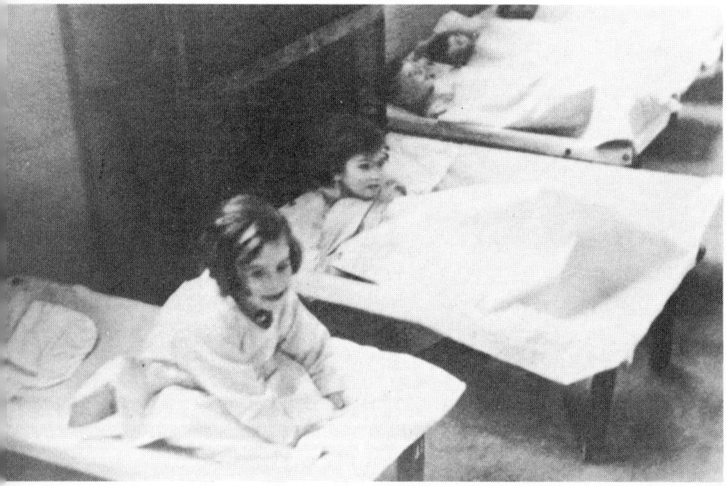

'We cannot permit the complete eradication of these people and in this manner. I, for one, am convinced that these crimes will not go unpunished. Can this really be the wish of the Führer? Now, I know full well that we are Dutch National Socialists, and since I continue to have faith in you as the leader of our movement, I must ask you one question before I tender my resignation. I shall put my question quite plainly, and without beating about the bush. Do you or do you not agree that these people should be eradicated in this barbarous manner? If your answer is yes, I cannot stay in the Movement one day longer.'

The nurseryman received no reply. Nor did he resign. As for his letter, its contents remained hidden in Mussert's files.

Further news of the massacre of the Jews of Poland reached Holland in February 1943. It came from an impeccable source, the young German engineer, Dr Kurt Gerstein, the poison gas expert who had seen the German murder squads in action in the east, and who passed on the details to a young Dutch acquaintance, J. H. Ubbink, with whom, as fellow members of a Protestant student organization, he had been on friendly terms before the war. Ubbink was at that very time sheltering Jewish fugitives and he sought out one of the leading Dutch resistance fighters, Cornelis Van der Hooft. A month later, in March 1943, Van der Hooft wrote down what he had learned. Although he himself was sceptical, he nevertheless recorded what he had been told. His report began:

'The following quite ghastly, unspeakably cruel and barbarous story has reached us from Poland, with an urgent request to bring it to the notice of all mankind. Its truth is vouched for by a high-ranking German SS officer, who made the following declaration under oath and with the request to publish it. . . .'

Van der Hooft hid the report in a chicken coop. It was never circulated. Nor was it published in the resistance newspaper, *Trouw*, with which Van der Hooft was in contact. In April 1944 he himself was arrested; and a year later he was shot during

Westerbork camp: the Jews celebrate the festival of *Hannukah,* the feast of lights, while *(below)* the Gestapo celebrate Christmas. Both these photographs are from the album of the camp commandant.

an evacuation march from Sachsenhausen camp.

Gerstein's story, passed on by Ubbink, was not the only one to reach Holland in the spring of 1943. Among those sent from Holland to Auschwitz, as well as Jews, were members of a Christian sect, the Jehovah's Witnesses. Six of them, all women, and all Dutch citizens, were released at the beginning of 1943. Incredibly, they had been released despite the fact that they had seen the gas chambers with their own eyes and seen the crematoria in which the corpses of the victims were then burned. Six witnesses returned to the sanity of the outside world, bearing their horrific message with them. They had seen the reality of the fate of tens of thousands of Jews, many of them from Holland like themselves. At Auschwitz, one of them recalled, 'we would sit all day long in the smoke of the crematoria, close to the gas chambers'. And yet their witness was to no purpose. 'Most people refused to believe us'.

On 22 January 1943 the two Presidents of the Jewish Council, Asscher and Cohen, received a note of concern from the 'foreign correspondence' section of the Council. The note pointed out that 'no message or other news had been received from women with children, or from the aged'. This was ominous: yet the main conclusion seemed to be that the Germans had broken their promise to keep families together. Separation, not extermination, was what seemed to be the cause for concern, as was the general paucity of letters from the deportees.

A total of 1,700 letters and postcards was received in Amsterdam from Auschwitz between July 1942 and the autumn of 1943, 1,000 of which arrived in the spring of 1943. So small a total began to worry the remaining Jews, now forced to live only in Amsterdam and continually rounded up and despatched to Westerbork for the rail journey east. In the autumn of 1943 the Dutch Government in exile in London received a secret anonymous report from a Dutch Jew still in Holland, in which the writer asked: 'but what are 1,000 letters when there are 60,000 deportees?' and he went on to ask: 'Where are the letters from the rest? And why, above all, is there no sign from all the children, the old and the sick?'

A deportation from Westerbork camp: a sequence of photographs from the album of the German camp commandant. The commandant himself relaxes in the sun when his day's work is ended.

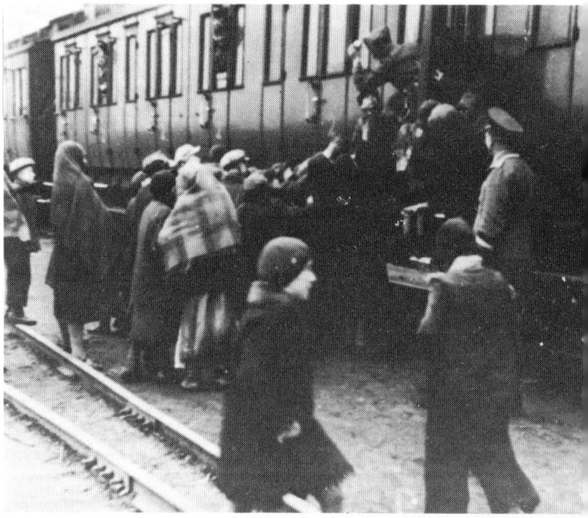

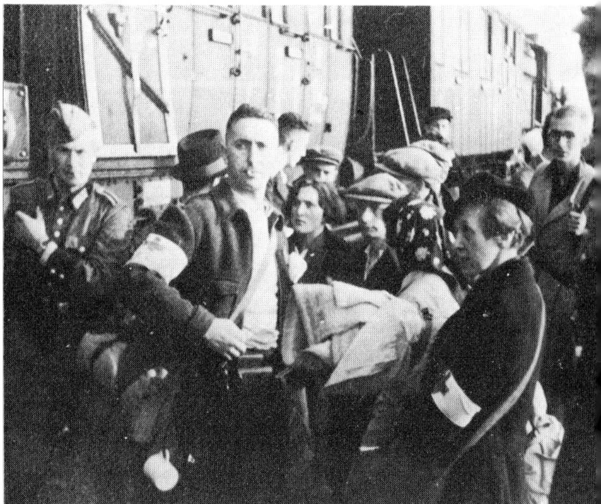

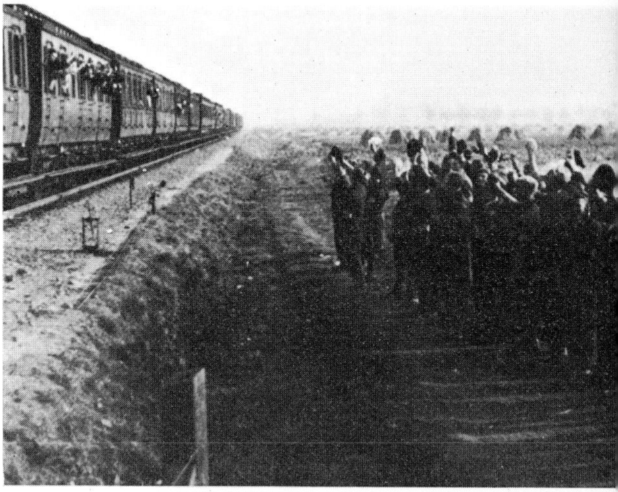

Dutch Jews arriving at Theresienstadt railway station with their meagre belongings.

Yet even this worried writer sought a rational explanation for the lack of letters. It was likely, he wrote, 'that the Jews in Auschwitz have been split into groups and taken to various camps with little or no chance of communicating with each other'. This anonymous reporter himself was seized, and sent to Auschwitz a few months later.

Not only did the tales of horror continue to leak out; they even found a public forum. For on 27 September 1943 the illegal Socialist underground newspaper, *Het Parool*, published an article by a leading member of the Dutch resistance, Frans Goedhart, who had just escaped from the concentration camp at Vught, in Holland. In it he gave details of the methods used in the gas chambers. But his warning came too late to alarm even those few Dutch Jews who remained in Holland, for two days later, on 29 September, the last anti-Jewish raid took place in Amsterdam and within forty-eight hours the Jewish Council itself was dissolved.

Even after so many tens of thousands, from Holland alone, had been murdered, the details of their fate remained unknown to those who stayed in western Europe. But one source of information did exist. In January 1942, in order to help run the concentration camp at Vught, a number of SS men and political prisoners had been brought specially from Auschwitz to Holland. In late 1943 two of these witnesses, an SS man, Joachim Perthes, and a political prisoner, Ernst Bandholz, gave two Jewish prisoners – Gerda Süsskind and Henri Glazer – a detailed account of the gassings. A similar account was also given by a Polish prisoner, Leo Laptos, who told another of the Jews at Vught, Dr Van der Hal:

Mauthausen concentration camp: the camp orchestra, itself made up of prisoners, is forced to lead another prisoner to his execution.

'... that when Jewish transports reach Auschwitz, most of the arrivals were immediately gassed and then cremated. He reported that the gas chambers were fitted out as bath huts and that people went there ostensibly to take a shower; that gas, not water came out of the taps and that, later, the floors were tilted so that the corpses dropped on to a belt which conveyed them to the crematorium.'

Shattered by this information, Van der Hal passed it on, in March 1944, to several Jewish doctors whom he met on his transfer from Vught to Westerbork. But although, as he later recalled, 'they were visibly shaken by my news', nevertheless, 'they simply refused to believe me'.

Van der Hal could make no impact on those to whom he spoke at Westerbork in March 1944. Even after his horrific report, which his fellow doctors were so reluctant to believe, a further 2,311 Jews, the remnant of Dutch Jewry, were deported from Westerbork to Auschwitz, to the gas chambers, and to the labour camps of the east.

There were other destinations also, equally terrible: Theresienstadt, Bergen-Belsen and Sobibor. Of the 4,879 Jews deported from Holland to Theresienstadt, 1,273 survived. Of the 4,000 deported to Bergen-Belsen, 1,100 survived. Of the 60,000 deported to Auschwitz-Birkenau, 500 survived. Of the 34,000 deported to Sobibor, only 19 survived.

The railways from Holland alone transported 106,000 Jews from their homes. Some of them were already refugees from Germany and Austria. More than 100,000 of those deported were never to return.

15

Sophia's Story

One Dutch girl who survived deportation was Sophia Hausman. Born in Rotterdam, she was thirteen years old at the outbreak of war in September 1939. Her family was a fairly prosperous one and, as she later recalled, 'we lived a good and contented life'. After the German occupation of Holland in May 1940, Sophia finished her schooling, and in 1942, when she was sixteen, she began to study nursing at a Jewish hospital in Rotterdam.

On 26 February 1943 the Gestapo came to Sophia's hospital. Staff and patients were forced into large trucks. Then, Sophia recalled, 'I tried to jump out in order to escape, but friends of mine grabbed me, because they did not want me to break my legs.' Her account continued:

'The lorries took us, the entire hospital, to Westerbork. Near the hospital there was an old people's home – they were taken on the same day as well. I stayed in Westerbork from 26 February until 15 March. On 15 March we were taken to Sobibor. In Sobibor we were a transport of 1,200 people from Holland, full of sick people, and it was very bad, the trip from Westerbork to Sobibor.

'We still travelled in an ordinary train. In Sobibor we were thrown off the train. Some of the people were brought in small wagons, evidently to the gas chambers; and those who could walk, we were taken to some large room for a selection.

'They asked "who can be a nurse", "who can sew", "who can work in the laundry". Thirty women replied: "I can"– and I was among the thirty, as was Miriam Blitz, about whom I'll speak afterwards.

'We were in Sobibor only two hours, and from Sobibor were taken to Lublin – after leaving all our possessions in Sobibor. That night, in Lublin, we slept on triple-decked wooden cots. There were Christian women from Poland there, and they were in a very good mood – I don't know why. Perhaps they had been drinking (for they were used to drinking lots of vodka) and were very happy and gay. We certainly were not happy – we had left our families and relatives.

'After that night we were transferred to Majdanek – with a dog which jumped on us and wanted to bite us. It was terrible. There I went (I meanwhile had my seventeenth birthday) to an SS man and told him I was a nurse – I was very proud – and said I wanted to work as a nurse. So he said to me: "Here it's forbidden to be ill, and we don't need nurses." Then we went to work with used clothing. It was a very large storeroom, full of clothes which came from the Jews. We found lots of money, diamonds there, and had to hand it in.

'There were also a great many Jewish women from Poland there, and some from Germany. I had studied quite a lot and had learned German well, so I spoke German. But a large part of our transport – of the thirty – were from poor families and hadn't studied, so it was very hard for them. We were given soup which it was impossible to eat at first. We immediately realized that the people there were not living from that soup but from the money they found in the clothing. In the evenings they would go to the fence. It was very dangerous.

'We were so hungry that we very quickly took part. We threw money and received bread from the Christians outside. If we threw more money we

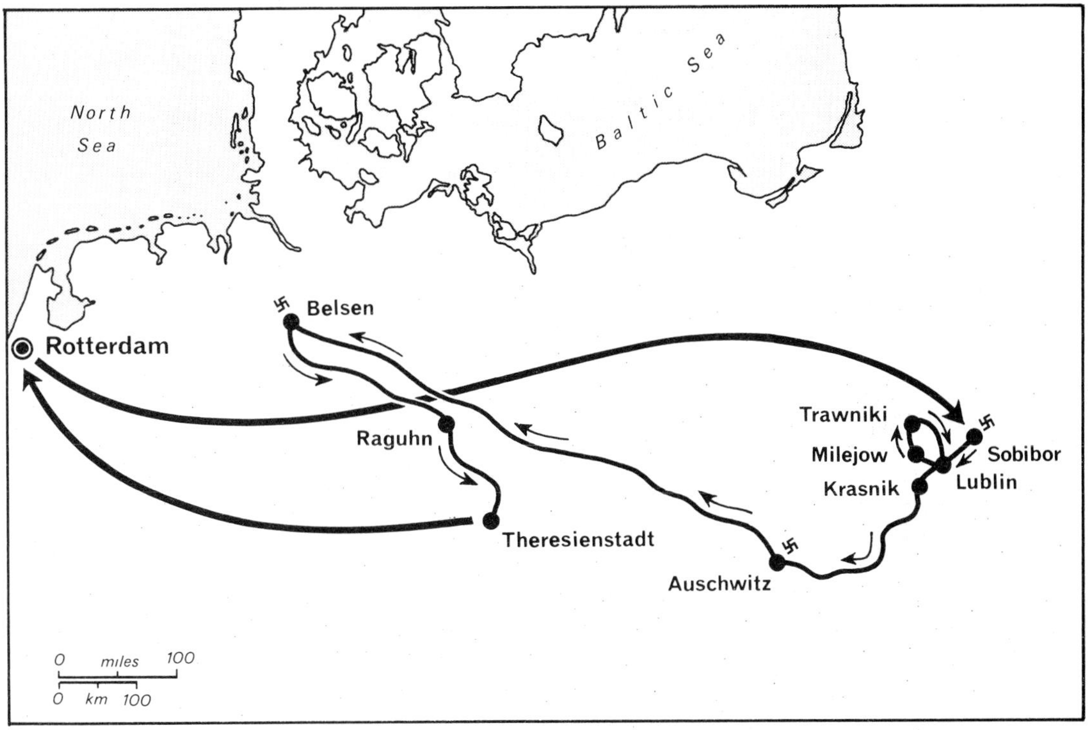

Sophia Hausman's journey.

even got butter. Sometimes we got a stone in return, instead of bread. And the German guards killed many people for this.

'Seven women slept in a very narrow bed, like sardines. It was very hard for us Dutch, because we were delicate – we had never suffered, had lived good lives, without anti-semitism. So we were delicate both psychologically and physically. . . .

'On one of the first days – I told you that I was from a very religious home – I stood in formation at the roll-call and prayed the morning prayer. Suddenly an SS man came and threw my prayer book out of my hands. That made a very sad impression on me.

'After a while we moved from the barracks to another camp in Lublin, and someone stole clothes – no one knows who did it. A Gestapo officer came on a big horse (I later heard he was killed in Italy) and said: "Because of this, twenty-five people must die"– because of the theft. And he pointed with his finger: "You and you and you". And I was among the girls. Of the twenty-five they wanted to hang five girls, and I was one of the five.

'They brought us to the Gestapo officer's room, all twenty-five of us (I recall that I was rather still), and we waited there. Each time they called another and another, until we five were left – I among them – and they said: "In a little while you will be hanging." Naturally we were very distressed, and they kept teasing us all the time. At the last moment – they must have got an order – they suddenly said: "All right, you can go." We returned to the barracks.

'I was with a friend all the time. She was five years older than I, also a nurse, and from the beginning to the end of the war, for twenty-seven months, we were together like sisters. She was like a mother to me, and we were like sisters in the best sense of the word. Even when she knew I would be hanged, she still kept a place in the bed for me. When we returned, the joy was great. My friend's name was Kato Pollack.

'Meanwhile there was an incident in which one of the thirty Dutch girls escaped. I don't know where she escaped to. I never heard of her again. It is very possible that she didn't succeed in escaping, because we did not hear of her anymore, not even after the war.

'One night a friend of ours went out to do her bodily functions and a German grabbed her and raped her. When she returned to the barrack she cried very hard and was totally hysterical. The next morning they called a big roll-call and killed her. Her name was Sophia Cohen.

'At the time I worked a lot with Miriam Blitz and we were good friends. For a while we worked at clearing horse dung from the streets of the Lublin ghetto. This was very good work, because we put potatoes among the horse dung, and then we had a rather good period.

'If a car went by with potatoes, we would quickly jump and steal. There was sometimes an opportunity to cook them on a kerosene stove.

'We Dutch girls were very attached to each other and helped one another. Each was together with her friend – otherwise it was impossible to live. Girls who were alone later, they died.

'Later, we once went on a big march. One of us was without her friend and was so hungry that she could not go on. They killed her *en route*. Another died of disease – we don't know exactly what it was, maybe typhus, maybe kidneys.

'After eight months the Germans came to call on us and said 'There's a chance of getting out of here." Not all the girls wanted to leave. Meanwhile there were already only twenty-eight of us, because one had died and one had escaped. There were girls who had boyfriends in the men's camp – about once every two weeks we were permitted to go to the men's camp – and they did not want to leave them. They stayed in Lublin and were killed.

'Once we also saw how a Dutch boy was hanged, because he wanted to escape. The entire camp had to go to the men's camp. We had to stand in a circle and were not permitted to close our eyes. We all saw it. His name was Jimmy.

'Sixteen of our girls said they wanted to leave. With us were also a few women from Austria, and if I'm not mistaken we were thirty all together. The Austrian women also brought their husbands. Miriam Blitz and I were ill. We had scabies. They told us that if it didn't pass within three days, they would send us back to Lublin. We understood that that would be very bad, because at the time they were killing all the Jews in Lublin. That's what we heard.

'We stayed in the barrack and that morning they took all the boys out. We heard shots from afar and we understood that all the women's husbands were being killed – in the morning we came to Milejow. We worked there. It was between Lublin and Trawniki. There was a jam factory there, where we worked, and we slept in the barracks.

'We were very hungry. They did not beat us there as in Lublin. We were thirty-two women from Poland and thirteen from Holland, there in Milejow. It was El Dorado in comparison with Lublin. We did not sleep so well, because we slept in stables, but the food and the *Wehrmacht*'s treatment were extraordinary. Many of us became ill, because we ate lots of uncooked onions, potatoes and seeds.

'Leaving Lublin saved us, because we heard that several days afterwards all the Jews in Lublin were killed.

'After five days the Ukrainians took us. They were even worse than the SS. They took us to Trawniki.

'Half an hour after we left Milejow we reached Trawniki. In Trawniki we found everything empty – it was terrible – empty of people, but very wealthy. We immediately saw that it was full of clothing and full of food and valuables. That is to say, apparently only a short while before many people had been there. We entered a very smelly barrack; it had the stench of dead bodies. The food was naturally excellent, because there were now forty-five women in a place where there were previously 10,000 people. We found money, gold, diamonds, insulin. We had to hand everything in.

'I even found pictures of Dutch people I knew. It means there were Dutch people there too, and we hadn't even known. We found a big grave there, and they wanted us to throw the dead bodies into it.

'The camp was full of dead bodies. They had been killed – shot – and we were required to throw them into that grave. That was our work. I myself did not do it, because my friend was like a mother and did not want me to do it. She sent me back and said I was ill. She herself did do it, as did Miriam Blitz.

'Once we stole several kilograms of butter, and I was severely beaten for it.

'Miriam Blitz was also very severely beaten, I no longer remember why. Her friend (she died afterwards) was so terrified by the beating her friend received that she later became a deaf mute (she was in shock) and died. We had a good life in Trawniki because of all the food we found.

'We had to arrange all the things that remained, make them into packets and the Germans took them to send to Germany.

'Miriam Blitz and I once planned an escape and even set a 5 am meeting in order to escape, because it wasn't so hard to escape from Trawniki. But at the last minute we decided not to do it, because of the language. We did not know how to speak Polish, and the Poles are very big anti-semites. The second reason was that I was together with Kato Pollack, and she was together with her friend, and the fact was that we did not want to leave them.

'After a while we were taken from Trawniki back to the camp at Lublin. They said it was because of the partisans. In the camp at Lublin things were very bad for us. They beat us and we were very hungry. There were Polish Communists there too, and they were very good to us. One of them kept sending me something to eat, until one of my girlfriends in fact stole him from me. Because in the final analysis, every man still wanted the women to sleep with him at some point, and I was still very young, from a religious home and very childish. So in fact she "stole" him, because she told him she did want to. And that's how my food supply ended.

'We worked in the sewing-room and actually did a little sabotage there. We sewed up the bottoms of SS men's trouser legs. We also turned their trouser pockets inside out, and we laughed about it. Even so, with all the suffering we also laughed a lot.

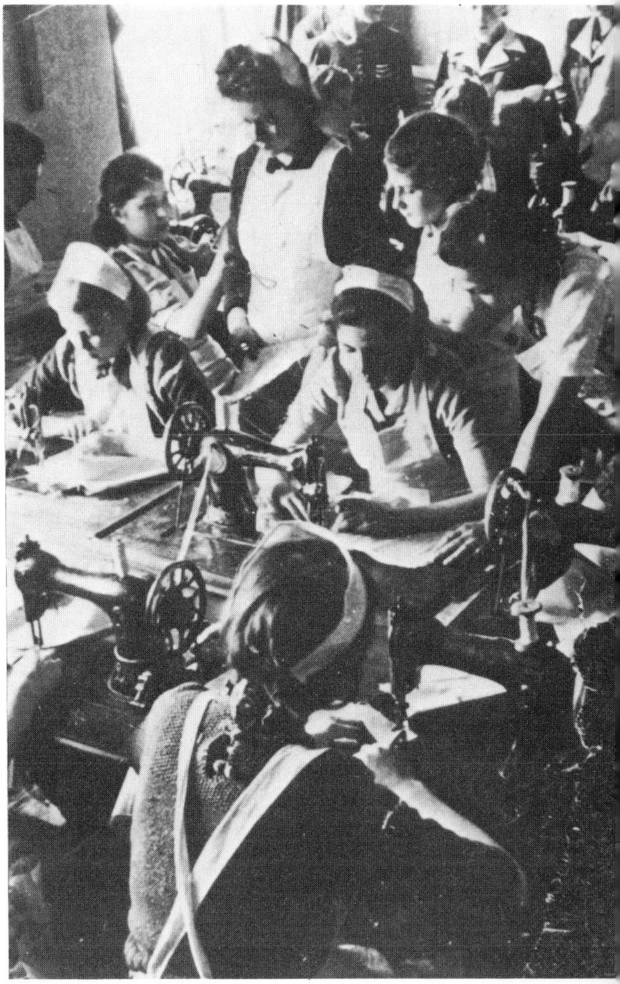

Jewish girls sewing in the Lodz ghetto.

'We had to leave there because the Russians were approaching. We left Lublin on foot, and it was awful.

'There were both men and women, and also Christians, because I remember that the Christian who was so good to me was killed on the way because he couldn't carry on. One of our friends, Clara Hompretz, was also shot. I too had a great deal of difficulty walking and my friend carried me on her back.

'There were also Dutch Christians on that transport. They too were in Lublin and were very good to us. We walked that way for a day and a night, in the rain. We had bread but could not carry it because it was wet and we had no strength for it, so we threw it by the wayside. Our shoes were also so wet that we could no longer walk in them. We took them off, and in the end we threw everything away. Finally, the Dutchmen also carried us on their backs, because they still had strength it seems. If we did not walk fast enough, the SS ordered the dogs on us, and they grabbed us by the legs. Don't think that the SS themselves didn't complain. It wasn't so easy for them either. They too had to walk.

'We reached Krasnik, in Lublin county, and were brought to a big hall. Slowly it became hotter and hotter. Afterwards we heard that they had actually wanted to burn us there. Heat and smoke rose from the floor. And suddenly it seems an order came, and they sent us out. They put us into railway cars and took us to Auschwitz.

'In Auschwitz they did not kill any of us. We had a shower, not knowing that the place where we were showering was also the gas place. We also got the numbers on our arm there. I was immediately transferred to the hospital. I could no longer walk because of the sores on my feet, and meanwhile I had a rather serious cause of jaundice.

'There was a selection in the hospital at the time, and after twelve days I returned to my friends. They gave me a compliment in the hospital: that I was so fat – because we found extremely thin people there.

'It wasn't so bad for us in Auschwitz. We Dutch were together. Twelve girls remained. We were given work on the excrement cart. It's hard to explain how filthy that work was, because we sometimes got all the excrement on us. If we did not throw it properly into the hole, we got it on our heads. We worked at that and were quite gay. We sang as we walked. We were outside the camp and had the possibility of stealing carrots. I remember that I once stole six carrots and was caught. For each carrot I stole I received a very hard blow with a stick. But in the end I got the six carrots back, so it wasn't so bad. I was happy with the carrots. My friend, Kato Pollack, kept trying to take the dirty work from me.

'I stayed in Auschwitz until November 1944. They did another selection and took several of our girls to the gas chamber, but by some miracle they came out and returned. But they did not return to us.

'In November we went to Belsen. At first we lived in tents. One night there was a heavy rain with strong wind, and all the tents collapsed on us. I was hit in the head by a big iron bar. There was a big panic.

'The initial period in Belsen was very very sad. We saw that the camp was full of dead bodies, which were put in railway cars and taken away. I also met Anne Frank there. She was with her sister. She was very weak, and evidently because of that she did not impress me. She died there as well.

'There was another Dutch woman there, who came from Auschwitz at the same time. She was not together with us, but rather came via Westerbork-Auschwitz, where she left her mother and came to Belsen. She was a very nice woman. Her name was Hetty Brandel, and she actually died of hunger. Nor could she tolerate the filth. She suffered very much in Belsen.

'We had already suffered so much that we were like the women from Poland – we weren't human beings any longer. We were like animals. Many of us were ill in Belsen. We had typhus. It also went to the head and people actually went mad from it.

'It was very sad that we did not work, because then we talked about food all day, and at night we dreamed about food all the time – actually nightmares. There was no other subject than food. Jews in the camp on the other side of Belsen tried to help us. There were many Dutch who knew us.

'From Belsen we went to Raguhn. The *Wehrmacht* were there and were very good to us, but there was no food. We worked in an ammunition factory there. I don't remember where we were as hungry as we were there. The cleanliness was extraordinary but we received almost nothing to eat. We spent a lot of time underground there, because the Americans were already approaching. When the Americans were very near, they transferred us to Theresienstadt.

'In Theresienstadt I was very ill. I got spotted typhus, and on the day they told me the war had

The exercise yard at Theresienstadt. To the left and right are the barracks, and at the back of the yard the wall of the old fort.

ended, the whole thing made no difference to me. At the end I was already nearly dead.

'On 14 July we were brought back to Holland, in French railway wagons. This was done very quickly, because the Russians came to Theresienstadt and they did not want us to stay with the Russians. I went back to Rotterdam. My friend was from The Hague and she wanted me to stay with her, but I wanted to look for my family. Meanwhile I was nineteen years old.

'I returned to Rotterdam, looked for my family and did not find them.

'The moment I came back I knew none of them would return. I was told all of them had died in Sobibor.'

16

A Belgian Story

On 2 September 1942 the first train left Belgium for Auschwitz, carrying in its suffocating sealed trucks the Jews of Brussels and Antwerp, Ostend and Bruges, Ghent and Liège.

Yet another Jewish community was about to be destroyed: a community which could trace back its origins more than seven hundred years.

Once more, a story of many centuries of spasmodic suffering, struggle and eventual prosperity was to reach a cruel climax. As early as 1261, following the death of Duke Henry III of Brabant, the Jews of Belgium faced sudden death. For the Duke had laid down in his last will and testament that all 'Jews and usurers' within his realms were to be expelled, to be, as he ordered, 'totally extirpated until not even one remains, unless they undertake to engage in commerce after the fashion of other merchants and agree to cease their practice of moneylending and usury'. The Duke went on to recommend manual labour for the Jews, in preference to usury.

The Jews of Brabant survived their Duke's deathbed orders; but in 1309 the Jews of neighbouring Louvain – men, women and children – had been massacred for refusing baptism; and forty years later, when the Black Death reached the province of Hainaut, the Jews were accused of poisoning the local drinking water, and again were put to the sword.

Two hundred years later, with the expulsion of the Jews from Spain and Portugal, the Belgian Jewish communities were revitalized. Antwerp in particular became the centre of growing communal and commercial life. In the nineteenth century several thousand Jewish refugees from central and eastern Europe, brought the sounds of

Lilian and Arnold Buschel in Antwerp during the German occupation of Belgium. They were deported from Antwerp to Auschwitz in September 1943.

Yiddish to the streets of Antwerp; Jewish schools flourished, while the diamond industry made Antwerp Jewry famous throughout the commercial world.

By 1900 there were 8,000 Jews in Antwerp: by 1930 more than 70,000 throughout Belgium. With the coming of Nazism in Germany, a further 20,000 German refugees found shelter among their fellow Jews in Belgium. On 10 May 1940, the day on which the German army struck across the Belgian frontiers, there were between 90,000 and 110,000 Jews living within those borders. Tens of thousands fled southwards, across the frontier to France. But eighteen days later the Belgian Government surrendered and an estimated 55,000 Jews were trapped.

For two years the burdens of Nazi rule had pressed heavily upon them, and their right to carry on their normal lives as citizens was progressively curtailed. Forced labour was imposed

Jewish schoolchildren in Brussels, photographed with their teachers a few months before the outbreak of war.

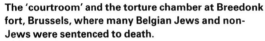

The 'courtroom' and the torture chamber at Breedonk fort, Brussels, where many Belgian Jews and non-Jews were sentenced to death.
Opposite: **one of the 'dormitories' at Dossin, the deportation centre in Brussels from which more than 24,000 Belgian Jews were deported to Auschwitz.**

in March 1942; the wearing of the yellow star in May. So it was that the first train, with 1,000 Jews, left Belgium on 2 September 1942. Within five weeks, 10,000 had been deported, among them a girl called Anny, whose mother and sisters remained in Belgium.

At Auschwitz, Anny was among those chosen to survive, at least for a brief while, as a member of the Auschwitz orchestra. She played the music which the Nazis demanded, as the SS examined the new arrivals and selected those who should live and those who should die.

Meanwhile, the trains from Belgium continued to arrive. Only once was there a moment of hope: convoy No 20, leaving on 19 April 1943, was attacked while still in Belgium by Jewish partisans, members of the Committee of Jewish Defence. The train was forced to stop and several hundred deportees escaped. The Nazis hunted many of them down. Even so, a few reached safety in Switzerland.

Inside Belgium extraordinary efforts were made to save those who had not yet been deported. Jewish and Catholic resistance groups worked together, the Red Cross did what it could, as did the Catholic Workers Youth Movement. As a result, more than 10,000 adults and 3,000 children were successfully hidden from the Gestapo. But for those who could not be hidden, the round-ups continued throughout 1943 and early 1944.

On 6 June 1944 the Allied armies landed in Normandy. The liberation of Europe had begun. Yet even then the deportation trains continued to roll eastwards, despite the pressing military demands of the battlefield. The arrival of one of those Belgian trains at Auschwitz has been described, not by Anny, the girl chosen to play music to the SS, but by one of her colleagues, Fania Fénelon, who had also been spared death in order to sing to the Gestapo while the death trains arrived.

'The doors of the railway carriages were open', Fania Fénelon recalled, 'and out of them tumbled men, women, and children. Few got up. Others came out shrieking, leaping over the dead.' This

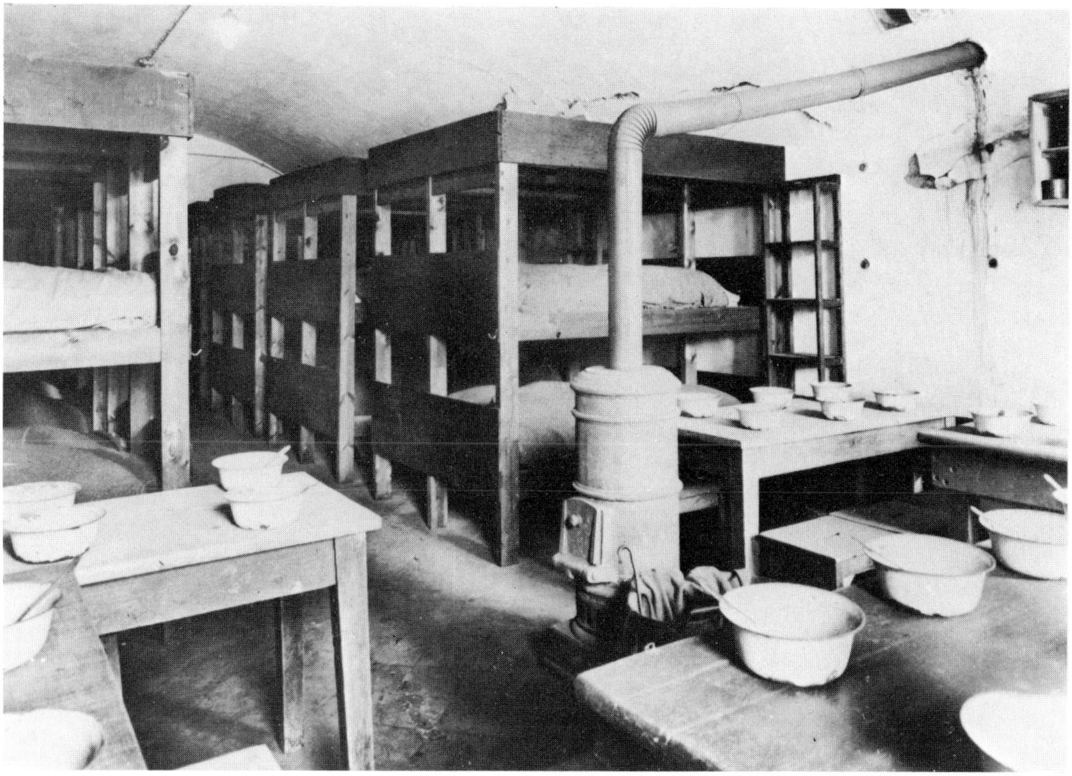

train, she learned, had been travelling, sealed, for twelve days, 'twelve days without air, food or water'.

The musicians remained in their block, rehearsing the quartet from *Rigoletto* to play to the SS later in the day. Rumour reached the block that this new transport had come from Belgium and, as Fania recalled, her Belgian friend and another girl from Belgium were looking intently at the new arrivals, 'as if all this sadness nonetheless brought them a whiff of their own country'. So the girls watched. Fania Fénelon recalled the sequel:

' "You know", remarked Anny, "they really look Belgian." Then, violent, irrepressible, a strangled shriek rose in her throat: "*Maman!* It's my mother, my sisters!"

'She threw herself forward. Down there on the ramp, her mother and sisters didn't look round. Brutally Florette planted her hand over Anny's mouth. Ewa, Little Irene and Lili pulled her back. Anny struggled desperately, wrenched away Florette's hand, shrieked, "Let me go. I want to go, I want to see them – to die with them. *Maman, Maman!*"

'Florette landed her a well-judged blow and groggily she allowed herself to be carried to her bed. We took turns mounting guard beside her. She cried all night and fell asleep at dawn.'

By the end of July 1944 the Auschwitz railway siding had received a total of 25,631 Belgian Jews, a statistic calculated, as were so many others, with all the care of Nazi clerical expertise. Only 1,244 of these Belgian deportees survived. It had taken thirty-one separate trains, and nearly two years, to complete this transfer. As convoy No 31 reached Auschwitz, the Allied armies, having broken out of the Normandy beachhead, were sweeping eastwards across France towards the Seine, the Somme and the Belgian border.

17

A Single Train

A Polish town with only 6,000 inhabitants, half of them Jews. A small Jewish community that could trace its origins back more than 600 years. For most of those years, a settled existence, with privileges granted and trading rights respected. For brief moments, persecution and fear. In 1374 the town's inhabitants had obtained, briefly, the special privilege 'of not tolerating Jews'. Four hundred years later their descendants had initiated a 'blood libel' charge: the false accusation that local Jews had used Christian blood to bake the Passover bread. Later, when part of the Russian Empire, the local Jews had suffered from the law which prohibited Jews from settling in the border areas. But the community survived, small, compact and timeless.

A typical story, this: the name of the town, Olkusz. It was of no particular economic importance as a town, overshadowed by the great coalfields and mining towns of Upper Silesia to the west, and by the city of Cracow to the east. Yet, like so many similar Polish towns and villages, its six-hundred-year-old Jewish life was soon to be brutally destroyed.

German troops entered Olkusz on 5 September 1939, only four days after the invasion of Poland. From the moment of their arrival, the Germans began to attack individual Jews in the street, to beat them for 'fun', to steal their property and to mock their religious feelings by public humiliation.

Within a month of the German invasion of Poland, the Jewish population of Olkusz was increased by the arrival of 800 men, women and children who had been expelled from the nearby industrial areas of Upper Silesia. These deportees, driven from their homes without warning and deprived of all their possessions, were among the hundreds of Jews who, as 1940 progressed, were seized in the streets of Olkusz during random Gestapo raids, and deported to Germany to forced labour camps.

Towards the end of 1941 the Jews of Olkusz were driven out of their homes and shops, and forced to move to a special ghetto set up in a suburb. Leaving the ghetto was strictly forbidden. Poverty and hunger increased.

In March 1942 three Jews slipped out of the ghetto illegally, in search of food. They were caught, and sentenced to death. To amuse themselves, the local German authorities not only ordered the hanging to take place on the Jewish festival of *Purim*; they also forced the Jews of Olkusz themselves to build the gallows and to carry out the hangings.

In Olkusz, in 1942, the Jewish festival of *Purim* was 'celebrated' by the Nazis by hanging two Jews who had been caught searching for food outside the confines of the ghetto.

Olkusz, 31 July 1940: after the identification parade, all the Jewish men were forced to lie down with their faces in the mud while waiting to be 'registered' by the German occupation forces. Later, the Jewish families of Olkusz were assembled for deportation.

These photographs were part of a series of sixteen, taken by a Polish photographer at the request of the Germans. Realizing the importance of the scenes, the photographer made a second set of prints, which he kept for himself until after the war.

Olkusz station, in German Ilkenau. The Jews are assembled for deportation. As they board the train, a soldier poses, while the man with a white bundle turns briefly to look down the train.

The deportations to forced labour camps continued. In the month of the *Purim* hangings, 150 women were sent out; a month later, a similar number of men; and a month after that, 1,000 more men and women. For this last deportation, the Germans again chose a Jewish festival, *Shavuot*, a time of feasting, of flowers, and of the spring harvest: one of the three pilgrim festivals of Judaism.

As the Jews of Olkusz were being deported, seven Olkusz-born Jews, who had been living for some years in France, were arrested in Paris and taken to Drancy. The first to be sent to Auschwitz, on 5 June 1942, was the forty-two-year-old Jacob Goldfield. Two months later Malka Rorcfeld was deported with her fifteen-year-old daughter Fryda. Of these seven Olkusz-born Jews, the last to be deported from Paris, the sixty-two-year-old Maurice Stark, reached Auschwitz at the end of March 1944.

Meanwhile, in July 1942 the able-bodied men left in Olkusz were sent to labour camps. Then all the Jews still in the town, more than a thousand women, old men, children, cripples and the sick,

together with their rabbi, were deported to Auschwitz: a single train, and a brief journey, only sixty-four kilometres, the sole aim of which was to destroy a whole community.

Following this final deportation, twenty Jews were left in Olkusz to 'clear up' the ghetto. All the belongings of its former inhabitants were taken as booty by the occupation forces. Then those twenty were themselves deported to Auschwitz, and murdered. The Jews of Olkusz were no more.

18

'Our Hope'

During the First World War, while the Austrian and Russian armies clashed in the Carpathians, a young Jew from the Austrian province of Galicia fled westwards to Prague. His name was Jacob Edelstein, and in the 1930s he became one of the leading Zionists in the new State of Czechoslovakia.

Appointed director of the 'Palestine Office' in Prague, Edelstein was active in seeking to secure visas from the British authorities for Jewish emigration to Palestine. It was not always easy to get these visas; the British restrictions were severe. But Edelstein's office did all it could to expedite Jewish emigration and to encourage Zionist youth groups to prepare for the practical tasks of life in Palestine as farmers and artisans.

Following the German occupation of Prague in March 1939, and the establishment of the Protectorate of Bohemia and Moravia, Jacob Edelstein argued with his Zionist colleagues that it was their duty, as leaders of the Jewish community, not to desert their flock. But what was to be the fate of the Jews of Bohemia and Moravia? In the winter of 1939 Edelstein himself saw the harsh conditions established by the German occupation authorities in Poland, at Nisko, in the 'Lublinland' reservation, and in the Lodz ghetto. As a result of what he had seen, he became convinced that deportation 'to the east' meant certain death.

Returning to Prague, Edelstein argued that the aim of the Jewish leadership, Zionist and non-Zionist alike, must be to hold the Czechoslovak community together as long as possible. Hope lay, he believed, in remaining in the Protectorate, in avoiding deportation and in doing whatever productive work the Germans would allow.

Such was the hope. But in October 1941 more than 6,000 Jews from Prague and Brno were deported by train to Lodz and Minsk. Edelstein was appalled, knowing that their fate would be a harsh one, so much so that they might not even survive the war. The deportations convinced him that action was urgent if the remaining 100,000 Jews of Bohemia and Moravia were to be saved. Thus was born the idea of setting up a special ghetto inside Czechoslovakia itself.

In the mountains north-west of Prague, near to where the river Eger flows into the Elbe, the Austrian Emperor Joseph II had planned a fortress town to guard the borders of his Empire. Built in 1780, and called Terezin, it had remained a small garrison town for 150 years, inhabited largely by soldiers and by traders who made a living by providing military supplies. Few Jews lived there: only three Jewish families were recorded in 1852 and less than a hundred Jews – most of them soldiers in the Czech army – by 1930.

In March 1939, following the German occupation of Prague, Terezin became part of the Protectorate. Of its 3,700 inhabitants, there were still a mere ten Jewish families living in the town, and there seemed no reason why this small remote place – now known by its German name of Theresienstadt – should become connected with the Jewish tragedy.

On 10 October 1941 the fate of Theresienstadt was transformed, for on that day a German document set out the new plan, to turn Theresienstadt into a Jewish ghetto into which all the Jews of Bohemia and Moravia would be deported. Thus, it seemed, Edelstein's hope of saving the Jews

The entrance to the Theresienstadt ghetto, with the Nazi slogan, 'Work Makes Free'.

from deportation to the east would be realized. Conditions were clearly going to be severe, with forced labour in the ghetto for all those over the age of fourteen. But at the same time the Germans wished to show the ghetto to the world as a 'model settlement'.

The Germans appointed Edelstein to be 'Jewish Elder'. He and his Council of Elders now set about trying to protect all those for whom life inside Theresienstadt still held out hope of survival. 'Did I do right', he asked in a letter a year later, 'to drag my best friends into chaos and persecution? Our pioneer training taught us always to be on the spot where the fate of the Jewish people had become tragic', and he went on: 'Who but we were destined to stand in the breach at the moment of the greatest affliction and the most fateful moments in history?'

Gradually the trains began to arrive at this remote corner of Bohemia. In six months, from November 1941 to May 1942, a third of the Jews of the Protectorate – a total of 28,887 people – were deported there. Yet even before the last trains had brought their deportees, the first trains had begun to leave Theresienstadt to the ghettos and death camps of the east, despite the hopes of Edelstein and his fellow Councillors.

By September 1942 there were more than 53,000 Jews crowded into the ghetto. Many were old people who had been brought by train from Austria and Germany, from Holland and Luxembourg. Some of the arrivals were German Jews who had been awarded the highest German military decorations in the First World War. Others were assimilated Jews who had tried to merge into the societies of which they had become an integral part.

Overcrowding in the ghetto was terrible: less than three square metres per person. Deaths from starvation were a daily occurrence. More than 33,000 died of starvation in forty-two months, an average of twenty-five people a day. At the same time deportations to the death camps continued: 13,000 were sent eastwards to their deaths in September 1942 alone.

Edelstein and the other leaders of the ghetto fought against the despair which these events created. They were determined above all to ensure that at least the 15,000 children of the ghetto survived into the post-war world. Helped by several

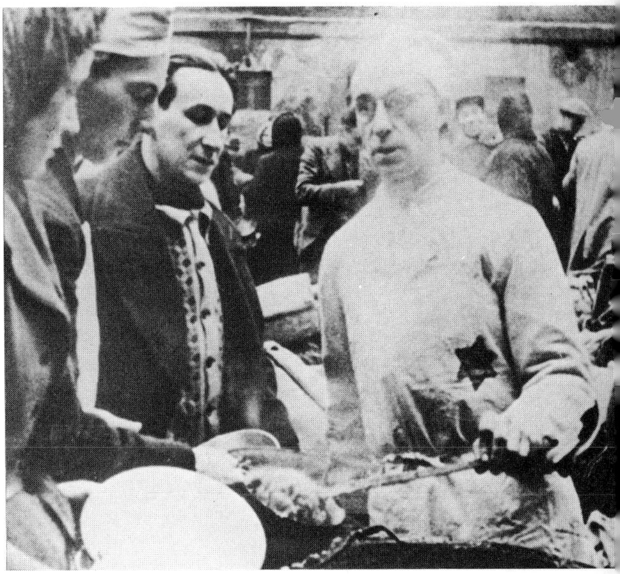

Dutch Jews arriving at Theresienstadt.

other Zionist and non-Zionist leaders, Edelstein made every effort to protect the children from being deported, by providing them with work outside the ghetto which the Germans would consider 'essential': paving roads in Bohusovice, coalmining in Kladno, and afforestation for girls and women in Krivoklát. Inside the ghetto similar 'essential' work was organized in special workshops devoted to electrical engineering, welding and woodwork; skills were taught and teenagers were apprenticed.

To save the children became the one hope of the leaders of the ghetto. In the summer of 1942 special children's houses were set up, aimed at shielding the children as much as possible from the scenes of hunger and deprivation around them. Three kindergartens were set up: one for Czech-speaking children, one for German speakers, and one for those whose language was Hebrew.

Inside the children's houses were workshops: sewing for the girls and shoe-repairing for the boys. Special Jewish instructors looked after the children's health and hygiene, sitting at night with those who were sick. One of these instructors, a girl, later recalled:

Theresienstadt and eastern Europe.

'As we didn't want our rooms to become like the other rooms in the ghetto where everyone lived their lives on their beds, surrounded by broken pieces of furniture and rags, we organized competitions for the best kept houses. We made cupboards and shelves from boards. Each house and each group was given a Hebrew name. The rough boards the beds were made of were planed smooth and coloured with coloured pencils or water colours.

'To ensure that the rooms be tidy and ready for lessons by nine o'clock, the children had to rise at six o'clock, for there was only one washbasin to every ten children and water had to be brought from the yard up to the second floor. Cleanliness was examined every day by the Youth Director and points awarded.

'Preparations for Sabbath were particularly thorough and occupied the entire day on Friday. The assembly on Friday evening was the most moving experience of the week . . . the most exciting moment being the presentation of the prize (an engraved board) to the best house of the week. These assemblies intensified the feeling of close relationship between our collective houses. (In the other youth houses no direct contact existed between each house.) At the end of the assembly a youth service was held.'

Among the names given to one of the children's

houses – whose official designation was house L 414 – was the Hebrew *Tikvatenu*, 'Our Hope'.

For the adults of Theresienstadt, there was little hope. Even births were 'forbidden' by the Nazis, and any pregnant woman who refused to have an abortion could be added to the list of those marked out for the next eastwards-bound train, together with her newly-born child. Despite this decree, a total of 207 children were known to have been born in the ghetto. Only twenty-five of them survived.

The efforts of the Zionists in the ghetto reached a climax in November 1942, when the Federation of Zionists' *Hehalutz* movement – 'the pioneers' – held their first formal conference inside the ghetto.

A street scene in the Theresienstadt ghetto.

Special committees were elected for Hebrew culture, education, aid for the sick and self-defence. Four months later, in March 1943, *Hehalutz* leaders instituted a 'helping hand' scheme whereby the children, working in units of five, carried out welfare activity on behalf of the old and the sick. Sometimes these small units would combine into groups in order to clean and repair a whole section of houses lived in by the crippled or the aged. A member of the *Hehalutz* Council, Shlomo Schmiedt, later recalled the minor tasks carried out by units and individuals under the 'helping hand' scheme:

'Among these "minor" tasks was standing in queues for food, the "purchase" of goods in the pseudo-shops of the ghetto, gathering the dregs of soup in the youth kitchens and dividing them up among the ever-hungry elderly people, washing their soiled underwear, darning, sewing, putting up shelves in their rooms, etc.

'At first, the old people were suspicious of the children, and even threw them out, because they could not imagine that they really wished to help. But later, when they learned that the children did not cheat them when bringing food and had not come to steal their belongings, they accepted their assistance gratefully.'

One of the adult workers of the 'helping hand' recalled how:

'The children would bring flowers to the old people hidden under their clothes (because it was forbidden to pick flowers from the garden). The old people, who were unable to believe that kindness still existed in the world, wept with emotion and when we had to leave them we would hear calls from the beds packed close to one another, "Come back again soon." '

The activities of the 'helping hand' were widespread. Scouting activities and physical training ensured a minimum of fitness. Hebrew classes and discussion groups maintained Zionist enthusiasm. The adults spoke of earlier summer camps in Europe and of life in Palestine. In the summer of 1943 a special Scout Day was the occasion for competitions in games, debates, dancing and Hebrew songs.

But the work of 'helping hand' was often sombre, for they helped to pack the meagre belongings of those who had been listed for the train journey to the east, and sought to console them on the eve of their departure.

During the summer of 1943 a special children's kitchen was opened in the ghetto. For the children, extra rations could sometimes be procured: once a week there was the chance of a small cake, or an eighth of a litre of skimmed milk. But hunger stalked the ghetto, killing thousands, and the children used to tell a story:

'Once upon a time there was a king who was hungry. He went to the service window and said to the cook: give me an extra portion – and he was given an extra portion.'

The overriding problems of food and survival failed to destroy the instinct for education. For the adults of *Hehalutz* the speaking of Hebrew was a central theme. A special 'language committee' arranged study circles for both beginners and advanced students. A library of Hebrew books was put together, and Hebrew plays produced. Despite opposition from those Jews who still argued in favour of assimilation, children of school age were provided with special Hebrew lessons, and a Hebrew kindergarten, attended by up to seventy children, was run by a nursery school teacher who had been trained in Palestine.

Preparation for Palestine was the aim, and the dream. One of the plays performed by the adult Zionists was one entitled: *Tevye the Milkman in Theresienstadt and His immigration to Palestine.*

Throughout the summer and autumn of 1943 a special 'Hebrew group' was active, consisting of some thirty-five *Hehalutz* members whose Hebrew studies were at an advanced stage. Although the Zionists were a minority in the ghetto, their activities flourished.

Jacob Edelstein approved of these activities. For him it was an article of faith that the children and youth should be prepared for the future immigration to Palestine. Not for them a return to Czechoslovakia, Austria or Germany when the war was over. Edelstein's Zionism was so passionate that one Jewish critic accused him of looking at Judaism 'through dark Zionist glasses, which unfortunately he was unable to take off'. At the same time he fought to protect those under his charge, and when the Germans asked him to help them prepare for the deportation of 20,000 ghetto inmates to Auschwitz, he refused. Later they discovered that he had failed to tell them of the children born in the ghetto, in an effort to save the lives of both mothers and children.

In November 1943 Edelstein was arrested by the Gestapo. His 'crime' was to have falsified the list of inmates in order to save the lives of several individuals marked out for deportation. He and his family were sent by train to Auschwitz.

Edelstein's deportation to Auschwitz cast a pall of sadness over the Zionists of the ghetto. But their activities went on, inspired by the hope that some of them must surely survive, and sustained by the vision of Palestine.

A month after Edelstein had been taken away, a special 'Hebrew Week' was held during the festival of *Hannukah*, with nightly programmes in Hebrew, a certificate of honour, and a special pin awarded to those who had made the best progress in Hebrew speaking. 'The persons wearing this pin', Shlomo Schmiedt recalled, 'undertook to speak only Hebrew amongst themselves!'

How long would the war go on? How long could the youth of Theresienstadt survive? Whatever the efforts of those inside the ghetto, the Nazi 'grand design' continued and the trains from Theresienstadt continued to be sent eastwards, some to Riga, Minsk, Lublin and Warsaw, others to the death camps of Treblinka, Sobibor and Auschwitz.

For the children, the deportations were a part of the uncertainty, the suffering and the unreality which marred their lives. In the summer of 1944 one of the adult instructors wrote:

'Among themselves they feel free, but they are still children of the ghetto. There is no freedom behind barbed wire fences. There is no freedom while wearing the yellow patch on the chest.

'The children's morality is the morality of the ghetto. Their reactions are totally different from our own at that age, or of the children outside the ghetto. They have seen their parents taken away before their eyes and know that they will never return. They have seen transports leave for the east; they have watched their friends pack their belongings and leave for the unknown. They have seen this not with the feeling of it being what they would expect after fourteen years of living in this world, but rather from the perspective of the last five years.

'These young people are never surprised. They accept with an equanimity arising out of their experiences over the past years, the various

Theresienstadt: children at play and *(below)* inside one of the men's barracks.

An old lady: a frame from a Nazi film aimed at portraying Theresienstadt as a 'model' ghetto. When the film was completed, those who had been shown in it were deported to Auschwitz.

instructions given them, the restrictions imposed on them. Here in Theresienstadt they have come face to face with death; they have watched thousands of inmates in their death-throes; they have watched the mentally unbalanced behind bars of the *Kavalirka* (the name of the building where the insane inmates of the ghetto were concentrated).

'The depressing, suffocating atmosphere of the ghetto has caused their laughter to be unlike the laughter of children of their age. And despite this, they have extraordinary stamina, a positive approach to life. They have lost one or two years, but in spite of everything they are ready, they will find their place in life, they will fulfil their task.'

In the east, the Red Army had begun its westward advance, crossing the eastern frontiers of Poland and Rumania in April, and driving the Germans from the Crimea in May. On 6 June 1944 British, French and American forces landed on the coast of France, opening a second front in Europe. Now, from both west and east, the Allies pressed in upon the Reich. But the German determination to destroy European Jewry was unaffected, even accelerated, by the Allied advance. At Auschwitz Jacob Edelstein had been kept in a punishment cell without light, food or water: without room even to stand up. Then, on 20 June 1944, having been forced to watch while his wife and young son were executed, he himself was shot.

On 23 July 1944 a special Red Cross Investigation Committee visited Theresienstadt. In preparation for its arrival, the Germans had set up false shops, a bank, a café, extra kindergartens and bogus schools. Flower gardens were laid out in the main street of the ghetto and the terrible overcrowding was lessened by the despatch of extra trains to Auschwitz.

Encouraged by the favourable impression which these preparations made on the Red Cross, a special Nazi propaganda film was made, entitled 'the new life of the Jews under the protection of the Third Reich'. Everything in the film looked most encouraging, even homely. The Jews need have no fear of Nazi rule. But when the film was finished, most of the actors were sent straight to Auschwitz and to their deaths.

On 25 August 1944 Paris surrendered to the Allied armies. Six days later the Red Army entered Bucharest. Vilna and Lvov were already liberated cities. That same August, in Theresienstadt, *Hehalutz* held their second conference, and approved the main aim of the Zionist movement in the ghetto: the upholding of human, national and Jewish values, the advancement of socialist Zionism, and education towards a collective way of life in Palestine.

The proceedings had not been without fierce disagreement. As Shlomo Schmiedt recalled:

'There was also a bitter argument over the pressing question of whether to permit members of *Hehalutz* to volunteer for transports and to join parents being sent to Auschwitz (we didn't know yet the significance of these transports!), or demand that they continue their work in the ghetto for the benefit of all.'

The conclusion finally reached was a democratic one: to leave the decision to each individual member. But now the Germans took their own decision: to end the charade of the showplace. No one would be impressed by it now in any case, as

A class of children at Theresienstadt, photographed with their teacher.

the Red Army, advancing westwards, was continually finding evidence of mass-murders and extermination camps. So the decision was made: to deport most of the Jewish Council to Auschwitz, and, in September 1944, to deport the children.

One of those who witnessed the fate of the children of Theresienstadt was the Polish woman who, after seven months at Auschwitz, had managed to write a letter to the President of the Polish Government in Exile. In her letter she wrote, in February 1945:

'I simply cannot describe what I have seen with

A deportation from Theresienstadt to Auschwitz. Two faces peer out, and a hand waves.

my own eyes. I saw 4,000 Jewish children below the age of ten, who had been brought from the Theresienstadt camp in Czechoslovakia, passing through our camp on their way to the gas chambers. Some of them cried, "Mother, Mother!" Others smiled at us and waved their little hands. Within a quarter of an hour they had all been suffocated by the gas, and their bodies were already burning in the crematory.'

Despite the hunger and deprivation inside Theresienstadt itself, the spirit of Jewish resistance had not died. Since January 1943 a German Jew, Paul Eppstein, had served as Jewish Elder. A former lecturer in Sociology at Mannheim University, and a prominent Jewish youth leader, Eppstein was forty-two years old when appointed to his difficult task. He, like Jacob Edelstein, stood up to the Germans, and as the final deportations were begun, he joined the secret organization of the ghetto's self-defence.

These efforts were in vain. On 27 September 1944 Paul Eppstein was arrested by the Gestapo and immediately shot.

Throughout September and October the trains moved eastwards from Theresienstadt to Auschwitz. Of the 15,000 children in the ghetto, 14,000 had been packed in cattle trucks and shunted to the gas chambers by the last week of October. Of those children between the ages of fourteen and eighteen who were deported to Auschwitz, scarcely more than 100 survived. Of those under fourteen, none survived.

Within the short space of two months, all the hopes and efforts of three years' work in the ghetto were destroyed. Then, at the beginning of November, on Himmler's personal orders, the gas chambers of Auschwitz ceased work. But the children of Theresienstadt were no more.

The Jews of Italy

Among the oldest Jewish communities marked out to die by Section IVB4 were the Jews of Italy, whose origins stretched back to the time of the Roman Empire. Theirs had been a troubled story, with no century free from persecution. The very concept of the 'ghetto' had its origins in a law proposed in Venice in 1516 which forced the Jews of the city to live in a single restricted area, away from the central business quarter. In 1555 Pope Paul IV had obliged the Jews throughout Italy to lock themselves in their ghettos at night, to sell all their property and to give up every trading activity except the sale of rags. But the Jews of Italy overcame these disabilities; their cultural life flourished; and in the first forty years of the twentieth century they obtained leading positions in Italian national and political life. One Jew was Minister of Finance for nearly twenty years, another was Minister of War, and yet another, Minister of Justice.

When Mussolini came to power in 1922, he allowed the 35,000 Jews of Italy to keep their social and legal equality. But on 17 November 1938, imitating Hitler, Mussolini introduced detailed anti-Jewish legislation, including severe economic restrictions and a ban on all marriages between Jews and non-Jews.

Between 1940 and 1942 all foreign-born Jews in Italy were interned and some 2,000 of them employed in special 'work legions'. But it was not until the surrender of Italy to the Allies on 8 September 1943, and the German occupation of Rome and northern Italy, that the 'final solution' was imposed, both on the Italian Jews and on the thousands of Jewish refugees from France and central Europe who had found refuge there.

At the end of September 1943 Captain Theodor Dannecker, who had organized the deportation of French Jewry, was sent by Eichmann to Italy. On 9 October 1943 Dannecker began his work, arresting and deporting to Auschwitz the Jews of Trieste. A week later, on 16 October, he seized 1,000 Jews in Rome. The Pope, learning of the arrests, sought to stop them. During 16 October the rector of the German church in Rome, Bishop Hudal, appealed to the German military commander:

'I have just been informed by a high Vatican official in the immediate circle of the Holy Father, that the arrests of Jews of Italian nationality have begun this morning. In the interest of good relations which have existed until now between the Vatican and the high German military command – which in the first instance is to be credited to the political insight and greatness of heart of Your Excellency and which will some day go down in the history of Rome – I would be very grateful if you would give an order to stop these arrests in Rome and its vicinity right away; I fear that otherwise the Pope will have to make an open stand, which will serve the anti-German propaganda as a weapon against us.'

The Bishop's appeal was in vain, The threat of the Pope's intervention did not deter the Nazis, and on 18 October a sealed train containing 1,007 Jews was despatched to Auschwitz. All but twelve of the deportees were gassed, or killed as slave labour. One of those who managed to survive was Meir Zvi Vaksberger, who had been born a citizen of the Austro-Hungarian Empire, in the Adriatic

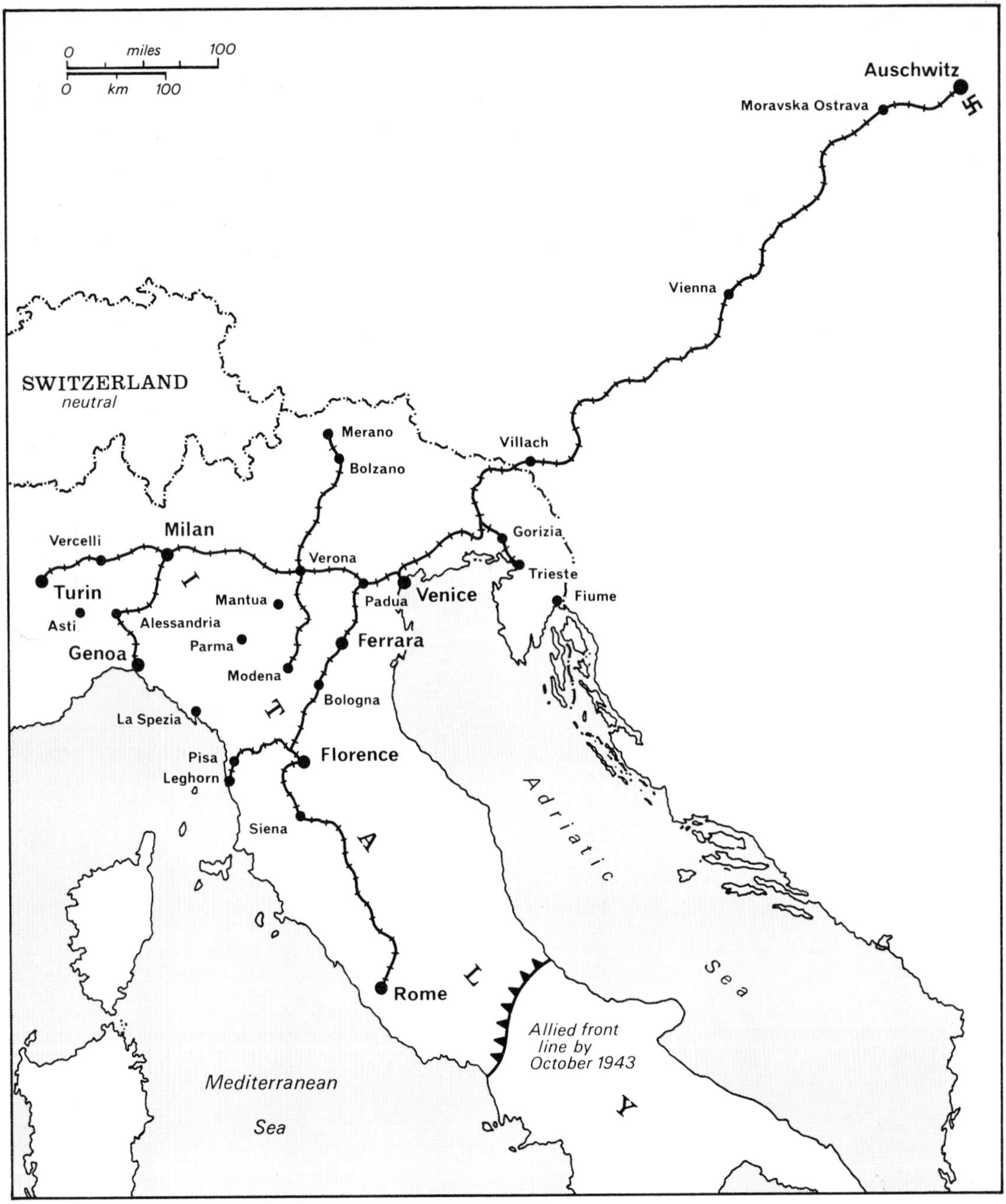

Some of the towns from which the Jews of Italy were deported to Auschwitz.

port of Fiume, in 1913. While he was still a boy, Vaksberger's home town had passed under Italian sovereignty, and he had studied at an Italian university. In 1943 Vaksberger was living in Rome. Immediately after the war he recalled how:

'On 16 October 1943 at 5 am a pair of SS men came with completed, filled-in tags to each individual family separately, according to designated addresses: you and your family are to be transported to a camp. Take along two blankets, food for eight days, and it is also "worthwhile" to take along gold and valuables.

'In ten minutes time, one had to leave one's home. One was loaded into lorries and taken to a military school. 1,300 Jews were crowded together in the military school; men, women and children.

'First of all the commandant ordered me, as interpreter (I was the only one who knew German) to announce to everyone that we were going to a labour camp beyond Germany, where everyone without exception would have to work. The older women would prepare the food for the workers and supervise the children. Since the cost of maintenance would have to be paid by the Jews alone, everyone without distinction must give his money, gold and all valuables to the commandant, for with that money food would then be purchased in Germany and distributed among all the Jews....

'On 18 October all 1,300 of us Jews were transported in cattle cars of 100 people to a wagon, to Auschwitz. There 300 strong men were selected by Dr Mengele and stood to one side, and the rest were sent straight off to the gas chambers.

'Of the 300 strong men another 100 were sent to the gas chambers because of a fiendish notion. Dr Mengele said to us that the camp was ten kilometres away from the station and, as he understands that we are tired from the journey, whoever finds it difficult to walk ten kilometres can travel in the lorry. 100 strong men got into the lorry. We never saw them again.

'In a few days I had the occasion of having a talk with Dr Mengele and I asked him: "Where is my family?" He answered me: "Don't you know what everyone knows, that all the weak people, women and children, being incapable of working, are not fit for the German regime." To my question, why aren't the 100 strong, healthy able-bodied men who got into the lorry suitable, he answered me: "People who are too lazy to walk ten kilometres, it's a sign that they have no desire to work – and they must be annihilated." Of the 200 Jews not gassed, only twelve men survived.'

The Jews of Genoa were deported on 3 November, those of Florence on 6 November, those of Milan on 8 November, those of Venice on 9 November, and those of Ferrara on 14 November. Within six weeks nearly 10,000 Italian Jews had been deported to Auschwitz, where more than 7,750 of them were murdered.

But 120,000 Italian Jews survived the war.

Above: **early in 1945 soldiers of the Jewish Brigade advance with the British army into northern Italy. Their truck bears the Star of David, now paraded in Europe as a symbol of pride, after more than five years during which it had been a symbol of humiliation and isolation.**
Below: **Italian Jewish children, who had been hidden from the Nazis, many by Catholic families, led by a soldier of the Jewish Brigade.**

Eichmann in Hungary

Among the Nazi leaders, successful deportations of Jews were a cause of boasting, and even envy. When, in March 1944, a convoy of cars and trucks assembled inside Austria for the journey across the Hungarian border to Budapest, the convoy's leader, Eichmann himself, had a 'record' which he hoped to break. As one of his Nazi colleagues later recalled, Eichmann wanted to prove that he could outdo 'the wonderous Obersturmbannführer Höffle who had deported the Jews from Warsaw – as to number and punctuality'. He hoped also, his colleague recalled, to avoid provoking the Jews of Hungary into 'a rebellion of the kind carried out in Warsaw', where hundreds of German troops had been killed during fierce resistance.

Eichmann and his convoy of 120 vehicles reached the Hungarian frontier on 19 March 1944, the day of the German occupation of Hungary. It was his thirty-eighth birthday. That night he slept in the Hotel Astoria in Budapest.

Eichmann's plan involved a massive mobilization of the local Hungarian Gendarmerie. Several hundred thousand Jews were to be deported to Auschwitz in as short a time as possible: for Soviet troops were advancing steadily westwards towards both Auschwitz and Hungary. Eichmann therefore instructed the Hungarian Gendarmerie Colonel, Laszlo Ferenczi, to 'load' 3,000 Jews on to each train: this meant forcing as many as seventy people into each goods truck. The first deportation was planned for 15 May. Meanwhile the Jews were driven from their homes and forced to gather in the main towns, uncertain as to their fate.

Beginning on 3 May, Colonel Ferenczi sent

Top: **part of the old Jewish quarter of Budapest.**
Below: **a Hungarian Jewish family, the Polláks.**

Eichmann daily reports of his 'progress'. There were always problems: once the deportations to Auschwitz had begun, six trains had been expected each day at the collection centres, but often only four would arrive. Eichmann insisted, however, that 'room' must be found for all those Jews who had been assembled. No one should be left out. Dividing Hungary into zones, the whole operation was to be conducted with precision and despatch.

The Hungarian Gendarmerie did not always relish the task that had been set them. It was carried out, nevertheless. One of those deported, a young Jewish woman by the name of Rachel R, recalled the deportations from the town of Szabad:

'In the middle of May we were instructed to pack our belongings and to prepare for the way. The Germans repeated this order three times, and the Hungarian authorities prevented them from carrying it out on each of the three occasions. But at last the German soldiers took us out of Szabad at night and made us march on foot to the railway station, where they put us on the wagons. There were 300 of us women.

'Since we went off in great haste, we were only able to take the most urgent things with us; and even those we were compelled to leave behind before we entered the wagons, for we were promised that they would be sent separately. I left behind a good raincoat, my mother's furs and other garments.

'Before the train left they also took away from us our jewellery and ready money. We were crowded 70 to 80 in a single wagon. Two pails were put in each wagon for our needs. One contained water and the other was for answering the call of nature. The pail of water was only filled again at Koszyce.'

Koszyce, known in Slovak as Kosice, in Hungarian as Kassa, in German as Kaschau, had itself been made 'clean of Jews' during May, when more than 11,000 Jews were deported to Auschwitz within three weeks, together with several local Christians who had sheltered Jews in defiance of Nazi rules. Now it was nothing but a railway junction through which Eichmann's deportees were transported towards their death. Rachel R's account of her own deportation continued:

Top: **the deportation of the Jews of Szombathely on 30 June 1944.**
Centre and below: **the Hungarian deportations continue.**

'At Koszyce there were many cases of suicide. Two people in our wagon also killed themselves. One let his blood flow and the other took poison (Andor Stern Kokanes). Apart from these there

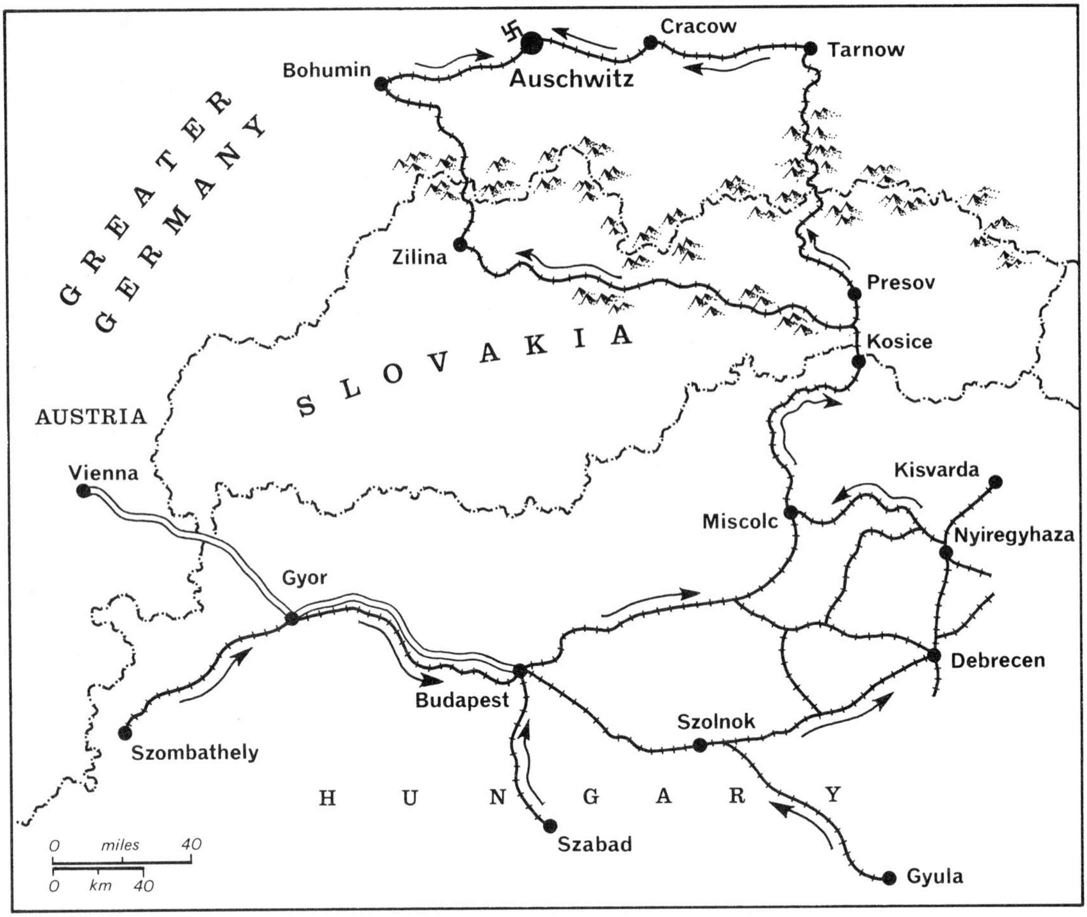

The deportation routes from Hungary to Auschwitz.

were six cases of natural death in our wagon. Four were children and two were old folk who died because of lack of air. The bodies were thrown out of the train at the station.

'After three days journey we arrived at Auschwitz, where we were received by German soldiers and Polish Jews. After the SS men separated the men from the women, the women were classified. Each young woman was asked her age and state of health. Little children were taken from their mothers, and lined up with the old folk.'

The children and old people were led away. Within a few hours they were dead. Rachel R and the other women went in another direction:

'From the station we were forced to run to the bathhouse. Anyone who fell behind in running was shot. After running for an hour we reached the bathhouse. On the way we saw a great fire and heard the terrifying and shaking cries of old people and young.

'A German soldier was good enough to explain to us that the building which we were passing contained the gas chambers and the crematorium, and that these were the cries of the people who were being put to death there. He even pointed out the crematorium to us.

'After the bath they shaved our heads. Rags and tatters were given to us instead of the dresses in which we had come. (The good clothes were sent to the storehouse.) A cross was marked on our clothes. When we had completed all these preparations we went out to the camp to which we had been assigned, and which was eight kilometres away.

'We were 800 women in all. We were guarded by an armed SS woman. There was no point in offering opposition or in trying to escape. On either side of the road stretched a barbed-wire fence, while there was a German soldier on guard every twenty metres along the road. We were forced to proceed at a quick march, and many of those who fell behind were shot by the soldier.

'The camp to which we were taken was a new one. There were huts there which had just been built out of packing cases. Beds were not to be found there, so we lay down on the floor.'

On the following day a doctor appeared. His mood was a kindly one. Rachel R recalled how he 'sweetly asked us how we were and how we felt, and promised to treat whatever we felt to be wrong'. Her account continued:

'At first many women went to him and asked for advice or treatment; and they were taken for treatment, that is, to the gas chambers. In the course of time we all came to know just what kind of treatment he gave, and nobody went to him any more, of their own free will. Then the doctor himself began selecting the sick and weak women. They used every opportunity they could of sending women away to the gas chambers. For the slightest transgression they would be sentenced to death by starvation.'

Life was grim in the huts. There was only one lavatory for 3,200 women. Washing was allowed only once a week. Yet on the wall of each hut was written: 'One single louse means death', and if any woman was found to have lice, she was dragged off to the gas chambers.

During the summer a sickness spread through the hut, resulting in a high fever and complete exhaustion. Anyone catching the sickness was at once sent, not to hospital, but to the gas chambers, together with whoever was in the bed next to them – even if the neighbour was still 'healthy'.

Rachel R survived the hunger, the doctor's 'selection' and the fatal fever. 'I succeeded in keeping myself clean', she recalled, 'with the aid of a rag which I tore off my dress, and I used to comb my hair with my fingers.' Meanwhile, the sickness spread and in less than four weeks more than 1,500 exhausted and emaciated women had been sent to their deaths.

In Budapest the Jewish leaders sought some means of escape or rescue from the daily deportations. On 30 June, while deportations were at their height, one small glimmer of hope flickered in the deepening gloom, for on that day a special train left Hungary, not for Auschwitz, but for the north of Germany. On board were 1,686 Jews, destined, not for death, but for release, in return for a ransom which had been collected from the Jews of Budapest.

The head of the SS, Heinrich Himmler, had himself approved of this 'deal', and three suitcases filled with diamonds, gold, platinum and foreign currency, valued at $1,600,000 had been delivered to the SS.

These few fortunate captives were eventually released and sent once more by train, this time to Basle in Switzerland. The first small group of 318 Hungarian Jews reached Basle on 21 August; the second, with the remaining 1,368, reached Basle on 4 December. Himmler was pleased with what he had done, calling this act a gesture of 'goodwill' towards world Jewry.

In a further act of 'goodwill' six complete trainloads of Jews were sent, not northwards to Auschwitz, but westwards to Austria. In these trains were 18,000 Hungarian Jews, part of an even larger 'deal' that was being negotiated between senior Nazi officials and a leading Hungarian Jew, Dr Rudolph Kastner, a former Associate President of the Zionist Organization of Hungary.

The prices to be paid for saving these 18,000 Jews had been discussed between Eichmann and a colleague of Kastner's, Joel Brand, as early as 8 May, a week before the deportations had begun. The arrangement was to be a barter one: 18,000

Hungarian Jews arrive at Auschwitz.

Jews on the one hand and, on the other, 10,000 trucks for use by the Waffen SS on the eastern front, 2,000,000 cases of soup, 200 tons of tea and 200 tons of coffee.

Joel Brand hurried to Istanbul, intending to put the plan to the British. He was arrested and put into solitary confinement, on the orders of the British authorities, who suspected him of being a Nazi agent.

Meanwhile, the deportations had begun. In vain did Kastner wait for some response from the Allies. As for Eichmann, he had no qualms about pushing forward the deportations with energy and despatch.

On 14 June Eichmann agreed to make a start on the 'barter' programme, in return for $5,000,000. Some money was at once paid over, together with fifteen tons of coffee. Thus it was that six trains, with their fortunate human cargo chosen after much anguish, were sent to relative safety. One of the special trains did not, however, reach Austria: an SS man, whether by mistake or as a little 'joke' is not known, switched it to the Auschwitz line and sent another train in its place. Among those who had been chosen to live, but was sent to Auschwitz instead, was the rabbi of Gyor, Dr Emil Roth.

Of the 'rescued' Jews, 1,000 died in work camps while they were still in Austria. A few were sent to concentration camps. But more than 16,000 survived the war.

Meanwhile, for more than 400,000 Hungarian Jews the deportations to Auschwitz were continued; not only the able-bodied men, but the sick, the blind, the deaf, cripples and new-born babies, were all driven to the collecting points. Hospitals, mental homes and homes for the aged were emptied out: their inmates marched or driven to the railway stations at which the trains had assembled.

The loading proceeded according to the carefully devised plan: seventy people to each goods wagon. After they had been forced inside, they were given a single bucket of water, and the wagon was sealed off. On 13 June 1944 the German Minister to Hungary, Edmund Veesenmayer, reported back to the Foreign Ministry in Berlin that the 'average' train could transport 3,150 Jews.

Guarded by armed Hungarians, the long trains – Veesenmayer reported that each one consisted of forty-five wagons – travelled northwards, as Rachel R had done, to Kosice, the Slovak frontier, and Auschwitz. Sometimes Hungarian guards

accompanied them all the way to their destination. But normally German guards took over at the Slovak frontier. At Kosice there was a further 'complication': the trains which had begun their journey there could only leave at night, as the railway yard in which the deportation trains were assembled was linked to the main railway by a branch line which ran across one of the main streets of the city. Even this night start did not prevent the local inhabitants knowing what was happening. Indeed, the German Consul in Kosice, Hans Josef Count Matuschka, recalled three years later how the population of the city often heard the crying of women and children who could not bear the intense, suffocating heat of the sealed trucks.

In desperation at these terrible events, and also in hope, the Jewish Relief Committee in Budapest contacted the Jewish leaders in Bratislava, who at once telegraphed to Switzerland begging the Allies to bomb the railway junctions between Hungary and Auschwitz. Two or three raids on the main junction on the Kosice-Presov-Zilina-Bohumin railway would, they argued, severely delay the whole complex deportation programme, and might – with the Soviet army already on the borders of Transylvania and with the Allies driving across France towards Germany – save tens of thousands, even hundreds of thousands of lives. But there was no response to this appeal.

As the trains moved slowly northwards across Slovakia, special 'arrangements' were made in the camp for killing as many Jews as possible, immediately on arrival. On some days as many as 10,000 Hungarian Jews were murdered in a single day.

Only a minority of those who reached Auschwitz were spared like Rachel R. For them there was the torment of hearing, day by day, the terrible fate of their fellow deportees. She later recalled:

'I spent seven months in that camp, and learned fresh things about it every day. I knew full well before long that the shrieks came from the gas chambers. All round the crematorium was a garden in which concerts were held in the daytime: and so the shrieks and wailings were heard only at night.'

On 11 July Edmund Veesenmayer was able to report to the German Foreign Office that a total of 437,402 Hungarian Jews had been deported from Hungary. By the end of the year, more than 300,000 of these deportees had perished, almost all of them in Auschwitz, as had in addition 28,000 Hungarian Gipsies, against whom the Nazis had also directed their hatred.

Rachel R survived. Yet her torment, like that of all the survivors, was almost beyond endurance. In her own hut, death was commonplace, and its circumstances were grotesque. On one occasion she wrote:

'A woman fell down and died. Her daughter, who was standing next to her, could not help her at all, and what was more, was compelled to restrain herself and not to show the slightest signs of grief; for the supervisors were on the watch the whole time. Any woman who dared to drop a single tear would be beaten, cursed and vituperated.

'The woman in charge of the hut repeats to us on such occasions: "What are you crying for? Don't you know that your mothers and your children were all burned long ago?" '

21

Sara's Story

On 1 August 1939, exactly a month before the German invasion of Poland, Sara Erenhalt celebrated her sixteenth birthday. Twenty-one years later, in her home in Israel, where she had settled when the war was over, she recalled the events of the intervening years. Her story illustrates many facets of the 'final solution':

'Our family was very large. There were eight sisters and a brother. Along with others we made for Stanislawow. In accordance with the Ribbentrop-Molotov agreement, in 1939 the Germans took one side of Przemysl, and the Russians the other. The bridge on the river San was the frontier.

'My family returned to Przemysl with the Red Army and remained under their occupation.

'From our side we could see Jews with yellow armbands, on the German side. It was known that the Germans were oppressing the Jews, confiscating their property and enforcing the wearing of the yellow armbands, but human life was not yet threatened.

'Shortly before the German invasion of Russia, I married Leon Pater. I was eighteen.

'The war broke out in June 1941. The Russians before leaving blew up a munitions store. My parents, as well as many other Jews, fled with the Russians, towards Russia.

'Near Stanislawow they were surrounded by Germans and had to go back. Again the family was reunited.

'The Germans had now taken over the whole of Przemysl and were merciless towards the Jews. They began by murdering about 1,000 people, including the chief rabbi of Przemysl.

'Our material situation under the Germans became much worse. My father, a tall, strong man, worked at the mill. He brought home wheat grains which we ground in coffee mills and this was our basic food. We were starving.

'Jews were allowed to move about town only during certain hours, from 8 till 10 am. Systematic actions and deportations began.

'During one action my husband was taken to Lvov, to a labour camp in Janowska, from which few people ever came back. I was in touch with my husband with whom I was able to correspond through my aunt in Lvov who had Aryan papers.

'In July 1942 I had a baby. Normally in peacetime this would have been a joyous event in the family, but at that time I was unhappy because I had brought into the world a being who would have to suffer along with me.

'When my child was two weeks old a great deportation took place. We wondered how to save the child at least. We decided to put the child in a crèche which then existed in the ghetto and, if I were deported, my sister would look after it, who as a working person might be allowed to stay.

'There was another idea – to hide in the shelter which my father had prepared beforehand in the cellar of our house. But there was the danger that if the Germans found us they would shoot us on the spot, as they had done with several other families.

'I went to the square for deportation with my parents and four of my sisters. My mother was then forty-four, and my father forty-nine. My sisters were almost children then.

'As she sat in the square my mother was grieving that I gave the child to the crèche,

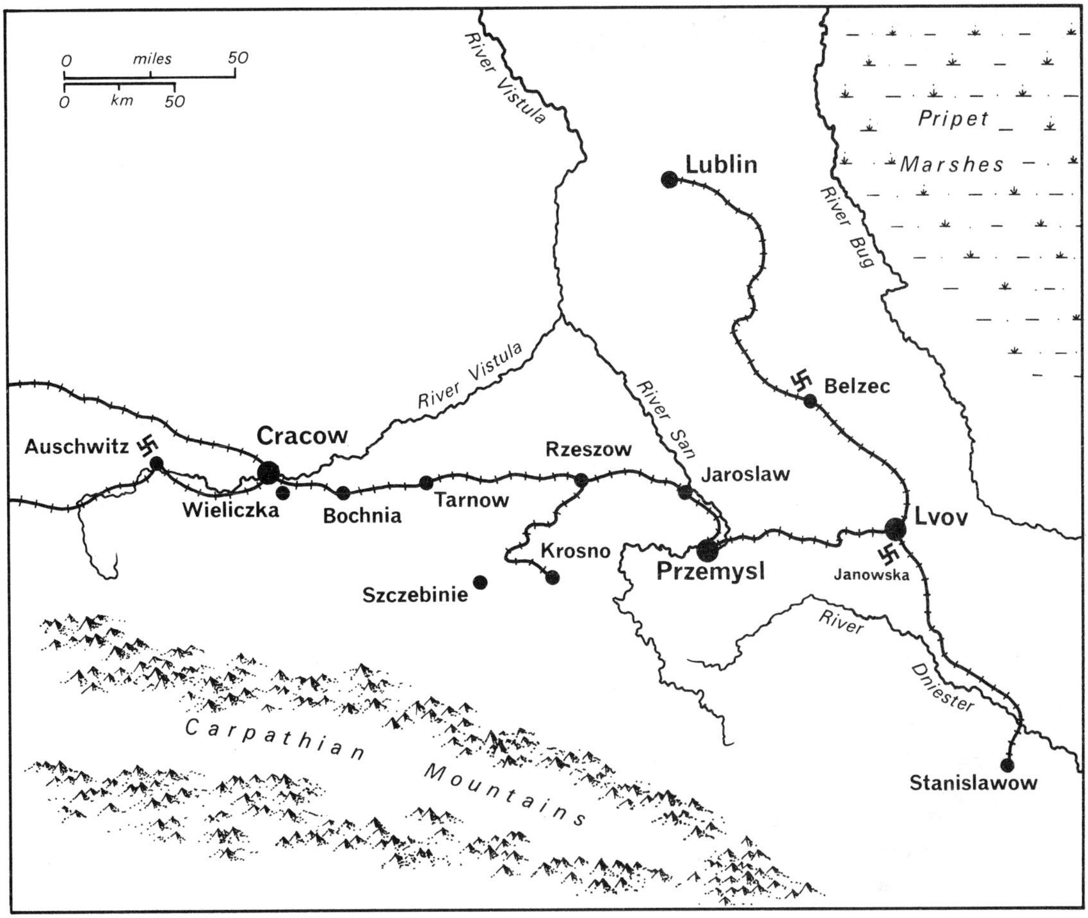

Sara Erenhalt's journey.

although before that we were afraid that precisely because of the child they would shoot us both in the square.

'At this moment the children from the crèche were brought to the square. At first there was deathly silence, then loud despair. Nobody could understand that the Germans could show such endless meanness and bestiality towards tiny innocent children.

'When I got over the shock I stood up and approached the group of children. I picked up my child and fed it. At this moment I noticed my sister who stood outside the square. I turned towards her instinctively, wanting above all to pass the child to her. I really don't know why I was so lucky. No one from the German or the Jewish police stopped me.

'My sister pulled me out of the square. I gave her my child and wanted to return to the square. I had a strange feeling that I should be able to save my parents. But my sister did not let me return to the square. She hid me and the child in the bunker which my father had prepared in our house.

'The people in the square were taken to Belzec. Nobody came back from there. At first there was a rumour that they were working there, and I believed it. Only in 1943 when I was sent to Auschwitz did I realize that none of those dear to me remained alive.

'In the meantime my husband, learning that I

German soldiers film the killing of Jews in the streets of Lvov; a few moments later *(below)* the bodies are taken away on handcarts.

remained in Przemysl, escaped from Lvov, from the famous death camp, and walked to Przemysl on foot. He walked at night, and in the daytime hid in barns, in the hay.

'He stayed in the ghetto illegally and hoped in time to make his stay legal.

'At that time my job was sorting out the clothes taken away from the Jews before deportation, and we lived on that.

'The necessity to sell clothes often meant that my husband left his hiding place and went into town. I threw parcels with clothes out of the window at a prearranged time and my husband collected them, and sold them on the Aryan side.

'Once I threw out a parcel in the usual way. A Gestapo man standing on the other side of the wire noticed me. He rushed in in a rage. He said he had arrested a man who picked up a parcel and threatened to shoot everyone if nobody confessed. I wanted to confess, I was sorry for those working with me. I believed that the Gestapo man could carry out his threat.

'As soon as the German left came Davidovitch, the head of the Jewish militia, and his deputy, Tajch. They demanded that the person who was guilty should confess, because otherwise there would be unpleasant consequences. Then I stepped forward and confessed. Everyone was amazed. I did not care any more. I believed that my husband had been taken, as the Jewish militia also maintained, although this was not so.

'My colleagues at work asked Kommandant Davidovitch to cover up the whole matter. It was quite exceptional that I was not denounced to the Germans. They explained to the Gestapo man that this parcel of clothes was meant for the children in the crèche, which had opened again.

'I was transferred, as punishment, to the non-working ghetto. There were two ghettos in Przemysl – one for those who worked and one for those who did not.

'The thought about my child gave me no peace. We spent all our time trying to find a way to save our child.

'My husband decided to leave the child with Poles. In order to do this he escaped into the Aryan side one day. He was noticed by the military police and arrested. They put him in prison.

'In May 1943 my husband was let out of prison. He was escorted by a Gestapo soldier and Jewish policemen. My husband evidently knew that he was being taken to his death. He threw himself at the German and knocked the revolver out of his hand, but at that moment the Jewish policemen came to the German's aid and my husband was shot in front of everybody. He was then twenty-four years old.

'This was the only time in Przemysl that a Jew showed resistance and did not passively go to his death, like everyone else.

'In September 1943 the ghetto for the non-workers was disbanded. At that time I was still with three of my sisters and my brother. My eldest sister was twenty-five. She was with her husband and her eighteen-months-old child.

'The action took us unawares in the night, but we still managed to hide in a previously prepared shelter. It was dug under an enormous house. Here were three shelters with seventy-five people. The Germans immediately discovered two of the shelters. Fortunately they did not find the third shelter where we were hiding.

'After the action we found ourselves in the bunker with no food, no light, and wearing only our underclothes. When things quietened a little our friends brought us bread and candles. They told us to stay until it would be possible to leave the shelter.

'Already before going down into the shelter my child who was then fourteen months old was ill and exhausted from starvation. I had no suitable food for him then, and staying in a dark airless place helped to kill my child. It died of suffocation. They carried me out unconscious.

'The child's death was a terrible blow for me. Life had no value. I wanted to die, but before that I wanted to revenge myself on the Germans. I got in touch with a group of five boys who had decided at any price to reach the partisans. On the day, the boys left early, but my sister did not wake me up and so prevented me from going with them. I stayed. None of those boys got back.

'It transpired that more than a thousand people had saved themselves this time in various hiding places. It was impossible to remain in the shelter any longer.

'My sister with her child, and another thirteen-year-old sister, went to the Aryan side to some Poles who promised to help them. The German police found them and returned them to the ghetto.

'I went over to the working ghetto. At that time the streets were covered with corpses and the Germans were shooting all the time. I walked and prayed that I might be shot in the back and have done with all this.

'In the working ghetto I was employed in the kitchen, but illegally. I was pleased with this job, because I could pass a little food to those hiding in the bunker.

'At that time I was looking after an eighteen-months-old child, whose parents were working for the Germans. I slept with this child in the cellar.

'The Germans realized that a lot of Jews were still hiding in bunkers and in order to flush them out they announced that they would employ the young in labour camps and put the old ones in old folks' homes.

'I, too, wanted to report there, but the kitchen workers did not let me. During a search I hid one more girl, Hinda Krebs, under planks which stood in the kitchen, against a wall.

'This was supposed to be voluntary reporting to the Germans, but the Germans searched every house and dragged people out.

'I was certain that my family was still hiding in the shelter. Later I discovered that my sisters answered the Germans' appeal and left the bunker along with others.

'The Germans gathered everyone in the school. They undressed them, shot them on the spot, and buried them in a mass grave near the school.

'The shooting lasted two days. There was not enough room in the mass grave, so the Germans poured petrol and paraffin on the bodies and burned them.

'After that action the Germans employed a group of 200 people to clean up the non-working ghetto. I was also in that group. I was working legally by then. In one house I found three people who hid under a pile of clothes during the action. I found out from them that none of my family remained alive.

'During that action the rest of my family had perished, three sisters and my brother. I alone remained, out of such a large family.

'I was taken, too, by the end of September 1943,

during the deportation of the working ghetto. There were about a hundred of us, mostly young people. We were taken to a camp in Szczebnie, near Krosno. A young man called Ela Sztryzener, a member of the sports organization "Hagibor" in Przemysl was among us.

'During the journey Sztryzener kept up our spirits, tried to make us see clearly, and explained that we must all help each other because in that lay our only chance of survival. At the end of his speech we sang *Hatikva* and we felt encouraged to face further struggles and an unknown fate.

'We arrived at Szczebnie. We found there Jews from Rzeszow, Tarnow, Bochnia, Wieliczka and also from Cracow and Przemysl.

'When we had been there for three days the Commandant of the camp, Grzymek, arrived and during the roll-call announced that he was now sending us to a resort where we shall be more comfortable than ever before. We discovered only later how much sadism and irony his words contained.

'We were taken on foot to the railway station. During the journey the Gestapo men pushed us and beat us with rifle butts.

'A goods train was waiting at the station. We were told before embarking to take off all our clothes and shoes and remain in our underclothes. They pushed us into the trucks like cattle, 200 per carriage. It was difficult even to stand. They closed the doors. We moved off.

'We did not know where we were being taken, but each of us had a foretaste of death.

'Among us was a woman who miraculously managed to board the train fully clothed. She was persuading me to run away, saying that she had some money with her which would help in our escape. She gave me her satin overalls.

'I felt completely resigned. None of my family were alive and life had no meaning for me. I had no strength left to make a decision and the escape did not materialize.

'We travelled for two days and two nights. It was stuffy in the train, there was no air to breathe. On the carriage roofs guarding the transport sat armed Gestapo men. After two days there were corpses in every carriage. They brought us in the night to the camp at Auschwitz. At the station we were told to disembark. In the light of a solitary lamp we looked like ghosts, with dishevelled hair, wearing only shirts, with tired faces.

'We were told to form groups of five. A group of Gestapo men stood there with the famous Mengele. He personally segregated the newly arrived people, placing some on the left and some on the right.

'I joined a group of 18 to 20-year-old girls. I thought that being with them would help me. I don't know what factors influenced them at the selection.

'I was sent to the right and the remaining group of girls to the left. Walking away I was certain that I was walking to my death. I looked back, towards the left, at the other group. I noticed in that group small children who were being put into lorries. Apparently they were told that they would have to go a long way and that was why they were being given a lift. But by then everyone knew that they were going to be killed.

'You could hear terrible screams from there, people were struggling before going into the lorries.

'All along the way I thought that it was because of the satin overalls that I was in the group of those still living.

'Our group was formed and we were led or rather, driven, at night, over stones and gravel. It was about three kilometres from the station to Auschwitz. We were half dead when they led us into the barracks and we were called in alphabetical order to be tattooed.

'I was given number 66952 and during many months I was only a number. Later we were told to undress completely and were taken to the bathhouse. After the bath we had our heads shaven and were given some kind of rags for clothes. To these clothes we had to stitch the star of David.

'The clothes were given to us by Jewish women prisoners, mainly from Czechoslovakia. They beat us horribly for the slightest reason. They were cross that we arrived without clothes or shoes and that they couldn't take anything from us. Maybe also because they resented it that we had, according to them, lived a life of luxury until now, sleep-

Jewish women from Hungary arriving at Auschwitz. Some were gassed within a few hours of their arrival, others died at slave labour; only a few survived.

ing on featherbeds, while they had already suffered eighteen months in this place.

'In new clothes, with shaven heads we looked so strange that we hardly recognized each other.

'SS-man Hessler came and told us that he managed to get for us excellent work in the "Union" factory, but that we must first go through quarantine. We already knew that quarantine meant 90 per cent dead.

'Out of the 1,500 women brought here, only 350 were taken into quarantine.

'We were led into a barrack which was inside a huge camp, surrounded by electrified wire fences.

'We were placed in a barrack with wooden bunks. In every bunk there were twelve women, each sleeping with her head by her neighbour's feet, only in this way was there room for all of us.

'Near this barrack there was the hospital. Mostly Jewish women worked there, and their supervisor was a German woman, a political prisoner. We came out only to be counted, this took hours, and they kept counting us.

'There for the first time I came across Jewish women from Greece, Italy and France. The Greek women were covered with boils. They lived in a separate barrack. One day we heard inhuman cries and screams, and weeping. The Germans had come to liquidate their barrack. They were all taken to the crematorium.

'After two days I met a girl I knew from Przemysl, Birenbaum. She was caught on the Aryan side and taken to Auschwitz.

'She pointed to the smoking chimneys of the crematorium and told us that we, too, were meant for the ovens, but until then we must be loyal to each other and help each other; then it would be easier for us to bear our suffering.

'Immediately after arriving I managed to pick up dermatitis. I had no medicine. I was very worried. I knew that Mengele paid special attention to full and clean bodies during the selections.

'I told my friend Birenbaum about my worry. She told me to rub the infected spots with ordinary wire. I listened to her advice with disbelief, but this really did help me, and saved me.

'Once a week we were taken to the bathhouse. There stood a German woman with a truncheon who rained blows at random at the naked bodies. In order to escape the beating I did not undress, and for two months I had not washed at all. All I did was drink the water in the bathhouse which was forbidden.

'By now we all had either typhus or bloody diarrhoea. Every day there were several dead bodies in our block. Some of the girls volunteered to carry the bodies into the trucks. For this they received a piece of bread. I never did this. I preferred to starve.

'Those women who survived the quarantine were transferred to the working camp "B", and from there they walked to work in the "Union" factory. The "Union" factory was three kilometres from Auschwitz. They made there fuses for guns.

'We were woken up at 3 am. Then we had the roll-call which lasted until 6 am. Then accompanied by Gestapo men and dogs we were taken to the factory. We worked 12 hours a day, with only two breaks of 15 minutes.

'In the morning we were given tea with bromide,

Jewish women at forced labour at Plaszow camp, near Cracow. At this, and similar camps, tens of thousands of men and women died as a result of the harsh conditions, or were murdered in cold blood while they worked.

at lunchtime water, which was called soup. At 9 pm we were given a piece of dry bread. The Germans added bromide to everything we ate, so that we would be confused and drugged. Indeed, people became daily more and more apathetic, without energy, with no will to live.

'At the factory there worked with me, on the same machine, a Jewish girl from France, Rachel, I do not remember her surname. She was born in Poland and left for France with her parents as a child. We became friends, we spoke Yiddish. After a while she began to trust me and introduced me to the underground organization. We were organized into groups of five. I knew only the girls in my five. But we did not know each other's names.

'Rachel told us what was going on in the world. She gave us courage, saying that the Red Army was approaching.

'Our main task was to accumulate as much explosive material as possible, i.e. petrol, paraffin, and also scissors.

'Our main objective was to tell everyone that we are all going to die in the crematorium, and when the Germans come to take us away we must set fire to the barracks, cut across the wire fences and allow at least a few of us to escape, so that the world would learn what goes on in the extermination camps.

'I stole scissors, and one of the girls hid them in the ground under her cot.

'I remember that during this period, during tongue examination, one of my friends, Tema Laufer, from Przemysl, who had just got over typhus was seen to have a white tongue and was taken to the sick bay. No one ever returned from the sick bay. She managed to hide several times during selection.

'But I was convinced that she was no longer alive. One day I received a note from her saying that she got out of sick bay, that she was in a so-called "recuperation hut", but was covered with lice, had no medicine and needed help.

'By then I was already in touch with the men's camp. There were boys from Przemysl there, Dawid Sztolc and Irek Warhaftig who were earlier members of the Zionist group, *Hashomer Hazair*. I told them I needed ointment, to treat dermatitis.

The boys got the cream and once on a free Sunday (we had one Sunday off in every five weeks) I got into Block "A", to Tema. She looked like a real skeleton, covered with boils. I treated her with the cream and left her to rest.

'After a while Tema got rid of the boils and returned to work in the "Union" factory. Tema Laufer is at present in Israel.

'When we were coming back from visiting Tema, I and a group of girls who were also visiting their friends, it was already dark. The gate of camp "A" was closed. Only now we realized what risk we were taking. How could we get back to our camp "B"?

'Fortunately there was a bombing raid that evening and all the lights were out. The girls, without thinking, began to climb the three-metre-high gate, bristling with electrified wire. We got across by a miracle. Suddenly the lights came on. The German policewoman cruelly beat those girls whom she managed to catch at the last moment.

'At the beginning of 1944 they were still bringing in Jews from Poland, and then they burned them alive, without any selection.

'At these times we were locked in our hut so that we would not witness what was going on around us.

'Later on, when they brought Jews from Hungary, we were allowed to move about the camp, so that the newly arrived Jews would see that there were living people around. The Germans told the people sent to the crematorium that they were taking them to the bathhouse.

'At that point our group, which was working at "Union" was transferred to a barrack which was near the men's camp, a few kilometres away, towards the town itself. Here the conditions were a little better. It was possible to have a wash after work. But the food was the same.

'We lived in a brick building. We slept on decent cots and we even had blankets. Before us, the barrack had been inhabited by SS men.

'We now often had some help from the men, who would often pass to us a little food.

'From this camp it was only a kilometre and a half to the factory. The road was specially built, with barbed wire on either side.

'Our camp at Auschwitz had an experimental block. The experiments were mostly carried out on Jewish women from Greece. One would see these mutilated and disfigured women, without breasts, without thighs. They also took women for artificial insemination. Sometimes after carrying out the experiments they sent the women to us, to the camp. They were like living corpses.

'By the end of 1944 one crematorium in Auschwitz was blown up. It was the work of men who were engaged in the underground organization. The explosives which they used came from the "Union" factory.

'At the factory two girls, Estusia and Regina Sofirsztajn, from Bedzin, had worked with explosives. Regina worked as a foreman. It was they who stole the explosives and passed them into the men's camp.

'The Germans carried out an investigation and found out that the explosives came from "Union". They arrested Estusia. For two weeks she was kept in a dungeon and tortured. Later three more girls were arrested. They were subjected to terrible tortures. One of them Jadzia Gerther, broke down and named the others.

'They arrested all five, including Regina, and later they were hanged in front of all the women who were working at "Union". I was also a witness of this terrible deed.

'The girls walked to their deaths semi-conscious, beaten and tortured. One of the girls, before she died, cried out: "Hold out, their end is near!" She died with the last word: "Revenge!" on her lips.

Estusia had a sister in the camp called Hanka. During the execution a woman overseer held her and forced her to watch her sister's death. . . .

'The bodies of the five girls were left hanging all night. At every opportunity the Germans said we should take a good look at them, because the same awaited us. All this happened six weeks before liberation.

'We were all nervous and tense. We could not know whether the Germans knew about the other girls. We lived in incessant fear. It seemed a pity to perish now, when the end of our suffering was in view.

'We knew the end of the war was near and the Germans too realized their defeat. They were hurriedly removing people from Auschwitz, leaving only the sick. Daily more and more Germans disappeared from the camp.

'We, factory workers, expected to be taken away at any moment. We made use of the general confusion and stole dresses and scarves from the clothing store. We began constantly to wear the dresses under our striped uniforms.

'One day the Germans took us – it was the 18th of January 1945, and the men as well, to the transport, straight from work and without any food. There was not enough room for us in the carriages. We were taken on foot in the direction of Germany.

'Only a few Germans escorted us. We were better organized, and we could have disarmed them without difficulty. But we were afraid of the local Poles.

'We walked for twenty-four hours. We were tired and hungry. We suffered from the cold, we had no shoes, it was minus 18°. The people could hardly walk, they dragged along. The Germans pushed us with rifle butts. Anyone who fell behind was shot on the spot. There were many victims along the way.

'I walked in a group of five girls from Przemysl. All the time we were only thinking how to break away and escape. We tried to stay in the last ranks.

'Our five were: Genia Ekert, Tema Laufer, Tusia Zak, Stefa (whose name I cannot remember) and I. Two sisters from Jaroslaw joined us.

'Along the way the Germans ordered a stop in the village of Poreba. They allowed us to find a night's lodging in the peasants' houses, saying that at 5 am we must be present in order to continue on our way.

'We all walked into one of the houses. Inside was a little old man. We greeted him with the traditional Polish Catholic greeting (*Niech bedzie pechwalony Jesus Chrystus*). We asked him to let us sleep in the barn. He replied: "You poor orphans, how can I let you sleep in the barn in eighteen degrees of frost?"

'It turned out that our host was a priest. He wore secular dress. We began to talk to the priest and asked him to hide us in his house. He immediately agreed to hide me and Genia. Genia looked like a peasant and introduced me as her daughter. We convinced the priest that we could not be separated from our friends, that we were always together in the camp, that they would perish on the way.

'The priest hesitated. He was probably afraid of the Gestapo men who were quartered in the same house, and he must have heard them remind us that we must march on in the morning.

'The priest knew that we were hungry and explained that the housekeeper could not manage to prepare food for all of us. Genia and I suggested that we would help out. He agreed. He allowed us to sleep in the barn on the hay and pointed out that we must not leave the barn until he allowed us.

'In spite of tiredness we could not sleep. In the morning we heard the whistles and calls of the Germans. But we stayed in the barn.

'One day we heard a loud conversation in Russian. We were certain the Soviets had come, and we were on the point of leaving our hiding place. But they were Ukrainians – members of the Vlasov army.

'There came two days' silence. The bombing stopped. Russians arrived.

'The first Russian who came into the priest's house turned out to be a Jew. I, who knew Russian, spoke to him and asked him if he was a Jew. He answered impatiently "What business is it of yours?" But when I told him that I was Jewish and that apart from me there were six more Jewish women there, he was amazed. He told us we had nothing more to fear and that we were the first Jewish women he had met at the front.

'He told us to leave immediately because there would be more fighting. On the following day we followed the Russians to Cracow.

'The priest wanted us to stay and said it did not matter that we were Jewish, what mattered was that Guardian Angels had sent us to him and that he had saved human lives. He also said that if we didn't find our families we could always go back to him and he would find us work. We had stayed with him for three and a half weeks. . . .'

22

The Death Marches

For many Jews who had been taken away by the Germans to slave labour and who had managed to survive the terrible conditions in these camps, the greatest torment came as camp after camp was disbanded.

Throughout the summer of 1944, as the Red Army advanced westwards, more and more groups of Jews, worn down and emaciated by two years or more of heavy labour, were marched away. Several hundred thousand died during these marches.

From the memories of the few who survived these marches, it is possible to realize just how terrible a part they formed of the fate of European Jewry. One of the survivors of such a march was Henech Abramovitch, a Polish-born Jew who was

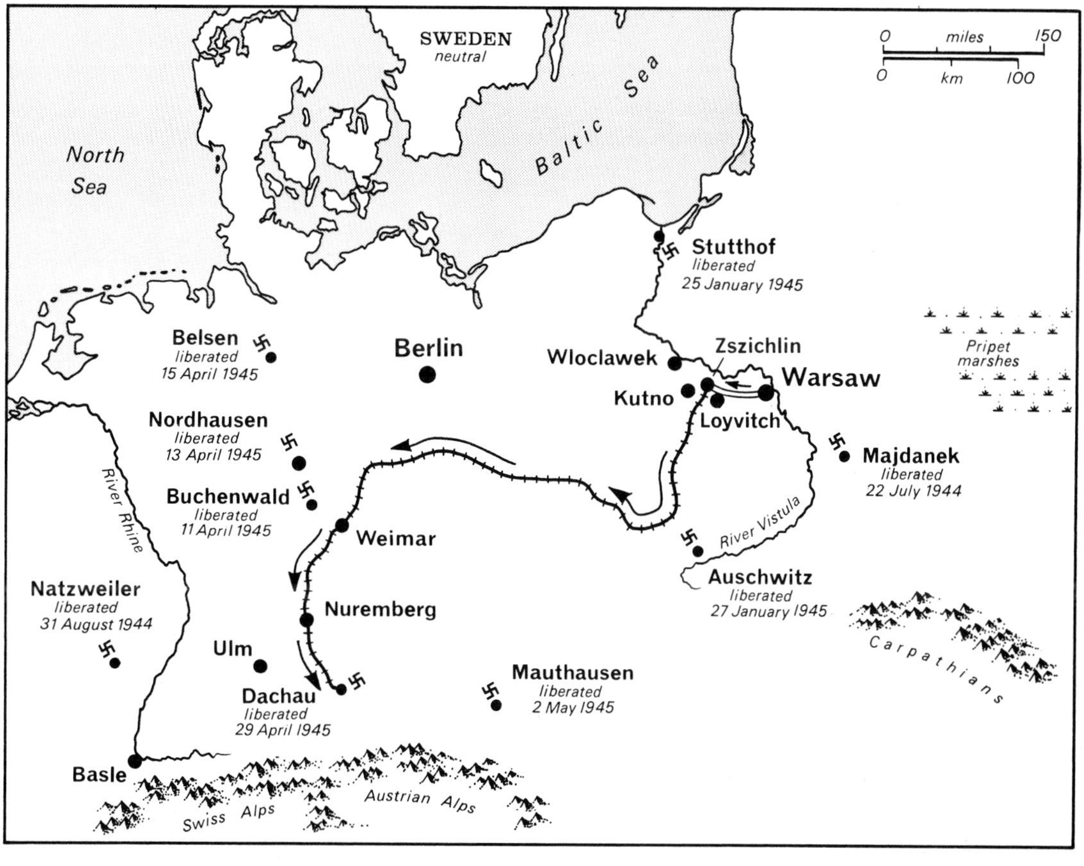

Henech Abramovitch's journey.

only twenty when the war began, and twenty-four at the time of the march itself. Immediately after the war, Abramovitch set down, in Yiddish, his own recollections of what, for so many, was to be their final journey:

'On 29 July 1944 the entire population of our labour camp, near Warsaw, a camp numbering 3,500 people, all Jews, among whom there were also a few dozen German *kapos*, was summoned to roll-call. The Camp Commandant Templ came to the roll-call and announced that the camp was to be evacuated. He also announced that everyone would march on foot to Kutno, some 130 kilometres away, and whoever did not have strength to march should present himself in order to be transferred by car.

'Two hundred and sixty men, almost all Hungarian Jews, presented themselves as not capable of walking. The 260 were led to the precinct and Camp Commandant Templ and a few other SS men shot them all.

'At 9 am each of us received a half loaf of bread and we marched out of the camp. It was very hot at the time and we marched until 6 pm. During the entire time we received no water. Marching by a ditch people bent down wanting to draw a little water. They were immediately shot by the SS guards.

'At 6 pm we remained where we were, in a field under the open skies, and spent the night. We received no water there either. The thirst tormented us terribly. We all had to lie down with our faces to the ground. The SS told us that whoever raised his head would be shot. We lay that way all night.

'On the first day of the march some forty people fell.

'The following morning bread was distributed, one loaf for eight people. The first 1,500 received bread; for the rest nothing was left. We marched off. Our thirst was terribly great, and in fact very many fell, not being able to march on. All of them were shot.

'We marched thus an entire day, until 6 pm. We spent the night there, not far from Loyvitch. Camp Commandant Templ promised us that in Loyvitch we would receive water to drink.

'The next morning we marched on. We no longer got any food. At 11.00 we reached Loyvitch. They led us to a body of water, to the stream which flows through Loyvitch. The first 100 men were led to the water, but instead of drinking water the SS began shooting at the groups. Up to twenty men fell there. So we drank no water and marched on.

'At 4 pm we stopped to spend the night in a swamp field. One of us understood that there must be water near the surface so he began digging with a teaspoon and was successful; at a depth of half a meter water appeared. Everyone followed his example and we stilled our thirst. Seeing this, the SS guards told each other that the Jews were a people to whom no other people could compare: fire does not burn them.

'Upon satisfying our thirst we began to feel our hunger. Being very tired, we slept through the night. The following morning we marched on. At noon the rains began and we marched in the most torrential rain. Around 5 pm we reached Zszichlin. The SS took us into a forest there, where we spent the night in the most torrential rain. We were totally soaked through. Many people fell that night. On the march from our camp near Warsaw to Zszichlin about 500 people fell.

'At 8 am we all assembled, and waited for the train to come. It came around noon and we were loaded ninety men to a closed goods wagon. Inside the wagons we were divided, forty-five men on each side, and in the middle of the wagon stood two guards and two *kapos*, Germans. We were given "rations", to each a piece of bread and some margarine, and we remained there all night in the wagons.

'It was terribly hot in the wagons – unbearably so. Our rain-drenched clothing steamed, and that caused an even greater and more suffocating heat. That night four Greek Jews cut out a piece of the floor and escaped. What happened to them I don't know.

'As a punishment, the entire wagon, with its eighty-three people, was locked and nailed up and throughout the journey we saw no light, ate nothing and drank nothing. Up to forty

As they advanced across Germany, the United States troops discovered many mass graves of Jews who had been murdered only a few days before, or who had died of starvation at the end of the 'death marches'. This photograph was one of hundreds taken by American soldiers during their advance, this one at Nordhausen on 13 April 1945, three weeks before Germany's unconditional surrender.

people died in the wagon that night.

'On 4 August, at 6 am, we left Zszichlin. The heat was very great. The thirst again began tormenting us. The *kapos* and guards had brought a few buckets of water into the wagon, but only for themselves. Our thirst was so great that people even drank their own urine. Some with gold teeth allowed them to be pulled out by the German *kapos*, in return for which they received a few swigs of water.

'Many people died in the wagons. In each wagon there were twenty to thirty dead people. We travelled that way for four days and four nights.

'On 9 August we arrived in Dachau. Getting out of the wagons, we all looked like corpses. Of the 3,500 people who had marched out of the labour camp eleven days earlier, only 2,000 reached Dachau alive – and even they were sick and broken.'

The murder of Jews continued until the very last days of the war. Hundreds of thousands of concentration camp inmates, transferred westwards as the Red Army now moved into Germany itself, died on the marches, froze to death in locked or open railway trucks, or were shot in the fields and ditches of the rapidly dwindling confines of the German Reich.

As the Allied armies advanced into Germany, they were shattered to discover camps such as Dachau and Belsen in which tens of thousands lay dead and where thousands of others were too weak to survive the liberation.

A British army review described the scene as British troops entered Belsen on 13 April 1945:

'Deaths were averaging 500 per day. More than half the total inmates needed immediate hospital treatment. 10,000 unburied bodies, typhus-infested, many in an advanced stage of decomposition, lay about the camp. Huts intended for 60 inmates housed 600. Feeding, toilet and sanitary utensils and equipment were non-existent....

Dachau: a survivor.

'The normal diet had been turnip and potato soup, plus a small portion of bread served only to those still capable of attending the cookhouse. The sick and those too weak to do so went without.

'There had been neither food nor water for five days preceding the British entry. Evidence of cannibalism was found. The inmates included men, women and children.

'A witness, describing the scene as the British troops moved in, says: "The inmates had lost all self respect, were degraded morally to the level of beasts. Their clothes were in rags, teeming with lice, and both inside and outside the huts was an almost continuous carpet of dead bodies, human excreta, rags and filth."

'Contact was made with the German Camp Commandant early the following afternoon, and an immediate reconnaissance was made which revealed a deplorable situation. Of this reconnaissance Lieutenant-Colonel Taylor says: "As we walked down the main roadway of the camp, we were cheered by the internees, and for the first time we saw their condition. A great number of them were little more than living skeletons. There were men and women lying in heaps on both sides of the track. Others were walking slowly and aimlessly about, vacant expressions on their starved faces."

'Another extract from Colonel Taylor's report says: "There was a concrete pit near the first cookhouse visited, with a few inches of dirty water in the bottom. This was the only water supply we saw and crowds were round it, trying to fill tins and jars tied to the end of long sticks." He added: "There was no sanitation of any sort in the camp, not even trenches for use as latrines. There were heaps of dead in every cage, and it was quite obvious that unless food and water arrived very soon, the whole camp would starve to death."

'The problem presented was not so much one of food supply but to provide rapidly the right food to the thousands of starving people of whom more than one quarter were physically incapable either of serving themselves or of digesting what at the outset could be supplied.

'The great convoy of food lorries which reached

the camp the morning following the entry of the British troops was made up of dried milk powder, rye flour, oatmeal, sugar and salt, together with tinned meat and vegetable rations. Not only did the meal thus provided turn out to be too rich and copious for even the fittest, but many of the inmates were unable to exercise restraint and a number of deaths from over-eating followed this original distribution.

'Quite early on, however, scales were worked out on a scientific basis by the senior medical officer and care was taken not to give them too much food....

'All stocks of food used were of German origin, and after the initial emergency convoy from army stores, *supplies were drawn from the well-stocked German supply depot discovered adjacent to the barracks.'*

On the same day that the British entered Belsen, 13 April 1945, units of the United States 3rd Armoured Division reached another concentration camp, at Nordhausen. There, as the United States Signal Corps recorded:

'The bodies of hundreds of slave laborers of many nationalities were found in conditions almost unrecognizable as human. All were little more than skeletons; the dead lay beside the sick and dying in the same beds; filth and human excrement covered the floors. No attempt had been made to alleviate the diseases and gangrene that had spread unchecked among the prisoners. Most of the men were dead when the camp was taken. The few still alive were removed to hospitals where all possible is being done to save their lives.'

The Jews welcomed their liberators, not able to believe that the ordeal was really over. Nor was it easy to return to the 'normal' world, from which they had been cut off for so long. A Rumanian Jewess, Rachel Hirsch, who had managed to leave Rumania for Palestine during the war years, has recorded how her brother David, who had emigrated to Palestine in 1939, and joined the British army, was stationed in Italy at the time of the liberation:

'In July 1945 he received word from a friend who had heard that our father was alive in Dachau. My brother immediately ran to his commander and received permission to go to Dachau.

'There he entered the office and found the list containing my father's name. He entered the shack and immediately noticed Father standing at the sink and washing dishes. Father raised his head when he saw the door open, and looked back again at the dishes, for he didn't recognize my brother and thought him a British soldier.

'My brother ran to him and embraced him and said in a voice filled with emotion: "Daddy, I'm your son David!" Father raised his head in amazement and said: "Pardon me, sir, there's some mistake here. My son is in Eretz Yisrael and he's not a soldier." My brother, in order to convince him, took out of his pocket some family pictures from home, and thus he finally managed to convince him that he was his only son.

'Then they burst out crying, not only they, but everyone around them, because Father had always told his friends in the camp that when he lay ill with typhus he had nightmares and also dreams of yearning, one of which was that his son came in an airplane, liberated the camp and said: "Father you can take ten people with you. Choose those who were most kind to you and take them." And as if the dream came true, his son had come to liberate him.

'He took Father to his camp in Italy, and took care of his physical and mental rehabilitation. Naturally he immediately wrote me the good news, and we went to Jerusalem to arrange an immigration certificate for him. That was in July, but he received the certificate only in November and then immigrated.

'So we were reunited in November, on a Friday evening, when my husband brought him from Haifa port.

'Our happiness cannot be described, nor can our sorrow when Father began to tell first of all that my mother and sister were no longer alive, and grandmother and all the family, all perished in Auschwitz. He rested for a few days, three or four, and immediately sat down to write his memoirs....'

Two Jewish children who survived the war. Born in Poland, they were photographed for their identity documents immediately after the war in a children's home at Ulm in southern Germany. Their whole lives had been spent in ghettos, in camps, in flight and in hiding.

Epilogue

The story of the deportations and the death camps has become a part of history. Yet, at the same time it has seemed almost to pass out of history, as being too horrific, too grotesque, to be written of in the same pages as 'Dunkirk', 'Alamein', 'Monte Cassino' or the Normandy landings. Those who had experienced the terror, and survived it, wished only to forget, or found that they could not easily convey their experiences to other people. Those who had merely read of the death camps in news bulletins, or seen brief snatches of film showing the liberation of the camps, found it hard to comprehend, or were even sceptical. Perhaps the depth of evil perpetrated on the Jews of Europe was such that ordinary people, leading normal lives, living in decent societies, will never be able to grasp it in all its enormity. As a Jewish lawyer who had survived the war in Poland wrote to a friend, from Warsaw, on 2 December 1945:

'I am sending you a photo of my adopted daughter. Look well at her and remember that such children were flung into the burning ovens. Just imagine that my little Tulcia is one of the few who was saved, and that hundreds of thousands of children like her were lost in the gas chambers when they were torn away from their parents.

'If you have a pathological imagination you may be able to picture this yourself, but if you are a normal person you will never be able to bring this chapter of horrors to life in spite of all your imaginings.'

Thirty-five years have passed since the events recorded in this book. The chapter of horrors recedes into history even as further historical research is in the process of revealing further horrors from that terrible epoch. For the Jews, those years will always remain the *churban* – the destruction; the *shoa* – the holocaust, the cataclysm, the darkness, the pit, the abyss, the catastrophe. But for much of the rest of the world there have been other catastrophes during these thirty-five years, bearing more directly on their own lives and futures, to blunt whatever impact the Jewish tragedy may have had.

Even in Poland, where three million Jews were murdered by the Nazis, the very fact that Jewish life was so effectively destroyed makes it difficult to recall it, as one travels through towns and villages which were once centres of Jewish activity, but which are now without a single Jew. The suffering of the Poles themselves during the war was so great as to predominate in whatever museums and memorials are established.

The Jewish community in Warsaw is now a mere 4,000, a shadow of its vibrant 400,000 of 1939. The ghetto, levelled to the ground by the Nazis, has been built on for the housing needs of Polish citizens. In 1978 a Warsaw-born Jew, Alexander Zvielli, revisited his birthplace after a thirty-nine-year absence and tried to retrace the site and scenes of what had been, only forty years ago, Europe's largest Jewish community. He found mostly monuments which told only of the non-Jewish victims, and wrote, on his return to his home in Jerusalem:

'The streets of Warsaw and the countryside are full of unpretentious little memorials commemorating the executions of hundreds of people. The local schools look after them. Actors come to pray for the souls of actors, professors for the souls of professors, and the schoolchildren sweep the pavements, lay fresh flowers and light candles. But who is going to light the candle for the unknown Jewish mother?'

The Jewish effort to record the events of those terrible years has persisted, despite the difficulties created by the scattered nature of the records, the many different languages involved, the fragments continually discovered, and the loss, during the war itself, of so much that would have made it possible to tell more. One of those who, at the time, believed that the Jews must preserve knowledge of their story was a young dental assistant, Moshe Posner, from Wloclawek, a town in western Poland.

Posner was in his mid-twenties when the war began. His dental practice was proving successful, more than he could have hoped for, and his dream was to become a great physician. Forced to leave his home town during the early deportations, he wandered across Poland, eventually reaching a small village near Lublin. There, at the soup kitchen of which she was in charge, he fell in love with the daughter of the head of the local Jewish council. They were married. Later, when the Jews of the village were being marched to the railway station, to be sent to Majdanek, she ran away from the march, and was shot. He ran after her, together with a friend, and managed to hide in a ditch while the Germans searched for him. Creeping away from the ditch, he and his friend dragged themselves into a nearby wood. But Posner could go no further, and, knowing that he would soon be killed, he said to his friend:

'For some time now this idea has obsessed me: does there *still* exist an eye which sees all this, and which hears all this, for future generations?

'I am tired. I cannot go on. One thing I demand of you; you have to make every effort to survive, to live.

'Guard yourself, as one has to guard every document, every piece of evidence, from this time of our universal destruction.'

Acknowledgments and Sources

In assembling the material for this book I am grateful in particular to the Chairman and staff of Yad Vashem, Jerusalem, who have made available to me over several years much previously unpublished material from their unique document and photographic collections. I am also grateful to the Keeper and staff of the Public Record Office, London, for permission to use several important Jewish eye-witness accounts of the Nazi persecution, copies of which have been preserved in the records of the Foreign Office. I should also like to thank the Director and staff of the Wiener Library, London, who enabled me to consult their own substantial library, archival and photographic holdings.

For the manuscripts of previously unpublished recollections, I am grateful to Yad Vashem, Jerusalem, for those of Henech Abramovitch, Sara Erenhalt, Sophia Hausman, Rachel Hirsch and Meir Zvi Vaksberger; and to the Public Record Office, London, for those of Edwin Van D'Elden, of Rachel R, of a survivor of the Jassy journey, of the woman who wrote to the President of the Polish Government in Exile, and of the lawyer who wrote from Warsaw to a friend about his adopted daughter Tulcia.

For the translations of many of the eye-witness accounts quoted in this book I should like to thank Halina Willetts (for translations from the Polish) and Taffy Sassoon (for translations from the Hebrew and the Yiddish). Each of the maps was drawn specially by T. A. Bicknell; the photographs, many of them copied from damaged or faded originals, were prepared by Zev Radovan of Jerusalem, and by Studio Edmark of Oxford.

I am also grateful to Judy Holdsworth and Penny Houghton who prepared the typescript; to Larry Arnn for his scrutiny of the proofs; to Michael O'Mara for his encouragement at every stage of the work; and to my wife for her valuable advice and guidance.

For the texts of many of the documents which I have quoted, I am indebted, as are all historians, to the prior and substantial researches of others. Above all, I should like to acknowledge the following works:

Reuben Ainsztein, *Jewish Resistance in Nazi-Occupied Eastern Europe*, London, Paul Elek Ltd (New York: Barnes & Noble Books), 1974.

Gideon Hausner, *Justice in Jerusalem*, New York, Harper & Row, Publishers, Inc., 1966 (London: Thomas Nelson & Sons Ltd, 1967).

Raul Hilberg (editor and translator), *Documents of Destruction: Germany and Jewry, 1933–1945*, New York, New Viewpoints, Watts Inc., 1971 (London, W. H. Allen & Co. Ltd, 1972). *Destruction of the European Jews*, New York, New Viewpoints, Watts Inc., 1961.

Serge Klarsfeld, *Le Mémorial de la Déportation des Juifs de France*, Paris, 1978.

I have also quoted from the documentary and factual material contained in a number of publications issued by Yad Vashem, Jerusalem, principal among them:

Blackbook of Localities Whose Jewish Population was Exterminated by the Nazis, 1965.

Jewish Resistance During the Holocaust, 1971.

Yisrael Gutman and Livia Rothkirchen (editors), *The Catastrophe of European Jewry: Antecedents – History – Reflections*, 1976.

Jack Robinson and Henry Sachs (editors), *The Holocaust, The Nuremberg Evidence, Part One: Documents*, 1976.

Rescue Attempts During the Holocaust, 1977.

Several of the essays published in successive volumes of *Yad Vashem Studies* have been of particular value: Shlomo Schmiedt's 'Hehalutz in Theresienstadt – its Influence and Educational Activities'; Adolf Berman's 'The Fate of the Children in the Warsaw Ghetto'; Louis de Jong's 'The Netherlands and Auschwitz'; and Yisrael Gutman's 'Adam Czerniakow – The Man and His Diary'.

In addition to material drawn from the above sources and publications, I have reprinted the text of certain individual eye-witness accounts, extracts from contemporary diaries, and personal recollections from:

Ehud Avriel, *Open the Gates! Dramatic Personal Story of 'Illegal' Immigration to Israel,* London, Weidenfeld & Nicolson Ltd, 1975 (*Open the Gates!*, New York, Atheneum Publishers, 1975).

Fania Fénelon, *The Musicians of Auschwitz*, London, Michael Joseph Ltd, 1977 (*Playing For Time*, New York, Atheneum Publishers, 1977).

Luba Krugman Gurdus, *The Death Train: A Personal*

Account of a Holocaust Survivor, New York, Schocken Books Inc., 1979.
Abraham I. Katsh (editor and translator), *The Warsaw Diary of Chaim A. Kaplan*, New York, Macmillan Inc., 1973.
Lionel Kochan, *Pogrom, 10 November 1938*, London, André Deutsch Ltd, 1957.
Ber Mark, *Uprising in The Warsaw Ghetto*, New York, Schocken Books Inc., 1976.
Emmanuel Ringelblum, (edited and footnotes by Joseph Kermish and Shmuel Krakowski), *Polish-Jewish Relations During the Second World War*, Jerusalem, Yad Vashem, 1974.
Gitta Sereny, *Into That Darkness: From Mercy Killing to Mass Murder*, London, André Deutsch Ltd (New York, McGraw-Hill), 1974.
Zosa Szajkowski, *Analytical Franco-Jewish Gazetteer, 1939–45*, New York, privately published, 1966.
Yuri Suhl (editor and translator), *They Fought Back. The Story of the Jewish Resistance in Nazi Europe*, London, MacGibbon & Kee Ltd, 1968 (*They Fought Back*, New York, Paperback Library, 1968).
Rita Thalmann and Emmanuel Feinermann, *Crystal Night: 9–10 November 1938*, London, Thames and Hudson Ltd, 1974 (*Crystal Night*, New York, Coward, McCann & Geoghegan Inc., 1974).

The recollections of Avraham Kochavi, Richard Böck and Willi Hilse are quoted from the verbatim transcripts of the Thames Television series, *World at War*. Jona Malleyron's 'Memories of Marculesti' are quoted from his letter to the *Jerusalem Post*, published there on 27 January 1978. Alexander Zvielli's reflections, quoted in the Epilogue, appeared in the *Jerusalem Post* on 5 May 1978. Moshe Posner's story and last words, with which the Epilogue ends, are translated from the Yiddish memoirs of O. Rapoport, *First Harvest After the Storm*, published in Buenos Aires in 1948.

I should like to thank the authors, editors, publishers and copyright holders of all the above works for permission to quote from them in this volume.

I am also grateful to all those who have made available photographic material, or who hold the copyright in the photographs:

Wilfrid Bade, *Deutschland Erwacht: Werden, Kampf und Sieg der NSDAP*, Berlin, 10 November 1933: 12
Bayerisches Pressebild, Munich: 214, 215
B. Alexander Bernfes: 167
Čekoslovenská Tisková Kancelář Illustrační Odděleni, Prague: 166, 173, 182, 187(bottom)
Centre de Documentation Juif Contemporain, Paris: 144
Editions Archives Centrales Iconographiques d'Art National, Brussels: 176, 177
Foto-Forbert: 7, 101, 102, 103
Foto-Grosman: 84(bottom)
Foto-Kasprowy: 84(top)
Martin Gilbert: 129, 130
Mendel Grossman: 85, 87
Imperial War Museum, London: 26
G. Kadisch, Ghetto-Bildersammlung: 39
Keren Hayesod, Jerusalem: 50, 193
Serge Klarsfeld, *Le Mémorial de la Déportation des Juifs de France*, Paris, 1978: 69, 127, 135, 136, 137, 138, 144, 145, 146, 149, 150
Z. Kluger: 193
O. Kraus and E. Kulka, *Továrna na Smrt*, Prague, 1946: 72, 73, 74, 75, 78, 147, 148, 198, 199, 205
K.Z. Museum, Dachau: 210
Landesbildstelle, Berlin: 9, 10(bottom)
Miriam Novitch, *Le Genocide des Tziganes sous le régime Nazi*, Paris, 1968: 70
The Orient Press Photo Co., Tel Aviv: 193
Hubert Pfoch: 118, 119
Photo-Acta, Brussels: 175
Photo-Diskay, Budapest: 194(top)
Photo-Hoffman, Munich: 11(bottom)
Photo-Oeder, Neu Isenburg: 212
Presse Illustrationen Hoffman, Berlin: 11(top)
Julia Pirotte, Reporter-Photographer, Marseilles: 152, 153
Raumbild-Verlag, Munich: 35
Rijksinstituut voor Oorlogsdocumentatie, Fotoarchief: 162
Savez Jevrejskih Opština Jugoslavije Istorisko-Muzejska Zbirka, Belgrade: 66
Louis Silvestre, Paris: 139, 141
Times Wide World: 21
United States Army Signal Corps: 211
Vandrey: 90
Verlag Heinrich Hoffman, Munich: 97
Wiener Library, London: 2, 10(top), 12, 13, 17, 18, 21, 22, 29(top), 52, 84, 105
Yad Vashem, Jerusalem: 7, 8, 9, 10(bottom), 14, 15, 16, 23, 24, 25(bottom), 27, 29(bottom), 31, 36, 37, 38, 44, 45, 46, 48, 51, 60, 61, 71, 80, 82, 85, 86, 87, 88, 89, 91, 100, 106, 112, 114, 115, 122, 123, 124, 125, 128, 154, 155, 157, 158, 159, 161, 163, 164, 165, 171, 174, 178, 179, 180, 183, 185, 187(top), 188, 189, 190, 194(bottom), 195, 202, 206
Żydowski Institut Historyczny, Warsaw: 94

Index

Compiled by the author.
Page numbers in *italics* refer to illustrations.
The accents on place names have been omitted, except for those in French and German.

Abramovitch, Henech: his recollections of a 'death march', 209-11
Agarici, Viorica: intercedes to save Jewish lives (1941), 46
Aglona: mental patients murdered at, 55
Ajaccio: a Jew born in, deported from France to Auschwitz, MAP 137
'Alamein': an important episode of the war, 214
Aleppo: MAPS 46, 137
Alessandria: Italian Jews deported to Auschwitz from (1943), MAP 192
Alexandria (Egypt): Jews born in, deported from France to Auschwitz, 132; MAP 137
Algiers: Jews born in, deported from France to Auschwitz, 132; Allies liberate, 151; MAP 137
Altdorf: labour camp at, MAP 76
Alytus: Jews murdered in (1941), 55; MAP 54
Amsterdam: the Jews of, 157; Jews deported from, *158*, 159, *159*, 166; MAP 160
Angers: Jews deported to Auschwitz from, 142; United States troops liberate, 156; MAP 130-1
Anielewicz, Mordechai: leads Jewish resistance in Warsaw, 111; killed, 114-5
Ankara: MAPS 46, 137
'Anny': deported from Belgium to Auschwitz, 176-7
Antonescu, Ion: and the resurgence of anti-semitism in Rumania, 42, 46-7, 48; seeks to impress the Allies, 50
Antwerp: Jews deported to Auschwitz from, 174; once a centre of Jewish commercial life, 174-5; MAP 137
Archangel Michael League: anti-semitism of, 42
Arles: Romans send Jewish captives to, 126; Jews deported to Auschwitz from, MAP 130-1
Arnhem: a report on the murder of Jews in the east reaches stormtroopers in (1942), 157
Ascher, Dr: deported to Lodz, 82
Asscher, A: sceptical of reports of the mass murder of Polish Jews, 161; receives a disturbing report, 163
Asti: Italian Jews deported to Auschwitz from (1943), MAP 192
Astoria Hotel, Budapest: Eichmann at (March 1944), 194
Astrakhan: Jews born in, deported from France to Auschwitz, MAP 137
Athens: German officials in, discuss methods of payment of cost of Jews deported by train, 68; MAP 46
Atmicetka: death camp at, 47, 48; MAP 47
Augustus: banishes a Jew to the Rhone valley, 126
Auschwitz (Oswiecim): Jewish deportees pass through (1939), 34; a concentration camp established at (1941), 63-4; and the 'final solution' (1942-5), 65; Jews of Salonica deported to (1943), 68; details of the 'death factory' at, 69-70; details of the arrival of a deportation train at, 73-4; a German recalls the murder process at, 76-8; the continuing deportation of Jews to, 83, 87, 132, 135-56; and the Jews of Holland, 158, 159, 160, 163, 166, 167; a Dutch girl recalls, 172; and the Jews of Belgium, 174, 176-7; and the Jews of Olkusz, 180; and the Jews of Theresienstadt, 186, 188-9, 190; and the deportation of the Jews of Italy, 191-3; and the deportation of Jews from Hungary, 196-7, 198-9; Jews from Szczebnie labour camp arrive at, 204; 'all perished in', 215; MAPS 28, 65, 67, 76, 130-1, 137, 160, 171, 184, 192, 196, 201, 209
Auserwald: a ghetto 'commissar', 104
Austria: Jews find refuge in, 13; fate of Jews in (March 1938), 15-16; anti-Jewish measures in, 17; refugees from, in Lublin (November 1939), 39; Jews deported from (1940), 40; Jews deported to Treblinka from, 123; Jews from, seek refuge in France, 127, 130; Jews born in, deported from France to Auschwitz, 135, 138; Jews born in, deported from Holland to the death camps in the east, 167; Jewish women from, at Lublin, 170; Jews from, deported to Theresienstadt, 182; Jews sent to, instead of to Auschwitz, 197, 198; MAPS 14, 19, 28, 41, 184, 196
'Auswitz': a mispelling, derived from unfamiliarity, 160
Avignon: 126; Jews deported to Auschwitz from, 154; MAP 130-1
Avigor, Rachel: born on Corfu, deported from Paris to Auschwitz (1942), 149
Avriel, Ehud: his recollections of the Nazi entry into Vienna (1938) quoted, 16

BBC: broadcasts details of the murder of 'hundreds of thousands' of Polish Jews (17 December 1942), 161
Baden-Baden: the humiliation of the Jewish community of (1938), *22*; the destruction of the synagogue of (1938), *24*; MAP 19
Baedeker's Guide: mentions Auschwitz (1905), 69
Baghdad: a Jew born in, deported from France to Auschwitz, MAP 137
Balanowka: death of Jews of, 49; MAP 47
Balkans, the: some Jews flee to (1940), 41
Baltic States: German occupation of (1941), 54
Bandholz, Ernst: a witness of the Auschwitz killings, 166
Baranovichi: and a railway junction deception at Treblinka, 119; MAP 117
Barcelona: a Jew born in, deported from France to Auschwitz, MAP 137
'Bari': a dog, taught to savage Jews on their way to death, 122
Bar-le-Duc: Jews deported to Auschwitz through (1942), 136; MAP 130-1
Basle: Jews from Hungary find safety in (1944), 197; MAP 209
Bastia: a Jew born in, deported from France to Auschwitz, MAP 137
Batum: Jews born in, deported from France to Auschwitz, MAP 137
Baum, Ignatz: born in Haifa, deported from Fance to Auschwitz, 132
Beaune-la-Rolande: Jews detained at, 129; Jews deported to Auschwitz from, 134, 140, 143; MAP 130-1
Bedzin: ghetto revolt in, MAP 112
Beirut: Jews born in, deported from France to Auschwitz (1944), 154; MAP 137
Bekes-Gyula: Jews deported to Auschwitz from, MAP 196
Belgium: Jews find refuge in, 13-14; under German rule, 62, 63; and the 'final solution', 66, 123; Jews from, in Paris, to wear the Star of David, 134; Jews born in, deported from France to Auschwitz, 135, 138; a deportation train shunted northwards to, 156; the fate of the Jews of, 174-7; MAP 117
Belgrade: air bombardment of (1941), 63; Jews murdered by gas near (1941), 63; MAPS 53, 56, 67, 117, 137
Belsen: Dutch Jews deported to, 167; a Dutch girl recalls, 172; British troops enter, 212-3; MAPS 65, 160, 171, 209
Belzec: death camp at, 65, 88-95, 111; 'nobody came back from there', 201; MAPS 65, 93, 201
Benzler, Fritz: seeks deportation of Jews from Serbia (1941), 63
Berlin: anti-Jewish boycott in, *8*; anti-Jewish slogans on road to, *10*; Jewish children leave, for safety, *17*; and the expulsion of Polish-born Jews from Germany (1938), 18, 20; the Jews of (1939), 30; a conference on the deportation of the Jews held at (1940), 40; receives report of Jewish train deaths in Rumania (1941), 46-7; Hitler's speech in, prophesying 'annihilation' of the Jews of Europe, 51; deportation of Jews to Lodz from, 81; Allies bomb, 151; MAPS 14, 19, 41, 53, 56, 67, 81, 117, 130-1, 137, 160, 184, 209
Berliner Illustrierte: publishes photograph of the deportation of Jews from Cracow (1940), *52*
Berman, Adolf: a witness to the fate of Warsaw Jewry, 96, 107, 109-10, 110-11
Bernard, Walter: photographs arrival of Jews at Auschwitz, *73*, *74*
Berne (Switzerland): a Jew born in, deported from France to Auschwitz, MAP 137
Bernhardt, Sarah: 126
Bessarabia: fate of the Jews of, 47, 48-9; MAPS 43, 47
Bialystok: Jews deported to Treblinka death camp from (1943), 68; 'bogus' greetings sent to Jews of Warsaw from, 111; ghetto revolt in, 114; and the railway junction deception at Treblinka death camp, 119, 120; Jews deported to Treblinka from, 121, *122*; sabotage of railway lines in region of, 123; MAPS 67, 112, 117
Biebow, Hans: urges Jews of Lodz to volunteer for work in Germany, 84-5
Biel, Max: an SS man, killed by a Jew at Treblinka death camp, 123
Bielefeld: Polish-born Jews expelled from (1938), 20; MAP 19
Bielsko: Jewish deportees pass through (1939), 34; MAP 28
Biglajzer, Bajla: deported with her four children from Paris to Auschwitz, 146
Birenbaum: a Jewess from Przemysl, at Auschwitz, 205
Birkenau: fifty-two letters reach Holland from, 159-60; MAP 76. *See also index entry for* Auschwitz (of which Birkenau was a part)
Biskra: Jews born in, deported to Auschwitz, MAP 137
Bismarckhütte: a labour camp at, MAP 76
Bizerta: Jews born in, deported from France to Auschwitz, 132; MAP 137
Blechhammer: Labour camp at, MAP 76
Blitz, Miriam: her story, as told by her friend, 168, 170, 171
Bloch, Marc: shot by the Gestapo, *154*
Bloch, René: deported to Auschwitz, 138
Blum, Léon: 126
Blumberg, Maiu: deported to Auschwitz when only fourteen days old, 155
Bobigny: Jews deported through, 136
Bobruisk: Red Army kills 16,000 German soldiers at (1944), 154; MAP 46
Bochnia: Jews deported to a labour camp from, 204; MAP 201
Bochum: Polish-born Jews expelled from (1938), 18, 20; MAP 19
Böck, Corporal Richard: describes the murder process at Auschwitz, 76-8
Bogdanowka: death camp at, 47; MAP 47
Bohumin: appeal to bomb railway line at, 199; MAP 196
Bohusovice: forced labour at, 183; MAP 184
Bologna: Jews deported to Auschwitz from, MAP 192
Bolzano: Jews deported to Auschwitz from (1943), MAP 192
Bompard camp, Marseilles: Jewish children in, before deportation, *151*
Bordeaux: Romans send captives to, 126; anti-Jewish exhibition at, *128*; Jews arrested at, 151; Jews deported to Auschwitz from, MAPS 130-1, 137
Bourlas, Leon: born in Constantinople, deported from Paris to Auschwitz (1942), 149
Brack, Colonel Victor: discusses using poison gas to kill Jews (1941), 64
Braila: MAP 43
Brand, Joel: and the negotiations between Hungarian Jews and the Nazis, for the 'barter' of Jews for jewels and money (1944), 197-8
Brandel, Hetty: dies of hunger at Belsen, 172
Breedonk Fort: the courtroom and torture chamber at, *176*
Bremen: Polish-born Jews expelled from (1938), 20; MAPS 19, 160
Breslau: 31, 66; MAPS 53, 67, 160
Brest-Litovsk: 'bogus' greetings sent to Jews of Warsaw from, 111; MAP 53
Briansky, Dr: shot near Warsaw, 98
Briol, Maria: deported to Auschwitz, 149
Britain: Jews find refuge in: 13, *17*; declares war on Germany (1939), 26; Eichmann prepares statistics about Jews of (1941), 64; Jews born in, deported from France to Auschwitz, 132, 135; troops from, enter

Belsen, 212
Brno: Jews deported to Lodz and Minsk from, 181; MAP 184
Brody: MAPS 93, 112
'Brownshirts': and the deportation of Jews through Germany (1939), 32, 34; and Jewish forced labour in Poland (1939), 35
Bruges: Jews from, deported, 174
Brünner, Alois: and the deportation of Jews from France, 155-6; disappears, 156
Brussels: the Jews of, deported to Auschwitz, 174; Jewish schoolchildren in, *175*
Bucharest: a Jewess, born in, deported from Paris to Auschwitz, 149; Red Army enters, 189; MAPS 43, 46, 56, 137
Buchenwald: concentration camp at, 17, 24, 26, 39, 156; MAPS 14, 19, 65, 130-1, 209
Budapest: deportation of Jews from, 121; a Jew born in, deported to Auschwitz from France, 154; Eichmann arrives in, to arrange for mass deportation of Jews from (March 1944), 194; a ransom paid, by the Jews of, 197; MAPS 56, 67, 117, 137, 196
Bug, river: 'liquidation' of Jews near, 47, 48; some Jews flee across, 79; Jewish partisans active east of, 125; MAP 47
Bühler, Dr Joseph: welcomes the 'final solution', 65
Bukovina: fate of the Jews of, 47; MAP 47
Bulgaria: Eichmann's representative sent to, 66; Jews reach Auschwitz from, 77; and the deportation of the Jews of Thrace to Treblinka, 123; Jews born in, deported from France to Auschwitz, 135, 154; MAP 67
Burger, Wilhelm Max: reports on the fate of the Jews of Lodz (August 1944), 87
Bursa: Jews born in, deported from France to Auschwitz, 132; MAP 137
Buschel, Lilian: a Jewish girl in Antwerp, and her brother, *174*

Cairo: Jews born in, deported from France to Auschwitz, MAP 137
Calarasi: a journey of torment to (1941), 45-6; MAPS 43, 46
Casablanca: Allied conference at, demands Germany's 'unconditional surrender', 151; Jews born in, deported to Auschwitz, MAP 137
Catholic Workers' Youth Movement: does what it can to help the Jews of Belgium, 176
Centre for Jewish Emigration: established by Eichmann in Vienna (1938), 52
Chagall, Marc: 126
Châlons-sur-Marne: Jews deported to Auschwitz through (1942), 136, 151; MAP 130
Chamberlain, Neville: 18
Chartres: liberated, 156; MAP 130-1
Chelmno: Jews murdered by gas at (1941), 63, 65, 83; MAPS 65, 81
Chemnitz: Jews deported through (1939), 31, 32; MAP 28
Chernigov: Jews born in, deported from France to Auschwitz, MAP 137
Chetovy, Moise: deported with his son 'in the hope of coming back soon', 156
Chicago: a Nazi 'alternative' to (1939), 30; a Jewish deportee originally on his way to (1939), 30
Chojnice (Konitz): Polish-born Jews expelled to, 20; MAP 19
Cholm: Belzec death camp on the railway to, 92; Jews trying to escape deportation shot at, 94; conversation in a beer hall at, about the murder of Jews at Belzec, 95; MAPS 93, 160
Churchill, Winston: his victory sign 'expropriated' by the Germans, 70; demands Germany's 'unconditional surrender', 151
'Clara': deported from Paris to Auschwitz, 72-4
Clemenski, Gertrude: commits suicide, 34
Cohen, Professor D: doubts that the Germans can commit 'atrocities' against Dutch Jews, 161; receives a disturbing report, 163
Cohen, Sophia: raped and killed, 170
Cologne: Polish-born Jews expelled from (1938), 18, 20; a former Gestapo deportation expert in retirement in (1979), 156; MAPS 19, 81, 137
Compiègne: Jews detained at, 131, 132, 133, 134; Jews deported to Auschwitz from, 134; MAP 130-1
Concentration camps: in Germany, 14, 15; in German occupied or dominated Europe, MAP 65; the liberation of, MAP 209
Constantinople (Istanbul): 198; Jews born in, deported from France to Auschwitz, 132, 146, 149, 156; MAPS 46, 56, 137
Copenhagen: a Jew born in, deported from France to Auschwitz, MAP 137
Corfu: a Jewess, born in, deported from France to Auschwitz, 149; MAPS 67, 137
Cornides, Wilhelm: learns about Belzec death camp, 92-5
Cossacks: persecutions by (1648-52), 42
Couruoble, Alice: witnesses the deportation of Jewesses from Les Tourelles, 139-40
Cracow: Polish-born Jews, expelled from Germany, find refuge in (1938), 20; Jewish deportees pass through (1939), 34, 35; Jews deported from (1940), 40-1, *52;* Jews deported to a labour camp from, 204; Red Army reaches, 208; MAPS 19, 28, 41, 53, 117, 137, 160, 196, 201
Cremenea: fate of Jews at, 49; MAP 47
Crimea, the: Nazis massacre Jews in, 69; Red Army liberates, 188; MAP 56
Crimean War: 152
Croatia: local fascists murder Jews of, 63; and the 'final solution', 64, 65; Jews from, in Paris, to wear the Star of David, 134; MAP 65
Cuza, Alexander: an anti-semite, 43
Cytrynowiec, Maurice: a schoolboy, deported to Auschwitz (1942), 140
Czechoslovakia: Jews find refuge in: 13, 16; Jews seek refuge in, 18; Jewish deportees pass through, 32; and the 'final solution', 66, 88; Jews from, seek refuge in France, 127, 130; Jews born in, deported from France to Auschwitz, 135, 138; Jewish women from, at Auschwitz, 204; MAPS 14, 19
Czechowice: a labour camp at, MAP 76
Czerniakow, Adam: becomes Chairman of the Jewish Council in Warsaw, 98; commits suicide, 107-8
Czernowitz: Jews deported from, 49; a Jewish boy reaches Palestine from, *50;* MAP 67
Czestochowa: Jews deported to 'Lublinland' from (1939), 36; ghetto revolt in, 114; MAPS 28, 112

Dachau: concentration camp at, *15,* 16, 17-18, 23, 39; Eichmann a corporal in, 51; Jews from a 'death march' reach, 211; Allied forces reach, 212; a survivor with his tin of food, *212;* MAPS 14, 19, 65, 209
Dagda: Jews murdered at (1941), 55; MAP 54
Daladier, Edouard: 18
Damascus: Jews born in, deported from France to Auschwitz, MAP 137
Dannecker, Theodor: organizes the deportation of Jews from Thrace and Macedonia, 123-4; organizes the deportation of Jews from France, 129, 134, 135, 136, 138, 140, 143; organizes the deportation of Jews from Italy, 191; commits suicide (1945), 156
Dante: his 'inferno' considered a 'quasi comedy' compared to Auschwitz, 148
Danube, river: Jews deported across, 18; Jews deported along, from Thrace, 124-5
Danzig: deportation of Jews from (1940), 40; MAPS 14, 28, 41, 137
Dardanelles: French Jews fight at (1915), 126; MAP 46
Darquier de Pellepoix, Louis: and the deportation of Jews from France, 143
Davidovitch, Kommandant: protects a Jewess in Przemysl, 202
'Death Marches': fate of Jews during, 162-3, 208, 209-11
Debrecen: Hungarian Jews deported to Auschwitz from, MAP 196
De Gaulle, Charles: enters Paris, 156
Denmark: Jews find refuge in (1938), 16; newspaper report in, of deportation of Jews from Stettin (1940), 52; under Nazi rule, 62
Der Stürmer: on public display, *9*
De Waarheid: reports extermination of Jews in the Ukraine, 159
Dijon: Jews arrested at, 151; Jews deported to Auschwitz from, MAP 130-1
Dniester, river: Jews released at, 49; MAP 47
Dortmund: Polish-born Jews expelled from (1938), 18; MAP 19
Drama: Jews deported to Treblinka death camp from the town of, 124; MAP 117
Drancy: detention camp at, *127,* 128, 129, 131, 132; and the deportation of Jews to Auschwitz from, 133-56; MAPS 130-1, 137
Dresden: Jews deported through (1939), 30, 31, 32; and the deportation of Jews by rail (1943), 66, 68; MAPS 28, 53, 67
Dreux: liberated, 156
Duisburg: Polish-born Jews expelled from (1938), 18; Allies bomb, 151; MAP 19
Dumanovka: death camp at, 47, 48; MAP 47
Dumbraveni: Jews flee to, 48-9; MAP 47
'Dunkirk': an important episode of the war, 214
Düsseldorf: Polish-born Jews expelled from (1938), 18, 20; MAPS 19, 81
Dvinsk: murder of Jews in (1941), 55, *61;* MAPS 53, 54, 56

Eastern Galicia: murder of Jews from, 88, 95; deportation of Jews from, *89;* MAP 93
Eckstein, Henry: born in London, deported from Paris to Auschwitz, 132
Edelstein, Jacob: and the future of the Jews of Czechoslovakia, 181; and the establishment of the Theresienstadt ghetto, 181-2; and the children of the ghetto, 183; and the hope of eventual immigration to Palestine, 186; executed, with his wife and son, at Auschwitz, 188-9
Eger: Jewish deportees pass through (in 1939), 32; MAP 28
Egypt: Jews of Warsaw resemble Jews in exile from, 99; Jews born in, deported from France to Auschwitz, 135
Eichmann, Adolf: his early career, 51-2; and the deportation of Jews to 'Lublinland', 52-3; receives reports of Nazi murder squads, 54-5; account of a murder squad given by a survivor at the trial of, 56; his own recollections of a murder squad at work, 62; and plans for a 'total solution of the Jewish problem' in Europe, 62-3; and the 'final solution', 63-6, 91, 123-4, 129, 132, 134, 135, 136, 140, 143, 149, 151, 152, 154, 191, 194-5; and the 'barter' of Jews for money, 198
Einsatzgruppen: Nazi murder squads, 54-6; their murder methods recalled by a survivor, 56-62; their murder methods recalled by Eichmann, 62; possible disgust spread by, 63; their area of operations, MAPS 54, 56
Ekert, Genia: sheltered by a Polish Catholic priest (January 1945), 208
Elbe, river: anti-Jewish sign over, *10*
Epernay: Jews deported through, 136
Eppstein, Paul: and the last months of the Theresienstadt ghetto, 190
Erenhalt, Sara: her wartime story, 200-08
Erfurt: a firm from, designs Auschwitz furnaces, 69; MAP 53
Erivan: Jews born in, deported from France to Auschwitz, MAP 137
Essen: Polish-born Jews expelled from (1938), 18, 20; and the deportation of Jews by rail (1943), 66; MAP 19
Esterwegen: concentration camp, MAP 14
'Estusia': arrested, tortured and hanged at Auschwitz, 207
Evian: international conference at (1938), 16-17, 18; MAP 14

Falesti: Jews flee to, 49; MAP 47
Fast: amuses himself 'by setting dogs on Jewish children', 122
Fénelon, Fania: recalls journey from France to Auschwitz, 70-4; recalls the arrival of a deportation train from Belgium, 176-7
Ferenczi, Colonel Laszlo: and the deportation of Jews from Hungary (1944), 194
Ferrara: deportation of Jews to Auschwitz from (1943), 193; MAP 192
Fez: Jews born in, deported from France to Auschwitz, MAP 137
Fiume: 191-2; Jews deported to Auschwitz from, MAP 192
Florence: Jews of, deported to Auschwitz (1943), 193; MAP 192
Flossenbürg: Jews deported to Auschwitz from (1943), 78; MAP 65
Forbert: a Warsaw photographer, 6
Forster, Albert: boasts about deportation of Jews from Danzig (1940), 40
France: Jews find refuge in, 13-14; declares war on Germany (1939), 26; under German rule, 62, 63; and the 'final solution', 65, 66, 69, 77, 126-56; Jewesses from, at Auschwitz, 205; MAPS 117, 130-1, 137
Frandji, Lea: deported with her three daughters from France to Auschwitz, 146
Frank, Anne: at Belsen, 172
Frank, Hans: and the 'resettlement' policy

(1939-40), 40; and the deportation of the Jews of Cracow (1940), 40-1
Frankfurt: Jews deported through (1939), 30; Jews deported to Lodz from, 81-3; Allies bomb, 151; MAPS 28, 81, 137
Franz, Kurt: sets his dog on Jews about to die, 122
Frick, Hans: and anti-Jewish discrimination on trains, 24
Fuantes, Fortunée: killed at Auschwitz, 156
Fuantes, Lucy: survives deportation, 156
Funk, Walter: and anti-Jewish discrimination on trains, 24

Ganzenmuller, Dr Theodor: Himmler's complaint to, 123
Gaza: a Jew born in, deported from France to Auschwitz, MAP 137
General Government: established in part of Poland (1939), 40; and the deportation of the Jews of Cracow (1940), 41; and the 'final solution' (1941), 65; MAP 41
Geneva: a Jew born in, deported from France to Auschwitz, MAP 137
Genoa: on the road to freedom, 40; Jews deported to Auschwitz from, 193; MAP 192
German Armaments Incorporated: provide gas chambers at Auschwitz, 69-70
Germany: pre-war Jewish life in, 9-15; and the Evian conference (1938), 16-17; and the invasion of Poland (1939), 26; turned into 'a huge military camp', 27; refugees from, in Lublin (1939), 39; Jews deported from (1940), 40; and the invasion of Russia (1941), 54, 83; Jewish clothing sent from Auschwitz to, 78; Jews sent to Belzec from, 88; Jews sent to Treblinka from, 123; Jews from, detained in France, 130, 134; Jews born in, deported from France to Auschwitz, 138; refugees from, in Holland, 157, 167; refugees from, in Belgium, 175; Jews from, deported to Theresienstadt, 182; MAPS 14, 19, 28, 41, 56, 81, 160, 209
Gerstein, Kurt: describes murder of Jews at Belzec, 88, 91-2; tells a Dutch friend of the mass murder of Jews in the east, 162-3
Gerther, Jadzia: tortured and hanged, 207
Gestapo, the: and the expulsion of Polish-born Jews from Germany (1938), 20; and the 'Night of Broken Glass' (1938), 23; and the deportation of Jews to Lublin (1939), 27, 28, 30, 31, 32-3, 34; its representative in Rumania, 47; Eichmann to head a special section of (from March 1941), 53-4; requests for gas vans from (1941), 63; and the deportation of Jews by rail to the death camps, 68; at Auschwitz, 76, 205; and the Jews of Lodz, 79; and the Jews of Warsaw, 106, 109, 110; and the Jews of Paris, 128, 131, 134, 135-6, 140, 143, 146, 147, 151, 152, 155, 156; and the Jews of Holland, 159, 168; at Majdanek, 169; at Theresienstadt, 190; at Przemysl, 202; at Szczebnie labour camp, 204; at the village of Poreba, 208
Ghent: Jews from, deported to Auschwitz, 174
Gipsies: to be deported (1939-40), 40, 52; murdered in Lithuania by the Nazis (1941), 55; placed in concentration camps in German-occupied Yugoslavia (1941), 63; shot, 63; brought to Auschwitz, 69, *70*, 199; murdered at Treblinka death camp, 121, 123; photographed by the Germans, *123*
Glaser, Miss: deported to Lodz, 82
Glazer, Henri: learns of Auschwitz killings (1943), 166
Gleiwitz: and Nazi deportation timetables, 66; MAPS 67, 76
Goebbels, Joseph: 24; 'every Jew is our enemy', 64; a photograph barred by, *105*
Goedhart, Frans: publishes details of gas chambers (September 1943), 166
Goering, Hermann: on the need to 'eradicate' Jews (1938), 18; on the status of Jews on trains (1938), 24-5; and the deportation of Jews from Germany (1940), 40; gives instructions to plan for 'a total solution' of the 'Jewish problem' in Europe (1941), 62-3
Gold: a musician, brought to Treblinka death camp to play music, 122-3
Goldberg, Robert: aged three, deported without his parents from France to Auschwitz, 147
'Golden Realm', the: Jews from Russia find refuge in, before the First World War, 96
Goldfield, Jakob: born in Olkusz, deported from Paris to Auschwitz (June 1942), 180
Goldkorn, Dr: accompanies orphans to the death camp, 110
Goleszow: labour camp at, MAP 76
Gollub, Max: his deportation ordered by Eichmann, 154
Golta region: death camps in, 47; MAP 47
Gomel: Jews born in, deported from France to Auschwitz, MAP 137
Gomolka, Professor: brought to Treblinka death camp to play music, 122-3
Gordon, Jakob: deported to Auschwitz with his family (1943), 78
Gorizia: Jews deported from, MAP 192
Gorki: a Jew born in, deported from France to Auschwitz, MAP 137
Gorlice: the Jewish school in, *88;* MAP 93
Gospic: concentration camp at, MAP 65
Graz: Jews taken to Dachau from (1938), 23; MAP 19
Greece: under German rule, 62; and the 'final solution', 66, 68, 77, 123; Jews born in, deported from France to Auschwitz, 135, 138, 149, 151; Jewesses from, at Auschwitz, 205; Jews from, escape from a train on its way to Dachau, 211; MAP 67
Griese, Funker: 'lectures' Jews of Lublin, *36*
Gross Rosen: concentration camp at, MAP 65
Grossman, Mendel: his photographs taken in the Lodz ghetto, *85, 87*
Grossman, Vassili: enquires into the facts about the Treblinka death camp, 119, 120-1
Grynszpan, Berta: reports on her family's plight (1938), 21-2
Grynszpan, Herszel: assassinates a German diplomat (November 1938), 22-3
Grynszpan, Marcus: expelled from Germany (1938), 19, 21
Grynszpan, Sendal: recalls his expulsion from Germany (1938), 18-19, 20-1
Grzymek, Commandant: 'sadism and irony' of his words, 204
Guertner, Franz: 24
Gurs: detention camp, 130; Jews deported to Auschwitz from, 140; MAP 130-1
Gyor: Rabbi of, reaches Auschwitz, 198; MAP 196

Haas, Hélène: aged eighty-two, deported with her husband to Auschwitz, 149, *150,* 151
Haifa: a Jew born in, deported from France to Auschwitz, 132; a woman united with her father at, 213; MAP 137
Hainaut: Jews massacred at, in the middle ages, 174
Hamaan, First-Lieutenant: his successful 'raiding party' (1941), 55-6
Hamburg: Polish-born Jews expelled from, (1938), 18; Jews deported from (1939), 26-7; MAPS 19, 28, 81, 160
Hanka: forced to watch the execution of her sister at Auschwitz, 207
Hanover: Polish-born Jews expelled from, 18, 19, 20; a Jewish shop front destroyed in (1938), *22;* MAP 19
Hanukkah: Jews 'celebrate' amid terrible scenes, 104; celebrated at Theresienstadt, 186
Harden, Georges: recalls the arrival of Jews at Auschwitz, 146-7
Hashomer Hazair (a Zionist group): two members of, in Auschwitz, 206
Hatikva: the Jewish anthem, sung by deportees, 204
Hausman, Sophia: her story, 168-73
Hebrew: illegal magazines published in, in Warsaw, 103; studied in pre-war Holland, 157; studied at Theresienstadt, 183, 186
Hehalutz (Zionist pioneers): hold a conference in the Theresienstadt ghetto, 185; urge speaking of Hebrew at Theresienstadt, 186; hold a second conference, 189
Heidelberg: Jews taken to Dachau from (1938), 23; MAP 19
Heinbuck, Hans: 'supervises' death of thirty children with an axe, 122
Heinrichsohn, Ernst: and the deportation of Jews from France, to Auschwitz, 148, 149; works as a lawyer at Miltenberg, a small town in Bavaria, 156
'Helping Hand': children's activities in the Theresienstadt ghetto, 185
Helsinki: MAPS 46,56
Henry III, Duke of Brabant: his dying wish, 174
Herskovitz, Rudolf: attempts to escape from a deportation train, 151
Hessler: sends Jewesses to 'quarantine' at Auschwitz, 205
Het Parool: gives details of gas chambers (September 1943), 166
Heydrich, Reinhard: 54, 62; and the 'final solution', 64-6
Hilse, Willi: recalls arrival of Jews at Auschwitz, 74
Himmler, Heinrich: 40, 68; orders the destruction of the Warsaw ghetto, 113; warned of disruption to his 'master plan for Jewish settlement', 123; orders destruction of gas chambers at Auschwitz, 190; agrees to 'barter' Jews for jewels and foreign currency, 197
Hirsch, David: finds his father alive, in Dachau, 213
Hirsch, Rachel: and her father's survival at Dachau, 213
Hitler, Adolf: 9-10, *11;* in Munich with admirers, *12;* enters Vienna (1938), 15, 16; at the Munich Conference, 18; and the assassination of a German diplomat in Paris, 23; and the creation of a 'ghetto state' (1939), 27, 28; the sun 'greater than' 32; prophesies 'annihilation' of the Jews of Europe (1939), 51; and the German invasion of Russia (1941), 54; and the discussions of his advisers to use gas to kill Jews (1941), 64; enters Warsaw, 96-7; his 'minions', 100; Mussolini imitates, 191
Hoess, Rudolf: 63-4, 135
Höffle, Obersturmbannführer: Eichmann seeks to 'outdo', 194
Hoffman, Ernst: photographs arrival of Jews at Auschwitz, *73, 74*
Hoffman, Heinrich: Hitler's personal photographer, photographs by, *11, 35, 97*
Höfinghoff: reports on methods of payment for Jews deported by train, 68
Hölbinger, Karl: takes part in gassing Jews at Auschwitz, 76-8
Holland: a motor-cyclist from, photographs German anti-semitic slogans, 11; Jewish refugees in, 16; German fear of local sympathy for Jews in, 63; and the 'final solution', 66, 76, 77, 123; Jews from, in Paris, to wear the Star of David, 134; fate of the Jews of, 157-67; Jews from, deported to Theresienstadt, 182, *183*; MAPS 117, 160
Hollender, Albert: a survivor of deportation from France to Auschwitz, 147-8
Hollywood: a deported Jew's sister in, 30
Hompretz, Clara: shot, 171
Hudal, Bishop: appeals to the German military authorities to halt arrest of Jews in Rome (1943), 191
Hungary: anti-semitism in, 9, 13, 15; Jews flee to, 16; murder of Jews in territory occupied by (1941), 63; and the 'final solution', 64, 66, *72, 73, 74;* a Jew born in, deported from France to Auschwitz, 135; preparations from mass deportation to Auschwitz from, 156; Jews from, reach Auschwitz, 196-9, 207; Jews from, murdered at the start of a 'death march', 210; MAP 196
Hyenas: Jews compared to, *10*

Inotesti: a terrible journey through (1941), 46; MAP 43
International Red Cross, the: in Lublin (1939), 38, 39-40; its representative in Roman intercedes to save Jewish lives (1941), 46; thought, mistakenly, to be at Auschwitz, 73; tries to help the Jews of Belgium, 176; visits the Theresienstadt ghetto, 189
Ireland: Eichmann's plan for the Jews of, 64
Iron Guard: anti-Jewish policies of, 43
Isopescu, Colonel: and the massacre of Jews, 47-8
Israel: recollections of a holocaust survivor in, 200-08; Tema Laufer in, 206
'Israel': Jews forced to take the name of, 17
Istanbul: *see index entry for* Constantinople
Italy: Germans fear local sympathy for Jews, 63; Jews reach Auschwitz from, 77; fate of the Jews of, 191-3; Jewesses from, at Auschwitz, 205; a soldier from Palestine in, goes to Dachau to find his father, 213; MAP 192
Iwanir, Herman: reaches Palestine (1944), *50*

Jacobi, Dr: organizes the deportation trains for the 'final solution', 66, 68
Jakubovitch, Samuel: aged nine, deported with his four younger brothers and sisters from

France to Auschwitz, 146
Janowska camp (Lvov): Jews deported to, 200; MAP 201
Japan: attacks Pearl Harbor, 64, 104
Jarnieu: writes of the 'invasion' of Jews into France, 128
Jaroslaw: Jews from, murdered at Belzec, 92; MAP 93
Jasenovac: concentration camp at, *66*; MAPS 53, 65
Jassy (Iasi): the fate of the Jews of (1941), 42-7; MAPS 43, 46, 47, 56, 137
Jedrzejow: 'pretty well intact', 35; MAP 28
Jehovah's Witnesses: their account of Auschwitz disbelieved, 163
Jerusalem: 126, 213, 215; MAP 46; Jews born in, deported from France to Auschwitz, MAP 137
Jewish Brigade: advances into Italy (1944), *193*; a soldier in, finds his father in Dachau (1945), 213
Jewish Fighting Organization: established in Warsaw, 111
Jewish National Home, in Palestine: 15
Jewish Relief Committee (of Budapest): appeals to the Allies to bomb the railway lines leading from Hungary to Auschwitz, 198-9
'Jewish State', the: a mocking masquerade at Treblinka death camp, 120
'Jimmy': a Dutch boy, hanged at Lublin, 170
Jonava: Jews murdered in (1941), 55; MAP 54
Joniskis: Jews murdered at (1941), 55; MAP 54
Joseph II, Emperor of Austria: and the foundation of Theresienstadt, 181

Kaisiadorys: Jews murdered at, 55; MAP 54
Kallmeyer, Dr Walter: an expert on euthanasia, 64
Kamenets-Podolsk: Jews murdered in (1941), 54; MAP 53
Kantorowicz, Mina: aged two, gassed at Auschwitz with her mother, two brothers and three sisters, 151
Kaplan, Chaim: records fate of the Jews of Warsaw, 98-9, 100, 103-8, 109-10, 111
Kaplan, Jacob: protests on behalf of French Jews, 128
Karlsruhe: Allies bomb, 151; MAP 53
Kastner, Dr Rudolf: negotiates with the Nazis for the rescue of Hungarian Jews, 197, 198
Katowice: on the railway line to Treblinka, 116; MAPS 117, 160
Kazan: Jews born in, deported from France to Auschwitz, MAP 137
Kedainiai: Jews murdered at, 55; MAP 54
Kerch: fate of the Jews from, MAP 137
Kielce: and the deportation of Jews to 'Lublinland' (1939), 35-6; MAPS 28, 117
Kiev: Jews murdered in (1941), 54; MAPS 46, 53, 56, 137
Killinger, Manfred von: reports on Jewish train deaths (1941), 46-7
Kishinev: 152; Jews born in, deported from France to Auschwitz, MAP 137
Kisvarda: Jews deported to Auschwitz from, MAP 196
Kladno: forced labour at, 183; MAP 184
Klar, Gertle: born in London, deported from France to Auschwitz, 145
Klarsfeld, Arno: born in Braila, deported from France to Auschwitz, aged thirty-eight (on 28 October 1943), 156
Klarsfeld, Serge: his memorial volume to Jews deported from France, 156
Klepper, Jochen: his views (1938) and fate, 17
Kletsk: ghetto uprising in, MAP 112
Klooga: concentration camp at, MAP 65
Knochen, Colonel Helmut: and the deportation of Jews from France, 132, 134, 136, 151; becomes an insurance agent, 156
Kobior: a labour camp at, MAP 76
Kochavi, Adela: 'bread! bread! bread!', 102
Kochavi, Avraham: his recollections of wartime Warsaw and the deportation of the Jews, 97-8, 99, 102, 108-9
Kohl, Lieutenant-General: 'approves 100 per cent' of the deportation of the Jews, and their annihilation, 134; and the shortage of rolling stock for deportations, 135-6
Kohn, Professor: brought to Treblinka death camp to play music, 122-3
Kokanes, Andor Stern: commits suicide, while being deported to Auschwitz (1944), 195
Königsberg: and the deportation of Jews by rail (1943), 66; MAPS 53, 67
Korczak, Dr Janusz: and the deportation of the orphans of Warsaw, 110
Koszyce (Kosice, Kassa, Kaschau): and the deportation of Jews from Hungary to Auschwitz, 195-6, 198-9; appeal to bomb railway lines at, 199; MAPS 53, 196
Kovno: Jews murdered in (1941), 54, 55, 56; MAPS 53, 54, 56
Kraslawa: Jews murdered at, 55; MAP 54
Krasnik: churches 'devastated' at (1939), 36; MAPS 28, 171
Krebs, Hinda: hidden by a friend, 203
Kremenets: ghetto uprising in, MAP 112
Kremer, Dr Johann: witnesses a 'special action' at Auschwitz (1942), 148
Kriva Palanka: Jews deported to Treblinka death camp from, 124; MAP 117
Krivoklat: forced labour at, 183; MAP 184
Krosno: a labour camp near, 204; MAP 201
Kruger, Friedrich-Wilhelm: warns of disruption to 'our master plan for Jewish settlement', 123
Krugman, Luba: recalls trains on their way to the death camps, 70
Krushin: ghetto uprising at, MAP 112
Kuetner: a Nazi executioner, killed, 125
Kuldichovo: ghetto uprising in, MAP 112
Kuntze: camp commandant, Compiègne, 133
Kutno: a 'death march' in the direction of, 210; MAP 209

Lakhva: ghetto uprising, MAP 112
Laptos, Leo: tells of Auschwitz killings (1943), 166-7
La Rose, near Marseilles: Jewish children deported to Auschwitz from, 152; MAP 130-1
La Spezia: Jews deported to Auschwitz from, MAP 192
Latvia: Jews born in, deported from France to Auschwitz (1942), 138
Laufer, Tema: in Auschwitz, 206; in Israel, 207
League of Nations: and the Jews of Danzig, 40
Le Bourget-Drancy: Jews deported to Auschwitz through, 136, *138, 139, 141,* 146, 147, 148; MAP 130-1
Leghorn (Livorno): Italian Jews deported to Auschwitz from (1943), MAP 192
Leguay, Jean: and the deportation of Jewish children from France to Auschwitz, 143, *144*
Leipzig: Polish-born Jews expelled from (1938), 20; deportation from Hamburg of a Jew from (1939), 26, 30; MAPS 19, 28, 160
Lejkin: representative of the 'Jewish jail' in Warsaw, 104
Le Mans: Jews deported to Auschwitz from, 142; MAP 130-1
Leningrad: siege of, 149, 151; MAPS 46, 56
Leon, Sadie: born in San Francisco, deported from France to Auschwitz, 154
Lerinville: Jews deported to Auschwitz through, 136; MAP 130-1
Les Milles: detention camp, 130, *131;* deportation of Jews to Auschwitz from, 144; MAP 130-1
Les Tourelles: Jewesses deported to Auschwitz from, 139-40; MAP 130-1
Lettich, Dr André: recalls a deportation to Auschwitz from France, 142
Lettich, Johnny: murdered at Auschwitz, 142
Levai, a historian: describes massacres of Jews, 48
Le Vernet: detention camp, 130; Jews deported to Auschwitz from, 140; MAP 130-1
Levy, Alice: born in Switzerland, deported from France to Auschwitz, 155
Ley, Dr Robert: his plans to drive out Jews and Poles from German-annexed areas, 52
Leyden: a Dutchman from, protests against the 'systematic and total extermination of Jewry, down to the smallest child', 161-2
Liège: Jews from, deported to Auschwitz, 174
Limbenii Noi: Jews flee to, 48; Jews put in a camp at, 49; MAP 47
Linz: on the road to freedom, 40; Eichmann's family move to, 51; and the deportation of Jews by rail (1943), 66; MAPS 28, 53, 67
Lisbon: a Jew born in, deported from France to Auschwitz, MAP 137
Lischka, Kurt: rises to the rank of Chief of the Nazi Police in Paris, 132, 134; in retirement in Cologne, 156
Lithuania: murder of the Jews of (1941), 55-9, 62; the Jews of, find refuge in Warsaw (after 1881), 96; the Warsaw ghetto troubled by lack of knowledge of the fate of the Jews of, 106; volunteer units from, in the Warsaw ghetto, 109; Jews born in, deported from France to Auschwitz, 138; and Holland, 157; MAP 54
Liverpool: a Jew born in, deported from France to Auschwitz, MAP 137
Lodz: anti-Jewish riots in (1935), 15; a Jewess appeals from (1938), 22; a high-level Nazi conference held at (1940), 52; murder by gas first experimented on near (1941), 63; the wartime fate of the Jews of, 79-87; Jewish girls in the ghetto workshops of, *171;* Czechoslavak Jews deported to, 181; MAPS 14, 53, 81, 184
Lom: deportees transferred to barges at, 124; MAP 117
London: Jews born in, deported from Paris to Auschwitz, 132, 145-6, 154, 155; MAP 137
Louvain: Jews massacred (in 1309), 174
Loyvitch: the SS kill Jews on a 'death march' who try to drink water at, 210; MAP 209
Lublin: Jews deported to (1939), 27-36; 'a vale of sorrows', 36-40; the mentally ill murdered in the region of, 63; Jews sent eastwards in labour gangs from, 88; murder at Belzec of Jews from, 88; Warsaw Jews told of massacre at, 105; Warsaw Jews asked to 'volunteer' for work at, 111; ghetto revolt in, 114; Red Army enters, 155; Jewish girls from Holland taken to, 168-9, 170, 171; Jews deported from Theresienstadt to, 186; MAPS 28, 53, 93, 112, 137, 171, 184, 201
'Lublinland': German plans to create a centre for Jewish deportees in (1939-40), 27, 36-40, 52, 79, 181
Lukow: on the railway line to Treblinka, 116; MAP 117
Luther, Martin: quoted by the Nazis, 29
Lutsk: ghetto uprising in, MAP 112
Luxembourg: under German rule, 62; and the 'final solution', 66; Jews deported to Lodz from, 81; Jews deported to Treblinka from, 123; a Jew born in, deported from France to Auschwitz, 135; Jews from, deported to Theresienstadt, 182; MAP 81
Lvov (Lemberg): regional centre from which Jews were sent to Belzec death camp from, 88; Jews await deportation from, *89, 90;* liberated, 189; Germans film killing of Jews in, *202;* MAPS 28, 46, 93, 112, 137, 184, 201
Lyons: Romans sent Jewish captives to, 126; Jews deported to Auschwitz from, MAP 130-1

Macedonia: Jews deported to Treblinka death camp from, 123, 125; MAP 9
Madagascar: Germans envisage possible Jewish deportation to (1940), 40, 79
Madrid: a Jew born in, deported from France to Auschwitz, MAP 137
Magdeburg: Jews deported through (1939), 30; MAP 28
Mainz: and the deportation of Jews by rail (1943), 66; MAPS 53, 67
Majdanek: death camp at, 65, 115; 'we don't need nurses', 168; a Jewish girl shot, in trying to escape deportation to, 215; MAPS 65, 209
Malleyron, Jona: his recollections, 49-50
Manchester: its Czechoslovakian counterpart, 33; a Jew born in, deported from France to Auschwitz, MAP 137
Mandel Georges: 126
Mannheim: the fate of a Jewish lecturer from, 190; MAP 53
Mantua: Jews of, deported to Auschwitz, MAP 192
Marburg: remarks of a professor from, at Belzec death camp, 91; MAP 53
Marculesti: Jews tormented at, 49-50; MAP 47
Marienbad: Jewish deportees pass through (1939), 32; MAP 28
Marijampole: a hundred mental patients murdered at (1941), 56; MAP 54
Marrakesh: Jews born in, deported from France to Auschwitz, 132; MAP 137
Marseilles: Jews deported to Auschwitz from, MAP 130-1
Marseillaise: sung by Jewish women deportees, 140
Matuschka, Count Hans Josef: recalls the torments of a Jewish deportation, 198
Maurois, André: 126
Mauthausen: a Jew led to his death at, *167;* MAPS 65, 160, 209
Memel: MAP, 41; Jews born in, deported from

France to Auschwitz, MAP 137
Mendelevitch, Githel: deported to Auschwitz, aged ninety-one, 152
Mengele, Dr: at Auschwitz, 193, 204, 205
Merano: Jews deported to Auschwitz from (1943), MAP 192
Meuter: amuses himself by 'setting dogs on Jewish children', 122
Miechow: 'pretty well intact' (1939), 35; MAP 28
Milan: deportation of Jews to Auschwitz from (1943), 193; MAPS 56, 192
Milejow: labour camp at, 170; MAP 171
Minsk: Eichmann recalls work of murder squads near, 62; and the deportation of Jews by rail (1943), 66; 'bogus' greetings sent to Jews of Warsaw from, 111; Jews deported to Treblinka from, 121; liberated by the Red Army, 155; and the deportation of Czechoslovak Jews to, 181; and the deportation of Jews from Theresienstadt to, 186; MAPS 53, 56, 117, 137, 184
Minsk Mazowiecki: on deportation railway route to Treblinka death camp, MAP 107; ghetto uprising in, MAP 112
Mir: ghetto uprising in, MAP 112
Mircesti: Jews massacred at, 45; MAP 43
Miscolc: Hungarian Jews deported to Auschwitz from (1944), MAP 196
Mittelstein, Fanny: London-born, deported from Paris to Auschwitz with her husband and four children, 154
Mizocz: Jews taken to be murdered at, *61;* MAP 53
Modena: Jews deported to Auschwitz from, MAP 192
Modigliani, Amedeo: 126
Mogilewer, S.: his journey from Hamburg to Lublin (1939), 26-40, 52; MAP 28
Monica, Mina: aged eleven, deported with her younger sister and brother from France to Auschwitz, 146
'Monte Casino': an important episode of the war, 214
Moravska Ostrava: Jews deported through (1939), 33, 34, 38; the Jews of, at Nisko railway station, 52; on the railway line to Treblinka, 116; MAPS 28, 53, 117, 192
Moscow: Jews rejoice at German failure to capture, 104; further German attacks still fail to capture, 151; a Jew born in, deported to Auschwitz from France, 154; MAPS 46, 56, 137
Munich: Jews taken to Dachau from (1938), 23; Allies bomb, 151; MAP 19
Munich Town Hall: celebrations interrupted at (1938), 23
Mussert, A. A.: informed of the 'total extermination of Jewry, down to the smallest child' (January 1943), 161-2
Mussolini, Benito: 18, 191
Myslenice: Germans burn Jewish property at (1939), *35;* MAP 53
Myslowitz: and Nazi deportation timetables, 66; MAP 67

Nancy: a Jewess born in, deported, 139; further Jews deported from, 154; MAP 130-1
Nantes: Jews deported to Auschwitz from, 142; United States troops liberate, 156; MAP 130-1
Naples: Jews from, deported from France to Auschwitz, MAP 137
Natzweiler: concentration camp at, MAP 65
Neu Bentschen: Polish-born Jews deported to (1938), 20; MAP 19
Neuberg (Mosel): Jews deported to Auschwitz through, 136; MAP 130-1
Neuengamme: concentration camp at, MAP 65
New York: a Nazi 'alternative' to (1939), 30; an account of 'Lublinland' published in, 40
Nice: Jews seized in region of, 155; MAPS 130-1, 137
Nieswiesz: ghetto uprising in, MAP 112
'Night of Broken Glass': 23; its aftermath, 23-4; in Danzig, 40; promotion for a Nazi active in, 132
Nisko region: German plans to settle Jewish deportees in, 52-3, 181; MAPS 53, 93, 184
Noé: detention camp, 130; Jews deported to Auschwitz from, 140; MAP 130-1
Noisy-le-Sec: Jews deported through, 136
Nordhausen: United States troops enter (on 13 April 1945), *211,* 213; MAP 209
Normandy: Allies land on beaches of (June 1944), 84, 154, 176, 188; Allies break through bridgehead in (July 1944), 155, 177; the landings an important episode of the war, 214; MAP 130-1
North Africa: Allied landings in (1942), 151; Jews born in, deported from Paris to Auschwitz (1944), 154
Norway: under German rule, 62, 63; and the 'final solution', 66
Novak, Franz: the Gestapo's transport expert, 140
Novi Sad: Jews and Serbs murdered in (1941), 63; MAP 53
Nuremberg: synagogue demolished in (August 1938), 17; deported Jews 'shunted' to (in 1939), 32; MAPS 14, 28, 209
Nuremberg Laws: 10, 16
Nyiregyhaza: Jews deported to Auschwitz from, MAP 196

Obeliai: Jews murdered at (1941), 55; MAP 54
'Ober Maidan': Jews told that they are to be deported to, 119
Oberstdorf: 'Jews not wanted' at, *10;* MAP 14
Odessa: MAP 46; Jews born in, deported from France to Auschwitz, MAP 137
Offenbach: a former deportation expert works as an insurance agent in, 156; MAP 53
Olkusz: 'pretty well intact' (1939), 35; the fate of the Jews of, 178-9; MAP 28
Olomouc: deported Jews pass through (1939), 33; MAP 28
Oppeln: on the route of deportation from Holland to Auschwitz, MAP 160
Oran: Jews born in, deported from France to Auschwitz, 132; Allies liberate, 151; MAP 137
Oranienburg: site of the Sachsenhausen concentration camp, 39; *see also index entry for* Sachsenhausen
Orléans: 126; Jews arrested at, 151; Jews deported to Auschwitz from, 154; United States troops liberate, 156; MAP 130-1
Oslo: MAP 56; a Jew born in, deported from France to Auschwitz, MAP 137
Ostend: Jews from, deported to Auschwitz, 174
Ostrowiec: churches 'devastated' at (1939), 36; MAP 28
Otwock: Jewish children killed during German air attack on (September 1939), 96; MAP 107

Padua: Jews deported to Auschwitz from, MAP 192
Palestine: Jews emigrate to, 9, 13, 15, 43, 96, 181; 'send the Jews' to, 19; a Jewish survivor reaches, 48, *50;* visited by Eichmann, 51-2; life in, spoken of at Theresienstadt, 185, 189; a school teacher at Theresienstadt trained at, 186; a Warsaw Jew visits, 99, 110; a soldier from, finds his father at Dachau, 213
Palmiry: Jews shot at, 98; MAP 107
Panevezhis: murder of Jews in, 55; MAP 54
Pappenheim, Bertha: dies in Gestapo custody (in 1936): 12
Paris: a Jewish woman recalls the journey to Auschwitz from, 70-4; the deportation of Jews from, 108, 133-56, 180; Allied armies approach suburbs of, 156; liberated, 156, 189; MAPS 19, 130-1, 137
Pariser Zeitung: reports arrest of Jews and non-Jews in Paris (1942), 135
Parisian Day: describes distress of deportees from Germany (1938), 22
Parma: Jews deported to Auschwitz from, MAP 192
Pasvalys: Jews murdered at, 55; MAP 54
Pater, Leon: resists, 202; shot, 203
Pau: Jews deported to Auschwitz from, 154; MAP 130-1
Paul IV, Pope: restricts Jews to ghetto areas at night (1555), 191
Pearl Harbor: Japanese attack on, 64, 104
Perel, Myriam: born in Tel Aviv, deported from Paris to Auschwitz, 146
Perthes, Joachim: a witness of the Auschwitz killings, 166
Pétain, Marshal: 127
Pfannenstiel, Professor Dr: mocks at Jews as they are murdered, 91
Pfoch, Hubert: witnesses the deportation of Jews to Treblinka (1942), 116-9, 120, 123; his photographs, *118, 119*
Philadelphia: a Nazi 'alternative' to (1939), 30
Pilsen: Jewish deportees pass through (1939), 32; MAP 28
Pinara: camp at (near Yampol), 49
Pinsk: the fate of the inhabitants of a small village near (1941), 56-62; MAP 53
Piotek, Esther: aged fifteen, deported with her younger sister and brother from France to Auschwitz, 146
Pisa: Jews deported to Auschwitz from (1943), MAP 192
Pissaro, Camille: 126
Pithiviers: Jews detained at, 129; Jews deported to Auschwitz from, 134, 140, 143; MAP 130-1
Piux XII, Pope: and the arrest of the Jews of Rome (1943), 191
Plaszow: a labour camp at, *206;* MAP 65
Plauen: the fate of a doctor from (in 1939), 30, 31, 32; MAP 28
Podul-Iloaiei: massacre of Jews on journey to (1941), 45; MAP 43
Poitiers: 126, 142; Jews arrested at, 151; Jews deported to Auschwitz from, MAP 130-1
Poland: anti-semitism in, 9, 15; expulsion of Jews from Germany to (1938), 18-22; German invasion of (1939), 26; German brutality against Jews of (1939), *27;* German plans to deport Poles from part of (1939), 40, 52; Eichmann in (1939), 52; Jews of, forced to wear the Star of David, 64; and the 'final solution', 66, 77; Jews of, seek refuge in France, 127, 130, 134; fate of Jews in, reported, 159-61; communists from, 'good to us', 171; Jews from, 'burned alive' at Auschwitz, 207; MAPS 14, 41, 107, 112, 201
Polanker: investigates the fate of Jews, Poles and Gipsies at Treblinka death camp, 121-2, 125
Politiken: reports on deportation of Jews from Stettin (1940), 52
Pollack, Kato: her story, as told by her friend, 169, 171, 172
Pollaks, the: a Hungarian Jewish family, *194*
Poltava: Jews born in, deported to Auschwitz from France, MAP 137
Pomerance, Milly: London-born, deported from Paris to Auschwitz, 155
Poreba (a village near Auschwitz): Jewesses helped by a Polish Catholic at, 208
Port Said: a Jew born in, deported from France to Auschwitz, MAP 137
Portugal: Eichmann's plans for the Jews of (1941), 64; some Jews born in, deported from France to Auschwitz, MAP 137
Posner, Moshe: his last words, 215
Poznanski, Pauline: deported with her three young children from France to Auschwitz, 146
Praga: Jews deported into the Warsaw ghetto from, 99; MAP 107
Prague: deported Jews pass through (1939), 32; Jews deported from, 33; 'Centre for Jewish Emigration' set up in, 52; and the deportation of Jews by rail (1943), 66; and the deportation to Lodz of Jews from, 81, 181; deportation of Jews to Treblinka from, 121; MAPS 28, 53, 81, 117, 137, 184
Presov: appeal to bomb railway lines at, 199; MAP 196
Prienai: Jews murdered at (1941), 55; MAP 54
Prostejov: Jews flee from (1939) 33; MAP 28
Protectorate of Bohemia and Moravia: Jewish deportees pass through (1939), 32; Jews deported from (1940-1), 40, 181; and the 'final solution', 64; MAPS 41, 184
Proust, Marcel: 126
Przemysl: divided between Germany and Russia (1939), 200; fate of the Jews in (after 1941, 201-3; Jews from, deported to Szczebnie labour camp, 204; MAPS 93, 201
Purim: Jews hanged during festival of, 178, 180
Pyrennees: 126, 130; MAP 130-1

Rabinsky, Benjamin: born in London, deported from France to Auschwitz, 154
'Rachel': deported to Auschwitz from France, an organizer of resistance in Auschwitz, 206
Rachel R: her recollections of being deported from Hungary to Auschwitz, 195-7, 199
Rademacher, Franz: comments on plan to deport Jews of Serbia to Russia (1941), 63
Radio Oranje: reports on the mass murder of Polish Jews, 159
Radom: Jews sent eastwards in labour gangs from, 88; on the railway line to Treblinka, 116; MAPS 93, 117
Raguhn: labour camp at, 172; MAP 171
Raseiniai: murder of Jews in, 55; MAP 54
Rath, Ernst Vom: assassinated (1938), 22-3

Ratibor: and Nazi deportation timetables, 66; MAP 67
Rau, Dr: and the deportation of Jews to the death camps by rail, 68
Ravensbrück: concentration camp at, MAP 65
Rawa Ruska: a German sees deportation trains pass through, 92, 94; MAP 93
Récébedou: detention camp, 130; Jews deported to Auschwitz from, 140; MAP 130-1
Red Army: advances into Rumania (1944), 50; reaches the forests of Lithuania, 62; enters Lodz (1945), 87; reaches Treblinka death camp, 121, 125; advances towards Germany, 154, 155, 189; reaches Theresienstadt, 173; reaches borders of Transylvania, 199; 'approaching' Auschwitz, 206; reaches a village in which seven Jewish women are hiding, 208; continues its westward advance, 209, 211; reaches Majdanek, Stutthof and Auschwitz, MAP 209
Rennes: Jews deported to Auschwitz from, 142; MAP 130-1
Rhineland, the: Jews taken to Dachau from (1938), 23; MAPS 28, 130-1
Rhodes: Jews born in, deported from France to Auschwitz, MAP 137
Ribbentrop-Molotov Agreement (Nazi-Soviet Pact): 200
Richter, Gustav: reports on 'liquidation' of Jews (1941), 47
Riemany, Erich: born in London, deported from France to Auschwitz, 135
Riga; Gestapo request gas vans for (1941), 63; an expert on euthanasia sent to, 64; Jews deported to, from Theresienstadt, 186; MAPS 46, 53, 137, 184
Rigoletto: the quartet from, played to the SS at Auschwitz, 177
Ringelblum, Emmanuel: his work, 111; his fate, 115
Ringelblum, Uri: killed, 115
Rivesaltes: detention camp, *129*, 130; MAP 130-1
Roethke, Heinz: and the deportation of Jewish children from France to Auschwitz, 143, 151; his request for leniency towards a Jewish inventor overruled, 154
Rokishkis: Jews murdered in, 55; MAP 54
Roman: a deportation journey reaches, 45-6; MAP 43
Rome: the Jews of, deported to Auschwitz (1943), 191; MAPS 56, 192
Roosevelt, President Franklin D: a rumour concerning, 99; demands Germany's 'unconditional surrender', 151
Rorcfeld, Malka: born in Olkusz, deported from Paris to Auschwitz with her fifteen-year-old daughter, 180
Rosenbaum, Alice: deported to Lodz, 82
Rosenberg, Mikla: cannot be freed, 59; shot, 62
Rosenthal: Eichmann insists on deportation of, 154
Roth, Dr Emil: sent to Auschwitz instead of to Austria and freedom, 198
Rothschild Hospice, Paris: elderly Jews deported to Auschwitz from (1942), 149, *150*
Rotterdam: the story of a Dutch girl from, 168-73; MAPS 160, 171
Ruhr, the: Jews taken to Dachau from (1938), 23; MAP 19
Rumania: anti-semitism in, 9, 15; fate of the Jews in (1941-5), 42-50, 66, 88; Jews from, in Paris, to wear the Star of David, 134; MAP 43
Rumkowski, Chaim: 'Elder' of the Jewish Council in Lodz, 81, 84, 87
Rzeszow: 92; Jews deported to Szczebnie labour camp, 204; MAPS 93, 201

SA, an instrument of Nazi terror: in Vienna (1938), 16; and the deportation of Jews to Lublin (1939), 32, 34
SS: and the expulsion of Polish-born Jews from Germany (1938), 21; and the deportation of Jews to Buchenwald (1938), 24; and the humiliation of the Jews of Lublin (1939), *36*; Eichmann joins, 51; Jewish deportees forced to build barracks for, 52; their work in the Nazi murder squads described, 58; at Auschwitz, 73, 74, 142, 146, 148, 196-7; at Belzec death camp, 91, 95; refuse to allow Jews being deported to be given water to drink, 92; and the 'round-ups' in the Warsaw ghetto, 111; and the Warsaw uprising, 113-4; at Treblinka death camp, 120, 121, 123; and Holland, 157, 162, 166; at Majdanek, 168, 169; 'sabotage' against, 171; 'they too had to walk', 172; demand music at Auschwitz, 176, 177; and the deportation of the Jews of Italy, 192; and the 'bartering' of Jews for trucks, soup, tea and coffee, 198; and the killing of Jews at the start of a 'death march', 210
Sabaoani: death of Jews reaching station of, 45; MAP 43
Sachsenburg: concentration camp at, MAP 14
Sachsenhausen: concentration camp at, *10*, 17, 24, 163; MAPS 14, 19, 65
Safed: a Jew born in, deported from France to Auschwitz, 135; MAP 137
Saint-Nazaire: Jews deported to Auschwitz from, 142; MAP 130-1
Sajmiste: concentration camp at, MAP 65
Salomon, Dr: and the deportation of elderly Jews from Paris to Auschwitz, 149
Salomon, Alice: insists on accompanying orphans from Marseilles to Auschwitz (1943), 152
Salonica: deportation of Jews to the death camps from (1943), 68; MAPS 46, 67, 137
Samothrace: Jews deported to Treblinka death camp from, 124; MAP 117
San, river: Jews deported across (1939-40), 52; divides German and Soviet occupied Poland (1939-41), 200; MAP 93
San Francisco: Jews born in, deported from France to Auschwitz, 135, 154
San Sebastian: a Jew born in, deported from France to Auschwitz, MAP 137
'Sarah': Jewesses forced to take the name of (1938), 17
Saumur: Jews deported to Auschwitz from, 142; MAP 130-1
Scharlottengrubbe: a labour camp at, MAP 76
Schmidt, Generalkommissar: declares that the destruction of Jews 'will continue until the last Jew has disappeared' (1942), 158; states that Jews deported from Holland will be 'clearing the rubble' in towns in the east, 159
Schmiedt, Shlomo: recalls the work of children in the Theresienstadt ghetto, 185-6; and the speaking of Hebrew at Theresienstadt, 186
Schneider, Gedalia: describes massacre of Jews in Transnistria, 48-9
Schneider, Moses: born in Auschwitz before the first world war, deported from Paris to Auschwitz, and murdered there (1942), 132
Schoenwald, Ottilie: recalls expulsion of Polish-born Jews from Germany, 18, 19
Schwerin von Krosigk, Count Lutz: 24
Seduva: Jews murdered at (1941), 55; MAP 54
Seine, river: Allied troops reach (1944), 177
Serbia: murder of the Jews of (1941), 63; MAP 53
Seroka, Baruch: killed at Auschwitz, 140
Seroka, Ida: killed at Auschwitz, 140
Seroka, Jacob: killed at Auschwitz, 140
Seroka, Nathan: the sole survivor of more than a thousand deportees, 140
Shar, Dr: falls ill, 49
Shavuot: Jews deported during the festival of, 180
Shimanski, Dr: accompanies orphans to the death camp, 110
Siberia: Germans envisage mass deportation of Poles to (1940), 40; Germans seek to avoid an analogy with (1942), 134
Siedlce: on the railway to Treblinka death camp, 116, 120; MAPS 107, 117
Siena: Jews deported to Auschwitz from (1943), MAP 192
Silber, Jonas: born in San Francisco, deported from France to Auschwitz (1942), 135
Silesia: Jews sent to Buchenwald from (1938), 24; Jews deported to 'Lublinland' from (1939), 36; Jewish forced labour camps in, 160; MAP 19
Skopje: Jews deported to Treblinka death camp from, 124; MAP 117
Slovakia: and the 'final solution', 64, *71*, 123; Jews from, in Paris, to wear the Star of David, 134; deportation trains from Hungary cross, 199; MAP 196
Smyrna: Jews born in, deported from France to Auschwitz, 132; MAPS 46, 137
Sobibor: death camp at, 65; Dutch Jews deported to, 167, 168, 173; Jews deported to, from Theresienstadt, 186; MAPS 65, 160, 171, 184
Socony Vacuum Company: Eichmann a salesman for, 51
Sofia: a Jew born in, deported to Auschwitz, 154; MAPS 15, 137
Sofirsztajn, Regina: a leader of resistance at Auschwitz, 207
Somme, the: French Jews fight in battle of (1916), 126; Allied troops reach (1944), 177
Sosnowiec: labour camp at, MAP 76
Soviet Union: its agreement with Nazi Germany (August 1939), 26; some Jews flee into area occupied by (1940), 41, 79; Germans invade (1941), 54, 83; Germans murder tens of thousands of prisoners-of-war from (1942), 158
Spain: Eichmann's plans for the Jews of (1941), 64; Jews from, deported from France to Auschwitz, MAP 137
Spandau: a Gestapo prison at, 39; MAP 41
Stalingrad: Germans exhilarated by victory at, 70; Germans driven back from, 151; MAPS 46, 56, 137
Stanislawow: Jews flee to (1939), 200; MAP 201
Star of David: deportation trains fly flags with (1939), 33; and the humiliation of an elderly Jew in Lublin, *36*; to be worn by all German Jews (1941), 64, 81; to be worn by all Polish Jews, 98; to be worn by all French Jews, 134, 135; to be worn by all Dutch Jews, 158; to be worn by all Belgian Jews, 176; becomes a symbol of pride, *193*
Stark, Maurice: born in Olkusz, deported from Paris to Auschwitz (1944), 180
Stettin: Jews deported from, 52; MAPS 28, 53
Stickgold, Jeannine: a schoolgirl, deported to Auschwitz (1942), 140
Streicher, Julius: and the destruction of the Nüremberg synagogue (1938), 17
Stroop, Brigadier: and the Warsaw uprising, 113-5
Stryj: ghetto uprising in, MAP 112
Stuschka, Lieutenant: his report from Belgrade (1941), 63
Stuttgart: Polish-born Jews expelled from (1938), 18; Belzec death camp commanded by a former police officer from, 91; MAP 19
Stutthof: concentration camp, MAPS 65, 209
Subotica: Jews murdered in, 63; MAP 53
Sudetenland: transferred to Germany (1938), 18; Jews deported through (1939), 32; Jews deported from (1940), 40; MAPS 14, 19, 41
Suhr, Major: his report from Belgrade, 63
Süsskind, Gerda: learns of Auschwitz killings (1943), 166
Sweden: details of the mass murder of Jews given to a diplomat from, 91
Switzerland: Jews find refuge in, 16; a Jew born in, deported from France to Auschwitz, 135; a few Belgian deportees escape to, 176; a few Hungarian Jews find safety in, 197; appeal to bomb railway lines to Auschwitz sent through, 199; Jews born in, deported from France to Auschwitz, MAP 137
Szabad: Jews deported to Auschwitz from (1944), 195; MAP 196
Szczebnie: a labour camp at, 204; MAP 201
Szolnok: Hungarian Jews deported to Auschwitz from, MAP 196
Szombathely: deportation of Jews from (1944), *195*; MAP 196
Sztolc, David: from Przemysl, in Auschwitz, 206
Sztrausberg, Jane: born in London, deported from France to Auschwitz, 146
Sztryzener, Ela: encourages deportees to sing the Jewish anthem, *Hatikva*, 204
Szydlowiec: churches 'devastated' at (1939), 36; MAP 28

Tangier: Jews born in, deported from France to Auschwitz, MAP 137
Targul-Frumos: MAP 43
Tarnow: Jews deported to a labour camp from, 204; ghetto revolt in, MAP 112; Hungarian Jews deported to Auschwitz through, MAPS 196, 201
Taylor, Lieutenant-Colonel: describes the scene at Belsen (on 13 April 1945), 212
Tel Aviv: a Jewess, born in, deported from Paris to Auschwitz, 146; MAP 137
Templ, Commandant: kills 260 Jews by a subterfuge, 210
Teschen: Jews deported through (1939), 34; MAPS 28, 196
Tevye the Milkman: a play performed in the Theresienstadt ghetto, 186
Theresienstadt (Terezin): Dutch Jews deported to, *166*, 167; exercise yard at, *173*; a Dutch girl transferred to, 172-3; the fate of the Jews

in, 181-90; MAPS 67, 160, 171, 184
Thrace: Jews deported to Treblinka from, 123-5; MAPS 67, 117
Tiflis: Jews born in, deported from France to Auschwitz, MAP 137
Tikvatenu (Our Hope): a children's barrack named, 185
Tiraspol: a thousand Jews murdered at (1944), 50; MAP 47
Tlemcen: Jews born in, deported to Auschwitz, MAP 137
Todt Organization: a German forced labour organization, 43
Topf and Company: design furnaces for Auschwitz, 69
Toulouse: Archbishop of, protests against the impending deportations of Jews, 149; Jews deported to Auschwitz from, 154; MAP 130-1
Tours: Jews deported to Auschwitz from, 142; MAP 130-1
Transnistria: Jews deported to, 49; some Jews allowed to return from, 50; MAP 47
Trawniki: labour camp at, 170-1; MAP 171
Treblinka: death camp at, 6, 65, 68, 106, 107-8, 111, 115, 116-25, 186; revolt at, 125; MAPS 65, 67, 107, 117, 184
Trieste: Jews of, deported to Auschwitz (1943), 191; Jews born in, deported from France to Auschwitz, MAP 137; MAP 192
Tripoli: Jews born in, deported from France to Auschwitz, MAP 137
Trouw: a resistance newspaper in Holland, 162
Trzebinia: Jewish deportees pass through (1939), 34; MAPS 28, 76
Tschounsky, Elizabeth: born in St Petersburg (later called Leningrad), deported from France to Auschwitz, 149
Tuchin: ghetto uprising in, MAP 112
'Tulcia': a girl who survived, 214
Tunis: Jews born in, deported from France to Auschwitz, 132; MAP 137
Turin: Jews deported to Auschwitz from, MAP 192
Turkey: A Jewish survivor reaches Palestine through, *50*; Jews born in, deported from France to Auschwitz, 132, 135, 149
Turner, Harald: 'the devil is loose here', 63

Ubbink, J.H.: told of mass murder of Jews in the east (February 1943), 162
Ueberall, Ehud: recalls arrival of Nazis in Vienna (March 1938), 16
Ukmerge: Jews murdered in, 55; MAP 54
Ukraine, the: anti-Jewish massacres in (1919-20), 9; German conquest of (1941), 54; work of volunteers from, at Belzec death camp, 95; the Jews of, find refuge in Warsaw (in the 1880s), 96; Warsaw Jews troubled by lack of news of the fate of Jews in, 106; volunteers from, in the Warsaw ghetto, 109, 111 and on the way to Treblinka death camp, 116, and at Treblinka itself, 120, 121, 122, 125 and at Trawniki, 170; Jews told that they are to be deported to, 119; fate of the Jews in, reported, 159, 161; MAP 56
'Union': a labour camp near Auschwitz, 205-8; MAP 76
United States: Jews emigrate to, 9, 13, 42, 43, 96; a Warsaw Jew visits (1921), 99; neutral (1939), 26; one Jewish family receives a visa for (November 1939), 39-40; two of its citizens murdered by the Nazis (August 1941), 55; at war with Japan (December 1941), 64; Germany declares war on (December 1941), 64, 129; aid from, to the Jews of Warsaw, 102, 104; Quota Act of, 126-7; citizens of, detained in France, 129; charitable help from, to the Jews of France. 129; its soldiers in Normandy break through, 155; its soldiers advance into Germany, 172, 212, 213
Universal Anti-Semitic Alliance: founded (1910), 43
Upper Silesia: Jews deported from, 178; MAP 76
Utena: Jews murdered in (1941), 55; MAP 54

Vaksberger, Meir Zvi: recalls his deportation from Rome to Auschwitz (1943), 191-3
Vallat, Xavier: and French Jewry, 128
Van D'Elden, Edwin: witnesses plight and deportation of Jews from Frankfurt, 81-3
Van der Hal, Dr: learns of Auschwitz killings (1943), 166-7
Van der Hooft, Cornelis: learns of the mass murder of Jews in the east, 162-3; shot during a death march, 163
Vascaut: Jews deported across Dniester from, *47*; MAP 47
Vatican, the: and the Jews of Rome, 191
Veesenmayer, Edmund: reports to Berlin about the Jewish deportations from Hungary, 198, 199
Velodrôme d'Hiver: Parisian Jews rounded-up at, *127*, 128
Venice: a ghetto created in (1516), 191; deportation of Jews to Auschwitz from (1943), 193; MAPS 56, 192
Vercelli: Jews deported to Auschwitz from, MAP 192
Vermin Combating Corporation: provides poison gas for Auschwitz, 70
Verona: Jews deported to Auschwitz from, MAP 192
Vichy: 127; MAP 130-1
Vichy Government: 128, 129-30, 143; German soldiers take over territory of (November 1942), 151; area of jurisdiction of, MAP 130-1
Vidas, Maurice: aged ten, deported to Auschwitz, 154
Vienna: Nazis enter (1938), *14*, 15; Jews humiliated in, 16; Polish-born Jews expelled from, (1938), 18; further Jewish expulsions from (1939), 33; the fate of a Jewess from (1939), 34; Eichmann in, *51*, 52; and the deportation of Jews by rail (1943), 66; Jews deported to Lodz from, 81; MAPS 14, 19, 28, 53, 56, 67, 81, 117, 137, 192, 196
Villach: Italian Jews deported to Auschwitz through, MAP 192
Vilna: Jews deported to Auschwitz from, 78; ghetto revolt in, 114; Red Army enters, 155, 189; MAPS 28, 46, 54, 112, 137, 184
Vistula, river: 99, 109; MAPS 53, 76, 93, 107, 113, 201, 209
Vitebsk: Red Army kills 20,000 German soldiers at (1944), 154; MAPS 56, 137
Vlasov's Army: reaches the village of Poreba, 208
Volkovysk: and a railway junction deception at Treblinka death camp, 119, 120; MAP 117
Von Eupen: his habit of 'trampling' Jews to death while on horseback, 122
Voronezh: Russians recapture, 151; MAPS 46, 137
Vught: concentration camp, 166; MAP 160

Wanhaufen: his habit 'to murder a few Jews before his meals', 122
Wannsee: leading Nazis discuss the 'final solution' at (January 1942), 64-6; effect of the discussions at 83, 84, 88, 158; MAP 53
Warhaftig, Irek: from Przemysl, in Auschwitz, 206
Warsaw: bombed (1939), 26; and the deportation of Jews by rail (1943), 66; some Jews find refuge in, 79; Jews sent eastwards in labour gangs from, 88; ghetto established in, 96; Jews born in, deported to Auschwitz from France, 132; 'death march' of Jews from a labour camp near, 209-11; MAPS 14, 41, 46, 53, 56, 93, 107, 112, 117, 137
Warsaw Ghetto: children in, *7*; news of Belzec death camp reaches, 95; the fate of the Jews in, 96-115, 121, 123; MAP 113
Warsaw Ghetto Uprising: 111-5; survivors of, deported to Treblinka death camp, 125; Eichmann seeks to avoid repetition of, in Hungary, 194; MAP 112
Weimar: Jews deported to Buchenwald through (1938), 24; MAP 19; Jews deported to Dachau through (1945), MAP 209
Weimar Republic: Jews in, 11
Weiss, Abraham: Eichmann insists on deportation of, 154
Weizsäcker, Ernst von: and the detention of foreign-born Jews in France, 129
Weller, Georges: recalls the conditions at, and deportations from Compiègne detention camp (1942), 132-3; recalls the deportation of children and old people from Drancy, 143-4, 152; himself deported, 154
Westerbork: a camp for illegal immigrants established at, 157; deportations to Auschwitz from, 159, 160, *161, 162, 163, 165,* 167, 168, *174-5*; MAP 160
Wetzel, Dr Erhard: and the use of poison gas to kill Jews, 64
White Russia: 54, 96; MAP 56
Wieliczka: Jews from, deported to Szczebnie labour camp, 204; MAP 201
Wilczynska, Stefa: accompanies orphans to the death camp, 110
Wilhelm II, German Kaiser: 11
Wilkia: Jews murdered at (1941), 55; MAP 54
Wirth, Christian: commands the SS at Belzec death camp, 91
Wloclawek: the story of a Jewish boy from, 215; MAP 209
Wöhler, General: demands 'Jews must disappear' (1944), 50

Yahia, Esther: born in Beirut, deported with her husband to Auschwitz, 154
Yampol: a Jew reaches, 49; MAP 47
Yevnine, Zeeb: born in Palestine, deported from France to Auschwitz, 135
Yiddish: Eichmann learns, 52; Warsaw a centre of, 96; illegal magazines published in, 103; heard frequently in the streets of Paris, 126; in Holland, 157; in Belgium, 174-5; a *lingua franca* in Auschwitz, 206
Yosselevska, Merkele: murdered, 59
Yosselevska, Rivka: her recollections of the work of a Nazi murder squad (in 1941), 56-62
Young Turk revolution: Jews emigrate to France after, 126
Yugoslavia: under German rule, 62, 63; the seizure of Macedonia from, 123

Zabrze: labour camp at, MAP 76
Zagare: Jewish 'mutineers' murdered at (1941), 56; MAP 54
Zagrodski: the recollections of a young mother from, 56-62; MAP 53
Zak, Tusia: on a 'death march' from Auschwitz (January 1945), 208
Zamosc: and Nazi deportation timetables, 66; MAP 67
Zarasai: Jews murdered at (1941), 55; MAP 54
Zausznica, Chaja: deported to Auschwitz with her eight children, 152
Zbonszyn: and the expulsion of Polish-born Jews from Germany (1938), 20, 21, *21*; MAP 19
Zdunska Wola: Jews die during deportation from, 83; MAP 81
Zelman, Annette: her 'crime' and fate, 139
Ziffer, Adolphe: killed while trying to escape deportation to Auschwitz (1942), 140
Zilina: appeal to bomb railway lines at, 199; MAP 196
Zionism: Eichmann studies, 52; Warsaw a centre of, 96; in Holland, 157; in Czechoslovakia, 181; at Theresienstadt, 182-3, 185, 186, 189
Zovednow: Polish tanks 'abandoned' near (1939), 36; MAP 28
Zszichlin: Jews on a 'death march' reach, 210-11; MAP 209
Zuckermann, Yitzak: comments on how news of the murder of Jews at Belzec was received in Warsaw, 95
Zurich: a Jewess born in, deported from Paris to Auschwitz, 155; MAPS 56, 137
Zvielli, Alexander: 'who is going to light the candle for the unknown Jewish mother?', 215